ESCALANTE

ALSO BY JAY MATHEWS

One Billion (with Linda Mathews)

ESCALANTE

THE BEST TEACHER IN AMERICA

Jay Mathews

An Owl Book
HENRY HOLT AND COMPANY / NEW YORK

Published by Henry Holt and Company, Inc.,
115 West 18th Street, New York, New York 10011.
Published in Canada by Fitzhenry & Whiteside Limited,
195 Allstate Parkway, Markham, Ontario L3R 4T8.

Library of Congress Cataloging-in-Publication Data
Mathews, Jay, 1945–
Escalante: the best teacher in America / Jay Mathews
p.   cm.
Includes index.
ISBN 0-8050-0450-5
ISBN 0-8050-1195-1 (An Owl Book: pbk.)
1. Escalante, Jaime, 1930–. 2. James A. Garfield High School
(Los Angeles, Calif.) 3. High school teachers—California—Los
Angeles—Biography. I. Title.
LD7501.L73M37   1988   88-11960
373.11'0092'4—dc19   CIP

Henry Holt books are available at special discounts for bulk
purchases for sales promotions, premiums, fund-raising, or educational use. Special editions or book excerpts can also be created to specification.

For details, contact:
Special Sales Director
Henry Holt and Company, Inc.
115 West 18th Street
New York, New York 10011

First published in hardcover by
Henry Holt and Company, Inc., in 1988.

First Owl Book Edition—1989

Designed by Katy Riegel
Printed in the United States of America
3   5   7   9   10   8   6   4   2

TO LINDA

ACKNOWLEDGMENTS

Jaime Escalante made this book possible, so I apologize for any discomfort or embarrassment he may suffer from my chosen subtitle.

There are many unusual people among the 2.2 million teachers in this country. I suspect several would be worthy contenders for recognition as the best, as indefinable and provocative as that adjective is.

Escalante has told me he does not think he is the best teacher in America. I insist on putting his name forward—more of a nomination than an election—for two reasons.

First, I have not yet encountered another educator in this country who has produced such spectacular results in such a difficult setting and who offers so many encouraging answers to some of the most important social and educational questions of our era.

Second, I want to provoke a response from readers. I hope they will confront their own views of what makes a good teacher and subject this story, and the educators they encounter in their own lives, to that test.

As Americans, we habitually put athletes and actors and musicians on the top of some kind of chart. If celebrating the best in a profession so much closer to our own lives requires a goad, then Escalante is a perfect candidate in my view, even if I have given him no say in the matter.

When it comes to teachers, nearly all of us have a personal best— a man or woman who changed our lives. For me it was a high school history teacher named Al Ladendorff, who showed me the delights of thinking and writing and questioning what I heard and read. Along with Jaime Escalante, he has my thanks.

Although this book bears the name *Escalante*, it is also the story of two other men, Henry Gradillas and Benjamin Jiménez. They, as well as scores of other Garfield teachers, administrators, and students, graciously assisted me in a project that took five years and required hundreds of interviews. I am also indebted to many officials of the Los Angeles Unified School District; East Los Angeles College; the ARCO Foundation; the Foundation for Advancements in Science and Education; the College Board; the Educational Testing Service; the Mexican American Legal Defense and Educational Fund; my Bolivian interpreter, Sandra Aliaga; and the Escalante family and friends who turned my research in La Paz and Achacachi into an adventure.

Nearly every person interviewed for this book has been given relevant portions of the manuscript to check for errors, but any mistakes remain my responsibility. Conversations and events that I did not hear or see have been reported as the participants remembered them, with emphasis on those elements found in more than one account.

All the names are real. Many Hispanic Americans do not use Spanish accent marks in their names, but some prefer them; for the sake of consistency and proper pronunciation, I have used them in all cases.

I want to thank my editor, Robert Cowley, who saw the importance of this story before even I did, and my agent, Diane Cleaver. Shirley Gray, William N. Curry, Judith Havemann, Fidel A. Vargas, Patricia C. Hager, Frank Sotomayor, Edith Jacobson, Jack Dirmann, Robert Hoffman, Harlan P. Hanson, and Fred A. Nelson read the manuscript and made helpful suggestions. I received valuable assistance from Lewis Diuguid, Terri Shaw, Noel Epstein, Steve Gold, John Kenelly, Bart Everett, Maria Tostado, Robert and Librada Mann, Daniel Shaw, Katharine Macdonald, Leslie Pendexter, Matt Lait, Richard Prosl, and Susan Brind.

My editors at the *Washington Post*, Alison Howard, Dan Balz, Robert G. Kaiser, Leonard Downie, Jr., and Benjamin C. Bradlee, were understanding and supportive. My wife, Linda, and my children, Joe, Peter, and Kate, accepted, with their usual wry amusement, my obsession with this book. My mother, Frances Mathews, a teacher for forty years, was also very helpful.

I have tried to tell this story of an educator and the transformation of his school as honestly as possible. I have gone back to his childhood, to the roots of his intensity and commitment, so that readers can ponder what makes exceptional teachers and decide for themselves if there is any hope of duplicating the process. I have also recounted many mistakes, disputes, and excesses, particularly Escalante's. Any readers struggling with their own schools should know that hard feelings and misunderstandings do not necessarily mean failure.

Much has been written about the decline of American education. It is a joy to describe one place where that shaky institution has experienced an unmistakable revival. And my happiness does not approach the thrill experienced by educators able to see beyond poverty and neglect to the real potential of young minds. I hope this book will impart some of that excitement to any who wish to set forth in the same direction as Jaime Escalante and the many other teachers in America like him.

ESCALANTE

INTRODUCTION

Some of the people I have tried to tell this story do not believe it. They are polite about it. They will listen for a few minutes, ask a question or two, then change the subject.

I cannot blame them. Many people tell stories of educational miracles. The stories are blessed with as much hope and hyperbole as real achievement.

Those accounts that do stand on solid ground usually celebrate the restoration of the national mean: A terrible school in a bad neighborhood finds a way to reach the standard of an average school in a good neighborhood. Marva Collins motivated inner city Chicago children to read beyond their grade level. George McKenna, a Los Angeles principal, doubled the number of Scholastic Aptitude Test takers at Washington Preparatory High School and cut its dropout rate. Such achievements are a credit to the educators responsible. But they do not come close to what happened at James A. Garfield High School.

I became interested in Garfield on December 7, 1982. I saw a story in the Metro section of the *Los Angeles Times*: 14 STUDENTS RETAKE TEST AFTER SCORES ARE DISPUTED—PRINCIPAL CHARGES MINORITY BIAS. Eighteen students at Garfield had taken the Advanced Placement calculus examination, and fourteen of them had been accused of copying.*

This news struck me as, if not unbelievable, at least mildly incredible.

It was not the cheating or the bias charges that surprised me. They

*The article proved slightly wrong. Twelve students retook the test.

1

seemed incidental, a sign that the *Times* had missed the point. How in the world, I wanted to know, did a place like Garfield find eighteen students willing to take the AP calculus test at all?

The school sat in the middle of East Los Angeles. It drew its student body from Latino families with little money or formal education. Many of the parents were recent Mexican immigrants who spoke little, if any, English. How could such a school find eighteen students with enough background in algebra, geometry, and trigonometry even to begin such a calculus course?

I attended an above-average high school in the middle-income northern California suburb of San Mateo, where the vast majority of parents were high school graduates and many had college degrees. My high school had won several academic honors and sent many of its predominantly Anglo students to college. Yet it did not have enough qualified mathematics students to form even one calculus class. My senior year, 1962–63, the four of us with the necessary prerequisites took calculus at night at the local junior college.

I knew the AP program had expanded since then. Some public schools in wealthy suburbs had begun to provide a small class or two in calculus. That did not explain Garfield. I drove over to see what was going on.

Garfield High School was built in 1925 at what is now 5101 East Sixth Street in East Los Angeles. It is a short block from Atlantic Boulevard, a raw stretch of telephone poles, used car lots, body shops, banks, bars, hamburger-burrito stands, churches, and service stations. Much of the rest of the area is residential. There are some sprawling, noisy apartment complexes, but most people live in small houses on crowded lots. Despite the lack of money, many East Los Angeles neighborhoods display tidy lawns, neat hedges, and other signs of care. Houses are often old, one-story wood frames or stucco looking better than they should because of fresh paint, decorative fences, and many well-tended flowers.

At least 80 percent of Garfield High School students qualify for the federal free or reduced-price lunch program, which means their annual incomes fall below $15,000 for a family of four. Many parents make much less than that. At least 25 percent of the students come from families that receive Aid to Families with Dependent Children, and that figure would probably be much larger if so many of the poor were not illegal aliens afraid to seek any government help.

But nearly all the people in East Los Angeles, like Americans any-where, prefer to rely on their own resources. The area is predominantly Roman Catholic. Families are often large, and family members go out of their way to help each other. That sense of family loyalty gives the community its emotional core.

More than 95 percent of the Garfield student body is Latino. Some of the families have recently immigrated to the United States from Mexico, often illegally. Even long-term residents usually speak Spanish at home. Few of the homes have many books in any language, or framed degrees on the wall from institutions of any kind.

But that first day, poking around the cracked asphalt walks and worn linoleum floors of Garfield High, I discovered that East Los Angeles did have one thing that was very special—Jaime Escalante.

I noticed his hands first. His thick brown fingers swept the air when he lectured and ground chalk into the blackboard with an audible crack. He had a stocky build, a large square head with prominent jaw, and a widening bald spot covered with a few stray hairs, like a threadbare victory wreath on a Bolivian Caesar. He looked oddly like the school mascot, a gruff bulldog, and exuded a sense of mischief that made me and, I discovered later, many others want to keep a close eye on him.

It took me some time to adjust to his accent. He seasoned his English with bits of Spanish and two Bolivian Indian dialects. He was almost fifty-two but had been teaching in America only eight years.

He was the man who had found and trained eighteen calculus students in a school where, by any reasonable measure, there should have been only one or two, if any. He told me immediately he was not satisfied with just eighteen. He seemed in a great hurry about everything.

At that time, in 1982, I wondered if his modest success might have been mostly luck. Perhaps an unusual number of bright students from a few particularly well-motivated families had managed to click on that one test. Other schools winning national acclaim had benefited from special admissions rules that let them take the best-motivated students.

I visited Garfield many more times. I talked to parents, teachers, administrators, and other people in the neighborhood. I looked at the national Advanced Placement test statistics and at welfare and income data for Garfield families.

I began to suspect that I and everyone else had seriously under-estimated both Escalante and his students. By 1986, a confirmed Garfield habitué, I was convinced of it.

In the spring of 1987 I surveyed 109 Garfield calculus students, youths who had gone further in mathematics and several other dis-ciplines than anyone else in the school. If any of Garfield's 3,400 students had special advantages at home, it would be they. Only 9 of the 109 raised their hands when I asked if anyone had even one parent with a college degree. Most of that small group were Asian American students who did not live in the Garfield district. Only 35 of the 109 said they had one parent with even a high school diploma.

No matter how talented Escalante might be, how could such a school produce eighteen students willing and able to risk a program as difficult as Advanced Placement calculus?

If that had remained the only question to be answered, this book would not have been written. The story of the 1982 calculus class, and the scandal that nearly overwhelmed them, provides mystery, heartbreak, and intrigue. It was what drew me to Garfield, but it was not what made me stay.

I wanted to know what would happen next. What unfolded before me, at first imperceptibly, was so much more important than 1982, and so unexpected, that I did not see it at first. Even after I had gathered and absorbed the essential statistics, it took me some time to realize what an unprecedented thing Garfield had done. No ordi-nary inner city school had ever achieved such national distinction in a major academic discipline.

Garfield had barely escaped losing its accreditation in 1975. Twelve years later it produced more Advanced Placement calculus students than all but three public schools in the country.

Yet the feat received little attention. The local Spanish-language press reported Garfield's progress nearly every year, but the national press largely ignored it. East Los Angeles was an isolated enclave; without the hint of scandal that had fueled the 1982 story, few re-porters were very interested.

I thought if I could describe in detail how Escalante taught and how Garfield had come so far, other teachers and schools with similar challenges might see something they could use. If I could honestly portray the setbacks, misunderstandings, and personal tensions that accompanied Garfield's achievement, perhaps others would not become disheartened when they found the path to learning particularly rough.

Garfield offers lessons for schools even in affluent neighborhoods. Calculus is an essential tool of modern science, but few American high schools teach it very well. Soviet students of calculus far outnumber their American counterparts. Japan and Israel have more successful programs for students this age. A study released in early 1987 by the National Research Council said that in most countries all advanced mathematics students take secondary school calculus, while in the United States only about one-fifth do. It said American mathematics education "lacks focus, challenge and vitality."

There are thousands of exceptional teachers struggling with students as disadvantaged and with resources as meager as those at Garfield. Like all good teachers, they sense potential in young minds but wonder if unimaginative administrators, deficit-conscious school boards, and distracted parents will give them the necessary support.

The problem is particularly acute in Latino communities and has led many commentators and politicians to suggest that the United States can no longer accept so many newcomers from Latin America. According to the National Commission on Secondary Education for Hispanics, 40 percent of all Latino youths who drop out of U.S. schools do so before the tenth grade. Forty-five percent of Mexican American and Puerto Rican children never finish high school. Seventy-six percent of all Latinos score in the bottom half of standardized achievement tests. Just in California, more than 13 percent of all high school graduates, but only 5 percent of Latino graduates, were eligible for admission to the University of California in 1983.

The story of Jaime Escalante and Garfield High School says to teachers, principals, parents, and students that those handicaps can be overcome. They can achieve results they never dreamed of. All they need is the drive and impatience and love that pushes a school and its students far beyond their assumed limits.

The world has plenty of books about automobile executives, fighter pilots, and politicians. I thought one about a teacher might do some good, particularly a teacher who had encountered so much trouble and disappointment. By the time this book was finished, people on every side of the debate over educational reform—the secretary of education, the National Education Association, several professors and politicians—had heard something about Garfield High and were arguing whether it was a useless exception to every rule or living proof that very high standards can work in inner city schools. Here is the entire story, an opportunity for everyone to decide for themselves.

Garfield encountered at a difficult moment in its long history a gifted immigrant educator who had no time for faculty room chat or gentle persuasion or waiting for the school board and the legislature and the governor and the voters to see the light and give his school the resources it needed. He found a young American teacher of very different background and temperament who shared his impatience. Blessed with a principal of unusual experience and resolve, they created a disciplined atmosphere where students could work. They turned very old methods of motivation into something very new.

Garfield remains a school with many problems. Its dropout rate is high. Some of its graduates have difficulty finding good jobs. These problems it shares with many other schools in Los Angeles and elsewhere, but they do not detract from what Escalante and Garfield have accomplished. No study has ever shown that high standards and high expectations *increase* the dropout rate. If anything, Garfield appears to have retained a few more students than usual in recent years. Standardized mathematics test scores and college admission rates for all students have also increased.

It was not easy, but Jaime Escalante fashioned a way to give American education in mathematics, science, and other difficult subjects a substantial boost. And, I think, he proved that the flood of new Americans from Mexico and the other Latin countries need not be the liability so many have feared.

Americans had similar fears about the immigrants of the last century, and we know how they and their children turned out. I have met a great many young people in the last six years who are ready to give America a new century even more productive than the old. All we have to do is consider what happened at Garfield High.

PART ONE

LIMITS

||1||

When Jaime Escalante was eight, a mischievous boy thin as the reeds lining Lake Titicaca, he received a packet of gum from his friend Armando. The two boys lived across a cobblestone alley from each other in Achacachi, a village on the Bolivian high plateau, the altiplano.

The sweet, dark gray sticks were Jaime's favorite. He hoarded them in the back pocket of his ragged shorts. He permitted himself a juicy bite only to celebrate his construction of another wood-scrap toy car or perhaps to end a satisfying day of soccer ball dribbling in the courtyard of his family's tile-and-adobe hovel.

His father was a stout, bright man whose frustrated ambitions had devoured a vital part of his soul. He stumbled home drunk that day and found his small son chewing contentedly on the prized gift. The father snatched it away.

"You stole this, didn't you?"

"No, Papa, no. Armando *gave* it to me."

The father struck the boy sharply across the face. "And you're a liar, too," he said.

The father walked unsteadily away, taking the gum with him, while two bright eyes watched his back. The boy was sick with anger that anyone, particularly his father, would doubt his word, but he did not know what to do about it.

In his eighth year as a physics teacher at the Jesuit-run San Calixto School in La Paz, Jaime Escalante decided not to accompany the senior class on its spring trip to Copacabana. He had already visited the

Lake Titicaca resort several times. When he was a teenager, he had often walked there with his friend Roberto Cordero—164 miles across the altiplano with the dust of passing trucks leaving an odor in their nostrils for weeks.

Bolivians told foreigners Copacabana was a religious shrine. Many faithful did come to pray to the huge statue of the Virgin and visit the chapels and cathedrals along the lakeshore. But there were also romantic boat rides and noisy festivals and nightly conversations awash in wine. The San Calixto graduating class of 1963, mindful of the resort's reputation, might have been forgiven for succumbing to a holiday mood.

The two priests detailed to chaperone the forty-seven resourceful teenage boys did not detect the *singani*, a potent local wine, smuggled into the hostel and mixed with Coca-Cola. When they discovered after midnight that more than thirty of their party were incoherent or at least intoxicated, they called a meeting.

The wisest course, they and their charges agreed, was to forget the incident. Father Trías, the school director, did not have a sense of humor on the subject of alcohol. "Nobody says anything, nobody gets hurt," said Jaime Delgadillo, the class's future banker and cost-benefit analyst. The air in the bus home, thin enough at 12,000 feet, was further reduced by many pairs of lungs holding their breath.

Sure enough, one of the more excitable boys told his mother, who complained to Father Trías. The director announced he would expel thirty members of the class. The golden senior year they had dreamed of was about to come to an abrupt end. They went to see Escalante.

"So, you *llockallas* had a good time, I hear," he said. "Did you bring me some of this potion? You idiots know better than to go drinking without me."

"Don Jaime, what can we do? We want to graduate. Can't you help us?"

"You're all failing anyway, what difference does it make?"

"Really, Señor Escalante. You've had a drink on a weekend, right? Is this fair?"

"Life is often not fair, *llockalla*. What would you like me to do?"

"Could you talk to the director please? You always get what you want from Father Trías."

"And what should I say, that it is *your* livers you are poisoning? That all the parents of all the other classes will be delighted to learn that advanced drinking has been added to the curriculum?"

"We figured you would think of something."

"You don't get the point, do you? This is about growing up, about becoming responsible for your actions. All of you went up there together, right? Am I saying this right? So why are you all coming back in pieces? The naughty drinkers get expelled, the rest of you slide through, even though everybody knew what was going on. You messed up *together*. You ought to take your medicine together. *You are San Calixto 1963*. Your pictures will go up on the balcony. Your plaque may hang on the wall. Where is your pride? Are you going to let some go and the others stay?

"I'm not going to help you. You're probably beyond help. But perhaps, it's a faint hope, you can help yourselves. Are you man enough, every one of you, to tell Father Trías that if he expels any of you, *all* will leave? I'm ready to do that. I'll leave with you. Are you *all* willing to say no class pictures, no plaques, that '63 will be an empty set? Think about it, if you still remember how to do that."

Trembling, they presented the suggested ultimatum to Father Trías. After some thought, the director changed the expulsion to a three-week suspension. They could return to take their final exams. Escalante invited the miscreants to the National Bolívar school, where he taught in the afternoon. He drilled them in trigonometry and physics. They all passed. They all graduated. All their pictures went on the wall. They had stayed together.

On the verge of leaving Bolivia and a bit sour on life there, the physics teacher had not really thought the boys could carry it off. He wondered about the hidden powers of children united to achieve something they really wanted.

‖ 2 ‖

The light green Volkswagen beetle had been with Escalante nearly every day of his eighteen years in California. The manufacturer had stopped making them, and parts were sometimes hard to find, but he refused to sell it. He drove it to his job at Garfield High School in Los Angeles and each Saturday to special classes at the University of Southern California. He taught mathematics to disadvantaged high school students, mostly Latino, the children of East LA.

Sometimes he would give one or two of his favorites a ride to USC. The first time Elsa Bolado stepped into the ancient VW for a Saturday ride she had the look of someone at a fear-of-flying seminar. "Are you going to drive this on the freeway, Kimo?" she asked, using the nickname given him by his students.

"Sure," Escalante said.

She smiled with sweet tenderness. "There is a better route, you know? Just take Atlantic down to Olympic, Olympic over to Figueroa, down Figueroa and you're there. Let's try it!" That way, the little car would rarely get near a highway ramp and never be forced to go faster than thirty-five miles per hour.

After the USC sessions, his Garfield group liked to stroll around the campus. They played Frisbee and soaked up the sight of trees and lawn and large brick buildings full of books. It was a place where they thought they might like to live and learn someday.

In 1979 Escalante had begun to prepare a few Garfield students for the Advanced Placement calculus examination, a test so difficult that fewer than 2 percent of American high school students ever attempted it. Students who passed an AP exam in calculus or any other subject earned college credit—saving time and money—at most of the nation's universities.

The first three years his students had done well, but there were very few of them. Now he had eighteen in his calculus class—a respectable number by the standards of nearly any high school. He wanted them to prove that Mexican American children with fathers who were fourth-grade dropouts could match the best seniors at Beverly Hills High.

When the pressure of after-school classes and Saturday drills became too intense, he collected what little lunch money his students had and led small expeditions to McDonald's on Atlantic Boulevard just north of the Pomona Freeway. They shared hamburgers and drinks and Escalante sketched equations for general discussion, between arguments over his devotion to the Lakers and distaste for the Dodgers. They scribbled definite integrals and delta epsilon proofs on napkins, and checked each other's results.

When this became a weekend ritual, the manager of the fast-food store intervened. "I'm sorry, I can't sell your group any hamburgers anymore. I think you ought to go to some other place."

Martín Olvera, an emotional boy, was indignant. "What's the deal? We pay for them."

"Yeah, but you're costing me lots of customers. You buy one hamburger and then you stay here over two hours. You take the chairs, you take the table. Nobody else can use them."

Olvera and the others left quietly. The man's expression, a mixture of weariness and astonishment, was something to savor, as tasty as large fries and a Coke.

Josie Richkarday, the only junior in the calculus class, lived in a two-bedroom house with seven other people. She would return late from cheerleading practice, fiddle with her homework for a while, then fall asleep on the dining room floor, in front of the heating vent. The uncomfortable position forced her awake at two or three in the morning, at which point, in the blissfully quiet house, she studied until breakfast.

Her ulcers had not come yet, but her mother sensed this difficult schedule would cost her something. "Your first priority should be your religion, your family and friends," she told her daughter. "What good is a nice B in some class if you're in the hospital? Lay off the studies. Go have some fun."

"Mom," she said, "this is fun. I know what I'm doing."

Luis Cervantes, a long-haired senior, usually spent his free time drag racing his avocado green Impala. But in the last weeks before the AP examination he found he became slightly apprehensive if separated from his calculus text. He took the book into the bathroom. Absorbed in derivatives and limits, he sat on the toilet for more than an hour at a time. His mother did not understand such behavior. "What's the matter with you?" she said.

When Escalante heard of Cervantes's devotion, he was delighted. He had his students prancing like racehorses. Other pursuits were forgotten. When Bolado was cautioned that her running was interfering with her mathematics, she dropped track. Raúl Haro put aside his beloved trumpet for the semester. Boyfriends and girlfriends were told to keep themselves busy, and call back in a month. Escalante delivered short sermons to justify the sacrifice: "You want to make your parents proud. You want to make your school proud. Think how good it will feel if you go to college and know you did the calculus AP. It isn't everybody who can do that. Wouldn't it be great if people noticed that East LA is producing such good students?"

Escalante passed out practice sheets of "free-response" questions—the problems requiring written solutions that constituted the last half of the examination. The Educational Testing Service, which administered the examination, released each year's free-response questions after the examination was over. He had more than a decade of material to work with.

"Look, we're going to fake the test, practice like this was it, but I want you to follow the instructions exactly like I do," he said. When he was excited, his words tended to slide together. The *k*'s in words like *fake* and *like* disappeared in the lush undergrowth of his Bolivian accent. "I want you to put the question on this side of the paper, and all the information you might need to solve it over on this side, then please go to the graph and the graph has to be in this corner. Understand?

"Okay, this leads to that and that leads to the graph and if you get stuck you have the time, the calculus all going to be over here and that way the picture is clear."

He checked their work. When he found a student who had not followed his form to the last decimal point, he would yell loudly, only a few inches from the accused's ear: "*Burro!* Why I waste my time? This got to be done. You don't understand me? *This is the way you have to do it!* Not that way, *my* way."

Cervantes began waking early in the morning, his mind pulsing with mathematics. The last week before the examination he dreamed he was doing a problem and could not solve it. He awoke with the numbers still fresh in his mind and rushed to his text to find the answer. This had to be the hand of God, he thought. This question was going to be on the test, and he, forewarned, was going to ace it.

The examination was held in Room 411, a large ground-floor classroom in Garfield's creaky old yellow stucco main building. It had three long conference tables arranged in a **U** shape along three sides of the room. Andreda Pruitt, the head counselor who proctored the test, placed three or four students at each table, widely spaced on alternating sides, and assigned the few extra students to individual desks scattered in corners. The eighteen youths sat and fidgeted. They tapped their pencils against the tabletops and studied their fingernails as Pruitt read lengthy instructions written in language suitable for sixth graders.

"All right. Now please open your examinations and begin."

Eighteen pairs of hands moved swiftly to the thin white booklets. Eighteen pairs of eyes scanned the first few questions and began the methodical, Escalante-taught process of marking the easy ones with a plus and the difficult with a minus. He had instructed them to do the pluses first, return to the minuses later. He called it "playing defense." Use their time efficiently and build confidence for the most troublesome problems at the end.

Within a few minutes, the tension in the room seemed to ebb away. The rapid filling of circles on the computerized answer sheets suggested rising self-assurance. Fernando Bocanegra was usually very insecure, but this time he thought, This is hilarious, this is really funny. Bolado had been trained to use the examination book as scratch paper, but the problems were so similar to those in Escalante's recurrent drills she hardly needed to scribble at all. Cervantes did two questions and said to himself, Geez, it's exactly like he told us, *noooo* problem!

Olvera had been indulging all morning in his usual brand of fatalism. It's either going to kick my ass, he thought, or I'm going to kick its ass. Now he had no doubt. A grade of 3 would be enough to win credit for introductory calculus at nearly every college in the country, but he was going to get the top grade, a 5.

When Pruitt collected the multiple-choice section ninety minutes later, the group had slipped into a celebratory mood. Pruitt had asked that Danish rolls, milk, and orange juice be brought in. The exuberant teenagers devoured the snack and told each other how smart they were. Pruitt called time. They sat down to take the ninety-minute free-response section—the word problems.

In Room 233, his headquarters atop the mathematics and science building, Escalante passed the three hours with a queasy stomach. Was there something he had not covered? Were they really as good as he thought they were? Nobody had ever tried to pull eighteen Garfield kids through AP calculus. Was he dreaming? He missed something on the board during an Algebra 2 lecture. "Are you nervous, sir?" a boy in the back asked loudly.

"No," he said, and corrected the equation.

Another boy approached him. "Are your kids taking the test, sir?"

He resented the reminder. "Get in your seat. Don't bother me. You don't need to be concerned about that."

Shortly before 12:30 P.M., Olvera appeared in the doorway. He raised his hands above his head, signaling a touchdown. "*Kimo!* That was a piece of *cake*." Cervantes followed: "No problem, sir." They all poured in, laughing and hugging and demanding a trip to McDonald's. Jesse López, teetering on three hours' sleep, asked for the rest of the day off and was dispatched with a firm Escalante handshake. The rest piled into the teacher's Volkswagen and assorted other cars for a four-block parade up Atlantic to lunch. Everything, they told Escalante, was cool.

Perhaps now, Escalante thought, Garfield had something going. Eighteen kids in AP calculus. Maybe twenty-five next year. "We killed them, Kimo." Wasn't that what Olvera said? "We killed them." Leticia Rodríguez was going to Princeton. Raúl Haro would study engineering at Cal Poly Pomona. Aili Tapio got into Harvard, and turned it down for USC because she liked the band. *Toot toot. Oom pah.* Too much band at Garfield, but he would fix that.

When, two months later, Escalante received the telephone call from Bolado, he had difficulty understanding what she was saying. Someone said they copied? Copied what? Ralph Heiland, the teachers' union representative at Garfield, called soon after and asked Escalante to come to the school.

Escalante slid into his VW and drove down Interstate 605 from Monrovia to the Pomona Freeway and then to Garfield. He found the tall, husky Heiland in his physics laboratory. The man looked even grayer than usual. "This is wrong, Jaime," he said. "This is an outrage."

He showed Escalante a copy of a two-page letter from Antonia Rosenbaum of the Educational Testing Service of Princeton, New Jersey. It was addressed to Jesse López, one of the Garfield calculus students:

> *Dear Mr. Lopez:*
>
> *I am writing to you because the ETS Board of Review believes there is reason to question your May 1982 Advanced Placement—Math Calculus AB grades. This is a serious problem, and I would like to talk to you by telephone after you have read this letter and the enclosed pamphlet.*
>
> *The Board of Review is made up of experienced staff members responsible for determining the validity of grades that are questioned. In reviewing your grades, they found close agreement of your answers with those on another answer sheet from the same test center. Such agreement is unusual and suggests that copying occurred. The Board doubts that the grades are valid for you because of these unusual circumstances. . . .*

Of the eighteen who took the test, fourteen received the same chilling message. Officials of the ETS eventually described it as one of the largest alleged test-security violations they had ever uncovered.

17

Kimo, what does this *mean*? What are they *saying*?" Bolado, a month from her freshman year at UCLA, was crying in Escalante's classroom. She was bright and beautiful and popular. She could have gotten into college without working so hard. Nonetheless, she had given her senior year to calculus. She had dropped track. She had endured the long drives to USC each Saturday. This unexpected journey into an uncharted bureaucracy 3,000 miles away seemed to her too much to ask.

Henry Gradillas, the Garfield principal, had spent much of his military and administrative career exposing youthful deception. When Tapio and Cervantes, in great distress, came to see him, he asked the question: "So, did you cheat?" No, they both said, enraged at him.

"Do you believe that?" Cervantes said. He and his friend Olvera had decided to ignore this roadblock on their triumphant march to the University of California, Berkeley. They would be doctors, no matter what happened. The ETS could shove its test.

"We're gonna take it to court, Jaime," said Heiland. A lawyer from the Mexican American Legal Defense and Educational Fund had expressed interest. The ETS continued to send telegrams asking if anyone wanted to take a retest. But how could they do that? It had been two months since any of the fourteen accused students had opened a calculus book. Some had jobs. Some had summer school. "And if you take it," Heiland reminded them, "it will just be a confession of guilt."

Escalante called Princeton, but no one would talk to him. "I'm afraid the teacher has nothing to do with this, sir," said Rosenbaum. He had suffered for these kids. He had had the gallbladder attack. He had pushed parents and intimidated administrators and fended off Fabiola's complaints about his few hours at home and the money he could be making in electronics. And now they had blown it, and he had blown it.

Every time he stuck his neck out, someone took a swipe at it. He could not abide being called a liar, a cheat. It was as if he were a child again, his treasured chewing gum snatched away. He had tried something very new in American education. Few people thought this many teenagers from such disadvantaged homes could master calculus. Now it was going sour, just as so many other teachers had warned him.

Maybe, he thought, he should get out. He was fifty-one already. Not much time left. He could always go back to Bolivia, or get a job in electronics again. No one really appreciated what he had been doing.

No. No, no, no. He had to show his power, his *ganas*. He had something to prove.

‖ 3 ‖

The people of La Paz live in a bowl of mountains, a concave receptacle ringed by snow and eucalyptus trees. The Andes valley is so steep and symmetrical that lost children or drunks need only head downward from wherever they are, following the tug of gravity, to reach the Prado, the main boulevard at the bottom of the bowl.

Adobe houses of pink, blue, green, and yellow dot the sides of the huge natural stadium like a Sunday soccer crowd ready for a game. They play good soccer in La Paz, but the real sport has always been politics. On the last day of the year 1930, the day Jaime Escalante was born in Bolivia's capital city, another election campaign was under way to try once more to supplant another rickety military junta. The price of tin had collapsed, and the new president, Daniel Salamanca, faced disaster. Jaime's parents, Zenobio and Sara Escalante, did their best to ignore it.

They were schoolteachers, poorly paid as teachers are throughout most of the world. As Bolivians they suffered the additional disadvantage of having to accept involuntary assignment, at least for a few years, in the more remote Aymara and Quechua Indian villages.

Achacachi, astride a garbage-strewn stream on the altiplano, the high plain, and located just east of Lake Titicaca, was better than most. The three rooms they rented from a La Paz doctor were barely 100 yards from a little village plaza with shops, a church, the mayor's office, plus park benches, old cypress trees, and the usual large iron bust of Antonio José de Sucre, first president of the Republic and Simon Bolívar's close comrade-in-arms.

Medical facilities, however, were inadequate. Sara left the village

20

that year for several weeks to stay with her relatives in La Paz and, in a hospital, give birth to Jaime Alfonso Escalante Gutiérrez. He was a good baby, like his sister Olimpia. Sara returned happy to have had a son, to be followed later by another daughter and two boys.

As a child, Jaime spent much of his time devising games for himself in the dirt *patio*, the inner courtyard found in most Achacachi houses, or strolling with Sara's father, a retired teacher and amateur philosopher named José Gutiérrez. The older gentleman, slender like his daughter and tall, took his grandson out to the plaza after siesta and distracted him with word games. "How do you spell that word, Jaimito? . . . And this one?"

In return Jaime would tease one of his grandfather's enemies, another pensioner known as "The Pig." No one called him that to his face. In Bolivia, one saved such insults for one's friends. But Jaime by age five had already developed a passion for getting under people's skin, doing anything to get a reaction. "Hey, *Pig*! Piggy, Piggy, Piggy, Pig!" he shouted across the square, as his grandfather pretended not to hear.

His father was another story. Jaime had seen Zenobio hit Sara more than once, and the father's wrath also occasionally fell on his small son. Jaime had inherited some of Zenobio's energies and black moods. The boy's dark eyes clouded with distant thoughts, a soft brooding, whenever something in the family troubled him. It would be many years before he learned to strike back directly at what he considered stupid and unfair.

When he was nine, with little warning, his mother left. His father had not returned home the night before. Whether it was drink or a woman, Sara did not know, but it did not really matter anymore.

"Jaime, I'm taking Olimpia and Bertha and José to La Paz." The boy, puzzled, saw the yellow truck, with bedding looped over the sides, waiting for passengers near the square. The truck bed, guarded by plank railings, could accommodate two cows, or two dozen people. His sisters and little brother were already walking toward it. She handed him a slice of bread. "You stay here and be with your father. Tell him when he comes home." She walked resolutely to the truck and pulled herself up and in. He watched her go, his beautiful slim mother with the black hair down to her shoulders.

Zenobio eventually appeared. Father and son regarded each other, each looking confused. Zenobio discussed the situation with other relatives. After some hesitation, he gave Jaime a bus ticket to La Paz and careful directions on how to find the house of one of his mother's relatives.

Jaime sat in the bus and stared at the altiplano through the thick dust kicked up by the rear tires. Aymara women in shawls and bowler hats stacked wet mud and sod for adobe bricks. Sheep tugged at stray blades of grass near the Titicaca marshes. Flat brown desert stretched in every direction toward fuzzy distant mountains. Shirtless boys in torn pants lay on their stomachs, chewing long strands of milkweed and watching cars go by until their fathers called them to supper.

Six hours later, the bus was screeching down a hill into La Paz's mountain bowl. Jaime hopped off with a few pieces of clothing tied into a towel around his back. He walked back up the hill, remembering his father's directions. Three blocks this way, two blocks that—he concentrated on the geographic puzzle. At the end was his prize, his mother looking out of a doorway, astonished. She enfolded him tightly in her arms.

If anyone ruled Bolivia in the 1930s, it was the thin urban crust of Spanish conquistador descendants. The vast majority of Bolivian Indians, the Quechua, once known as the Incas, and the Aymara, their old adversaries, squatted on the altiplano or in the steamy eastern tropics. They had a few crops and the blessed insulation of the mud-based adobe to keep them alive. Later revolutions would pull the Indians up a little, pull much of the middle class down. But in Jaime Escalante's childhood Bolivia was two very distinct countries. He spent most of his life on the rough edge between them.

The first day he reported for elementary school in La Paz the other boys stared, and then laughed at him. He wore the long pants and long-sleeved shirt of the Aymara children. He impressed them all the same with his skill at arithmetic, as well as soccer, basketball, and particularly handball. He could perform thick-fingered magic with the small orbs of hard rubber. La Paz was a garden of delights after the simplicity of Achacachi and its single square.

When the rains came in the soggy January summer, small rivers poured down the cobblestones outside their home on Graneros Street and flooded the neighborhood *frontón*, the handball court. Jaime brooded and tried to calculate when the clouds would part so he could find some convenient excuse to leave the dark, concrete, ground-floor apartment. "May I buy you something at the store, Mama?"

"How nice, Jaime. Yes, we need a loaf of bread and one of these medicines. I will write it down. Here are the three pesos." The thin bills disappeared into his moth-eaten pants pocket.

"And, Jaime, this time don't dawdle."

He skipped down Graneros Street, turned left, and strode fifty yards toward the market a half mile away before the soft sound of rubber against concrete stopped him. He turned abruptly left and began to climb the stone steps to investigate. It was a handball game. Señor González, Jaime's friend, fired three quick corner shots to his opponent's right and left, winning a game.

"Your turn, Jaime," he said. González thought the boy had possibilities, but there was a code to games on the *frontón*. First, you had to have some money. It was not to purchase balls. Jaime made his own, with rubber stripped from old tires, cooked and molded around a small stone. He needed money for wagers, and that day he had his three pesos, and an aching desire to play. It was a dangerous combination. In another year he would be difficult to beat. But that day the three pesos disappeared quickly. Jaime walked back down to the street, thinking dark thoughts.

"Olimpia," he said to his elder sister. "You have to help me. I am dead."

She saw he was empty-handed and guessed the truth. "Where is the money, Jaime? Where is the bread, the medicine?"

"I spent it on bets at the *frontón*. Can you lend me some, please?"

"This better not happen again, ever."

"Oh, I promise," he said, smiling with relief.

"Are you sure, Jaime?"

"Yes, I'm sure," he said. "Next time I win."

Olimpia was his confessor; Bertha, his acolyte. His mother insisted he take the younger girl on many of his forays into town. In the Plaza San Francisco, a lively spot full of architectural beauty, he taught Bertha how to leap aboard the moving streetcars without the conductor's noticing. Jaime demonstrated, then Bertha tried, her pigtails bouncing, her face twisted with fear and concentration. "You *burro*! You missed. Try again." He yanked on her hair to underscore the point, a favorite pedagogical device in his later years, and pushed her toward the next car ascending the steep thoroughfare.

As he approached his teens, Jaime became absorbed in a series of engineering experiments. He built wooden vehicles to coast down steep, bumpy Graneros Street. One of the little cars tipped over and landed Bertha, his test pilot, head first in an open manhole. She pulled herself out and wept at the mud and excrement entangling her hair.

He explored the delights of electricity. Holding a small generator, he shook hands with an unsuspecting Bertha and gave her a shock she remembered years later. He stood on a metal plate that set his hair dancing straight up while his sisters screamed in terror. He set off small fires and dropped a volatile fluid on Olimpia's right foot, burning it to the bone.

Life would have been a constant joyful search for knowledge except for the occasional appearance of his father. Zenobio and Sara had reached an accommodation that required their children to tread lightly. The three eldest never called him Papa, just *he* or *him*—"Where is he?" "Don't let him see you."

Zenobio arrived one afternoon, slightly drunk, and found Jaime, then twelve, hunched over a book. "They tell me you're a good student." It was a challenge, not a compliment.

"I don't know," Jaime said. He had learned to be suspicious of any interest his father showed in him.

"Yes, yes. You're going to prove it to me. Come here." One small bulb lit the room. His father had settled in a rocking chair in a corner. "Get the newspaper," he said. "Read this headline. Every word, please."

Jaime read: "Government Opens Talks over Trade Surplus."

The man jumped out of his chair, leaned over, and slapped the boy across the forehead.

"No, no, no. That's not the way to read it. You hold the paper *this* way." He folded it, then hit the boy again. "Now read it again."

Jaime remained silent. He stared at the concrete floor.

"See? You can't read. You can't even remember. Why do they say you're so smart? You're nothing but a little *thief*. You probably cheat on your tests, too, don't you?"

"No, Father. You could ask the teacher."

"And you talk back to your father also, don't you?" The man struck the boy hard with his hand just above his left ear. "Don't you ever lie to me. It will go harder for you next time."

Sara Escalante eventually moved the family from Graneros Street to a place high on the western slope called Sopocachi. In La Paz, unlike

Hong Kong, Hollywood, and most of the other hilly cities of the world, the wealthy occupied the lowlands, the poor stayed high. The new house sat below a steep dirt road that would eventually acquire cobblestones and be christened Méndez Arcos Street. The hillsides offered grass and shrubs for the neighbors' cows and sheep to nibble. The Escalante dogs—Jalisco the dachshund, Fifi the frenetic white mongrel, and a succession of other favorites of Sara—prowled the slopes. Farmers in scattered adobe huts grew corn and *cebada*, a cattle feed, on the rugged terrain.

Visitors to the Escalante household stepped down off the road and followed an adobe wall to a red metal door. Later Sara added a second story, allowing entrance from a level closer to the road. But at the beginning it was just another hovel, lifted out of the crowded squalor of Graneros Street to the chilly, arid waste of Sopocachi.

The move meant a longer walk to school, where Jaime had acquired a reputation as a wit, raconteur, and durable street fighter. He resisted hard academic labor, except for mathematics and science, where he found new problems as hard to resist as a steaming *salteña*.

His curiosity often got the better of him. When a handball disappeared down a drainage pipe high up on a wall during one schoolyard game, Jaime climbed a makeshift ladder to reach it. In his eagerness to see what else was stuck in the crevice, he remained on the teetering perch a moment too long. The fall broke his arm and left a scar on his forehead that would never quite disappear.

When Jaime was fourteen, his mother managed to find enough money to send him to San Calixto, a prestigious Jesuit high school just up the hill from the Palacio Quemado, Bolivia's presidential palace. The Jesuits, then as now, tried to teach social concern and Christian charity to children whose families considered money and social standing a bulwark against a hostile Andean environment.

From the outside, the school presented high flat walls of plastered adobe, casting deep shadows on the narrow streets. But anyone who ventured inside discovered a hidden little world of sunny courtyards, gushing fountains, dwarf peach trees, commemorative plaques, and strategically placed basketball hoops.

To Jaime it was heaven, a place where quick wits and passion for odd corners of human knowledge could charm the priests and let them forgive his many transgressions.

The priests lived around the central courtyard of the old mansion of Andrés Santa Cruz, Bolivia's third president and the man whose gift to the Society of Jesus had given the school its start. An enormous glass roof let the sun bathe the gray decorative tile of the patio floor. Sometimes a violent hailstorm shattered several panes and sent shards whistling down past the arched columns holding up the wraparound second-floor balcony.

The school had 750 boys, scattered over two more courtyards tacked onto the west of the Santa Cruz mansion. Classrooms opened onto patios or second-floor balconies, but the windows were tiny and the air inside dark and oppressive.

Handball remained Jaime's first love. An enormous wall, 50 feet high, dominated the north end of the high school patio. If, during a break, he was playing very well, he would signal a confederate to stick a twig next to the clapper of the classroom bell to silence its ring and extend the recess.

His knotted, thick-fingered hands and supple shoulder muscles had acquired exceptional strength and speed from all his hours at the *frontón*. By the time he reached San Calixto, his reputation had inspired a number of arranged fistfights.

"Hey, Jaime, this *llockalla* out here says he can beat you," announced his aide-de-camp, the slim, thoughtful Roberto Cordero.

"Oh, I like that. That is very good. He has *ganas*, no?"

The word meant "urge" or "desire." It was an Escalante favorite. Years later it would become central to his view of what a teacher ought to encourage in a student.

"The guy's right out here," Cordero said. "I think his friends have money."

"All right. One shot. Hold my jacket, please."

His group shared food at lunch, eating off one plate. For weekend homework they convened at a member's house Saturday at 9:00 A.M. and proceeded through all the lessons, more or less completely, until 7:00 P.M., with Jaime and other specialists occasionally lecturing beside a small blackboard.

Sara had become accustomed to erratic behavior from her son. She thought he was brilliant, but far too imaginative. When her children presented their report cards, Jaime would first shuffle them back and forth. "Here is Bertha's, Mama. Here is Olimpia's. Here is mine." His quick hands, honed on the *frontón*, could switch cards when attention wavered so that a confused Sara sometimes suspected she had never really seen Jaime's card, but had two separate glances at Olimpia's.

If she found his real grades, she delivered her set speech: "I know you think you're funny. I know you like jokes. I know that. But *they're* not going to understand you. Look at this: 'Jaime talks too much.' 'Jaime likes his jokes.' This is a bad recommendation. People aren't going to say you do this because you have a good sense of humor. They're going to say this guy is not well educated. Or worse, they're going to blame me!" She would pause for dramatic effect, a trick Jaime never forgot, then focus her stare at him. "I don't want to hear anything more about it. This is the last time I'm going to sign this. Next time this happens I'm sending Uncle Arturo to school with you."

He adored puzzles, natural and man-made. He preferred to read ahead to the problems in his textbooks rather than circle around each concept like a vulture, picking at the dry carcass the instructor had dumped before him. He sat on the grassy hillside near the Sopocachi house, a textbook propped on his knees, his eyes glancing at the city far below, and worked through the problems toward the back of a book. He would set a goal. He would finish this book, and all the problems in the back, in six months. He borrowed advanced books from Olimpia, who was deep into chemistry. Invited to a friend's house, he would scour the shelves for books. "Can I take this book?" he asked a cousin who had brought him over for the afternoon. "No, no," the boy answered. "Don't touch anything. That belongs to somebody." It was physics, a new adventure for a fifteen-year-old. He slipped it inside his shirt and took it home to his hill.

In his fourth-form year at San Calixto, the equivalent of the American tenth grade, he fell under the spell of a new physics teacher from France, Father Descottes. The man was thin and gray and sarcastic, but he made magic in a laboratory with an electric motor, a set of premeasured weights, a compass, and a small pendulum. Jaime volunteered to keep the laboratory clean if he could learn more about the instruments, and borrow some of the priest's books.

Higher mathematics began less happily. Father Luke, the advanced algebra teacher, had been shoveled into the department with little preparation. He stuck to his textbook like the sailors in his Bible hugged the Mediterranean shore. If a storm pushed him into the dark seas of theory, he was lost.

"But how did you come up with that figure, sir?" Jaime asked.

"It is very clear if you refer to your notes, Escalante."

"Why is that the better solution, sir?"

"Because I say so."

Physics became Jaime's real love. A sour-tongued layman named Lincoyan Portus, his body seemingly as thin as a map of his native Chile, arrived to teach the works of Isaac Newton. Portus would begin each class with a story, usually obscene or at least in questionable taste. He would interrupt himself for snap quizzes, oral and on the spot. If the answers were not sharp, he said, "You sound like you had shit for breakfast." A good student paid attention.

"Escalante!"

"Yes, sir."

"Did you do your homework?"

"Yes, I did my homework."

"You paying attention?"

"Yes."

"Can you repeat the joke I told yesterday?"

"Certainly." And then Jaime would tell it, with embellishments he often thought improved on the original. Teachers who did not appreciate such creativity sent him out to the patio to stand with his arms extended until told he could relax. He sent one proctor into an uncontrollable rage by objecting to a twenty-peso fine for damaging a desk during a fight. "You should divide that by three, sir," Jaime said. "One who should pay is this guy here, he messed me up, and his friend over there, who was coming to help him."

"I don't think we can do that."

"You can't divide by three, sir? I can help you."

Uncle Arturo, his guardian angel, was forced to make one final appeal when Jaime was caught tossing a string of firecrackers under the gown of the school director during an impromptu graduation celebration. Uncle Arturo was a fat, balding man who won his nephew's admiration with his concern and his inexhaustible optimism. "You've got to understand," he told the director. "The kid's active. He doesn't do anything wrong. He does many things at home. He makes his own tools. He goes to the junkyard. He makes some stuff. He's a good carpenter. He just flies off the handle too quick. He's a good boy. I tell him, Anything you going to do, count to ten before you do it. I tell him, Sometimes you don't even count to one, you just explode. But at least the kid does something. That's the kind of men we need these days, don't you think, Father?"

That same year, 1948, more than 5,000 miles away on the eastern fringe of the American city of Los Angeles, a boy four years younger than Jaime was completing junior high school. He had no certificates to boast of. He was bright, but no one cared. His father, a carpenter, expected him to follow in some manual trade. He took wood shop and metal shop, basic English and mathematics. He had asthma. When it rained, he stayed home. He was as thin and frail as the European war orphans whose pictures he saw in the *Los Angeles Times*.

His doctor ruled out regular athletics, so he joined the Reserve Officers' Training Corps, the high school junior military program, to get some mild exercise. He liked its orderliness. Then he too encountered a high school science teacher who offered an alluring opportunity to clean up a laboratory, this one full of plants and small animals. Those pungent smells, plus the drumbeat ROTC drills, would become a part of his life. His name was Henry Gradillas, and in three decades he and Jaime Escalante would form a partnership—a difficult one, to be sure—to help similarly undirected or misdirected young men and women discover things within themselves they had not suspected were there.

Two blocks to the west of San Calixto, down the steep cobblestone alleys toward the Prado, lay the Palacio Quemado, the ornate residence of the president. The name meant "The Burned Palace." It had been torched in one of the many nineteenth-century uprisings. The Bolivian government never had very much power, but what it had was centered on this square. The huge white building with the four wide columns across from the palace was the Congress. On the next side was the cathedral. In the center of the square stood a statue of Pedro Domingo Murillo, the revered martyr of the aborted 1838 rebellion against Spain. Close by was the lamppost where a mob had hung President Gaulberto Villarroel in 1946 while Jaime, stunned, looked on.

A circular walk ringed the statue, giving the shoeshine boys a chance to approach anyone walking past the square. Jaime enjoyed talking to them. He came often to the square for conversation, a soda, and a *salteña*. The big knot of thick yellow pastry dough, held with a piece of thin paper, dripped hot juices and bits of onion, beef, tomato, garlic, baby peas, beans, and egg from its steaming core. Few of the other San Calixto boys cared to speak to the small, skinny shoeshiners, but Jaime joined them in discussions of the relative merits of different *salteña* stands, the fortunes of La Paz's soccer teams Bolívar and The Strongest, the weather, his and their personal handball exploits (often embroidered), and the odd people they saw come and go.

Sara frowned on this. Teachers had a bare toehold on respectability in the stratified society of La Paz. It did no good to tarnish the family reputation, and their meager financial worth, by consorting with street beggars and small merchants. Her daughters echoed her disapproval. But Jaime thought he could learn something.

He had the same attitude toward the carpenter who sublet a small room from Sara and the tailor who lived across the street. He used whatever he learned about construction and fabrics to build his own addition to the house—a room for himself off the kitchen with two little windows, adobe walls, and a tin roof. He found a way to tap in to the local power lines and shed more light on his books.

Sara took her children to 5:00 A.M. mass whenever she could. Even in chilly weather she would drag them out for the walk down the hill to the church, and then back up for breakfast. One day she could find only a single piece of stale bread in the cupboard. "Today we don't have much to eat," she said. "You divide this into four equal parts. One for Olimpia, one for Jaime, one for Bertha, one for José, one for me." Years later, her son would remember being appalled that his mother did not know how to divide properly.

Zenobio's visits grew less frequent. His moods became more violent. Rarely was he sober. Jaime realized his father was an intelligent man, but he had seen what happened to intelligence with nothing to prop it up.

One afternoon Zenobio collapsed on the couch of the little house in Sopocachi. Sara was very calm. "Here, Jaime," she said. "Here is the prescription. Go get the medicine, please."

"Yes, Mama."

They put him in a bed. He died the next day.

At the funeral, Jaime learned one more thing about his father. Zenobio had been raising a second family. There were two boys and a girl. They stood, very small and sad and somewhat frightened, in a corner of the funeral hall.

Jaime's sisters wept. He felt tears come to his eyes. This surprised him. Why would he cry for such a man? He thought about it, as he looked at his mother in her black dress. He was crying with relief. He was glad his father was dead.

4

With his father dead, and his other relatives unable or unwilling to lend him any money, Escalante put aside his dream of attending engineering school. He found some odd jobs while he thought about his future. Then, like nearly every Bolivian, he tasted a bit of revolution.

He did not tell his mother he was going. A wave of strikes and leftist uprisings in Sucre, Potosí, and other southern valley towns had forced acting president Mamerto Urriolagoitia to order a general mobilization. Escalante was nineteen. He and his friends liked the idea of an adventure, if brief and not too dangerous. When had there ever been a long war in Bolivia? The recruiter said: "Here is your uniform. You have one hour to dress and say good-bye to your family." Escalante took the bus up the hill to the house and changed. His mother was not there. He left no note. He asked a friend to drop by and tell her where he had gone.

After a few brief and inconclusive stops along the way, their battalion reached Sucre, the center of the rebellion. They joined in some desultory battles, but they were little more than observers. The rebels did not attack in force. The government army lobbed a few shells into the most suspicious parts of town, then withdrew. A few leaders were caught and imprisoned. Most of the young recruits, including Escalante and company, were discharged. They commandeered the next day's train and soon were dipping down into the mountain depression that sheltered La Paz.

It was one in the morning when the train pulled into San Francisco Station. Escalante still had his rifle, his pack, his eating utensils clanging together on chains attached to his belt. The buses did not run at that hour. He began to climb the hill to Sopocachi. If he was to face his mother, it was best that it be at night, in full gear, with his rifle in his hands.

The neighborhood was still wildly rural. He rattled up the grassy hill with all the grace of a three-year-old coming home to display a new toy. He leapt over a low fence below the house and continued on. Bertha heard the noise and looked out a small window. There was almost no light. All she could see was a dark, moving clump, a nondescript monster making horrible noises as it headed toward the house. She thought, If only Jaime were here.

She woke Sara, who took a look and reached for a shoe to throw at the invader. It came closer. Bertha screamed in terror. The monster immediately stopped, seemingly puzzled. It spoke: "I'm *Jaime*! I'm Jaime. Don't be scared!" The women felt a prickly astonishment pass over them, then shouted with delight. "Jaime is home. Jaime is *home*!"

Escalante's impulsive decision to wear every piece of military equipment he possessed, and prove he had been to war, had its desired effect. Sara went limp with relief. It was some time before she mustered the strength to pull herself off her chair and scold him. "Jaime, you didn't write one letter. You left without saying one thing to me, and all my life I sacrificed for you."

For once, he had a serious reply: "Mama, someday you're going to hear something from me. That's all I can say. I have to do things my way."

At loose ends again, Escalante met Cordero at their favorite Prado café. He bought four *salteñas* and a beer, but it did not make him any happier. "Jaime," said his friend, trying to change the mood. "You always like to work with physics and math and chemistry. Why don't you sign up at Normal Superior, become a teacher?"

"Ahhh, no. I don't want that."

"Look, it's a chance. Something to try. You can always change if you don't like it. Today they're giving the entrance test. I'm going to take it. I want to be a chem teacher. Let's both go over there."

Escalante sighed. He rarely contradicted Cordero. His friend was smart. "Okay," he said. "Can't hurt to give it one shot."

The test proved easy for two San Calixto boys. The acceptance letters arrived. They began to attend class in Normal Superior's old mansion on Campero Street, a short distance from the Prado if one had to relieve a severe thirst.

A dull brown adobe wall topped with shards of glass surrounded the little courtyard in front of the narrow lot. In the middle a fountain sent up a feeble spray from a bottle-shaped spout, with a peach tree and an old eucalyptus offering shade. The old yellow building with its Doric columns and balcony did not have enough room, and there were continual problems with the water and electricity.

Not many months after Escalante arrived, the dean complained to a group of students that he could not get the lights to work properly. Escalante volunteered to scale the roof and check the power connections. He scrambled across the steep sheets of tin like a small dust storm on the altiplano, tearing out wires, throwing away cables, cutting and splicing and . . . "Oh, Lord," said a young woman below. "He's hanging from the edge." His feet jerking in search of a foothold that was not there, Escalante eventually pulled himself back up and returned to safety. All had been fixed. The dean beamed. "You looked like a cat up there, Jaime. *El Gato*, that's you."

One of the instructors at the Normal, Umberto Bilbao, had taught one of Escalante's elementary school classes. He remembered with affection the little boy with the fiery imagination and the talent for creative mischief. During Escalante's second year at the Normal, Bilbao joined the Education Ministry and took charge of recruiting. When a physics instructor died suddenly at the American Institute, Bilbao went to the Normal for a replacement. The law required private schools to hire at least 60 percent of their teachers from the Normal. But Normal graduates qualified in physics were few. Two women in the senior class begged off; they were having enough trouble completing their requirements for graduation. Two juniors agreed to help. They suggested Escalante, already known as a self-proclaimed Einstein. Bilbao called him.

"Can you teach?"

Escalante smelled pesos. Sara could not afford to put all her children through school. "I can teach anything you want me to. No problem."

"Let's go see the principal."

The institute sat on a ridge on Landaeta Street on the far northwest slope of the city. A high adobe wall surrounded the neatly landscaped grounds first established in 1907 by an American Methodist missionary, Francis M. Harrington. Cobblestone walkways led past tall eucalyptus trees, six-foot-high hedges, and irrigated lawns—a rarity in La Paz.

Escalante had no idea where the former teacher, inaccessible in his grave, had left off. He would have to face a class of both boys and girls, an innovation of the American-educated administrators that he was not accustomed to. He had never had a course in teaching technique. He had just begun his second year at the Normal, taking the usual blend of science and mathematics. The teaching courses would not begin until the following year.

The principal, Mr. Yoder, seemed distressed at this news. "You know you must be prepared over here. You must understand both the subject matter and the students, even if this is just a temporary assignment."

"Oh, yes," Escalante said, looking at the floor. "I know all that, sir." The principal had challenged the Escalante canon, his absolute confidence in his own abilities. He gave the man a determined look. "Could I ask one favor, sir?"

"Certainly."

"Next week I am going to invite you to come to my class. But not this week, give me the one week."

He was twenty-one years old, and did not look any older than some of the high school's seniors. He had no textbook, but neither did his students. They would have to study whatever notes they took on his lectures. He assembled his own assortment of worn physics books, and the personal notes that he had kept from each San Calixto class. These were treasures as priceless as a reporter's telephone directory or a bookmaker's bet sheet.

At his first class at the American Institute he picked up a piece of chalk, large and flat and irregular in shape, and began to write on the board. Words. Diagrams. Questions. Experimental results. Years later he would wonder why any of them paid any attention. He showed them his back for most of the period, turning only two or three times to see if they had had enough. He often looked at the clock. When the time expired, he chalked up a few problems for review, said *"Hasta mañana,"* and left.

He would eventually learn that a simple show of competence would usually suffice at the beginning of a class. Years later, when he found himself in an American school system rich with textbooks, he was glad he had learned the value of teaching from his own notes. In Bolivia he never had the luxury of switching restlessly from one publisher to another, as American schools often did. He handed the material back to his students in the exact fashion he had learned it. He gave them all the shortcuts he had stumbled upon and the little pieces of insight that had helped him unravel convoluted concepts.

His class technique improved. The first day he brought a few notes. The second day, in a typical act of hubris, he brought only the class roll, a white sheet of paper with twenty-eight names. He memorized the lesson and practiced it on his walk to school. Each weekend he spent hours framing his explanations and exercises. Although his presentation was still stiff and humorless, his students listened.

The final examination was approaching. He could not absolutely control what questions they would be asked, and he found that a powerful incentive for careful teaching.

The American education system he would encounter two decades later periodically fretted over its lack of accountability. If the teachers always tested their own students, how could a parent or a college admissions officer be sure they were really prepared? In a crude way, Bolivia in the early 1950s had overcome that problem. Secondary school final examinations, although often short and limited, were nearly always given by another instructor, usually from another school.

One of the first things that would attract Escalante to the Advanced Placement examination in the United States would be its implacable objectivity—it was a test written by anonymous outsiders. He could no more control or predict its questions than he could read the mind of the examination proctor from National Bolívar who came to test his class at the American Institute. Escalante and his students became part of the same team, fighting a common foe, rather than adversaries in a war in which the teacher always had the upper hand and the students often contemplated revolt or desertion.

Four weeks before the proctor arrived, Escalante gave a practice test. More than ten of his twenty-eight students failed. He was crushed. He had poured his soul into the course. He had ignored his Normal classes. He had missed his afternoon and weekend handball games. He had stuffed as much information as he could into every spare minute.

That, he decided, was the problem. He had led the students far beyond the material the proctor would demand. He had left them weak on the basics, where the man was sure to probe. He had mentioned absolute value. He had shown them the sign for it, single vertical lines on either side of the number, but he had only explained it once and had not drilled them at all. If this got back to the Normal, he was certain he would be ruined.

He addressed the class: "Look, a lot of you are failing. We've got to do something. I want everybody to come back here at four o'clock every Tuesday and Thursday. We'll get you in shape, no?" They had come to believe he knew what he was talking about. They thought the 40 percent failure rate was their fault. They could not handle a tough teacher. Now he was offering peace. That seemed, to them, like a good bargain. Few missed the after-school sessions. When the proctor arrived to present his questions, the answers leapt out of their mouths.

If Escalante was not at school, he was usually with Roberto Cordero. For all their physical and temperamental differences, the muscular, square-jawed, often distracted Escalante versus the delicate, mustachioed, calculating Cordero, the two young men fit together well. For four straight December summers, they hiked the 328 miles to Copacabana and back.

They formed *El Piquete*, "The Group," a small core of Normal students who chose to spend their drinking time together. La Paz, the great bowl of sin and lights to rural Bolivians, was by international standards a very backward place. Shops, bars, and restaurants closed by 10:00 P.M. Young women had to be safely home not long after. If a man was to enjoy a drink with his friends, he had to do it in the afternoon. They would visit a bar, drop in at one of their parents' homes, or best of all take a bottle and picnic basket out to a remote glade. Señora Macha, the lady with the drink stand near the Normal, would supply the national beer, *Cerveza Boliviana Nacional*. They sat at one of her little tables and provided the entertainment. They serenaded many an unwilling customer with the club song:

> *We're from El Piquete*
> *and we really like to drink.*
> *You arrogant ones who abandon us,*
> *someday you'll die and stink.*

And, like most Bolivian college students, they organized their own little rebellion, inspired by thoughts of the crumbling main building of the Normal, where Escalante had risked his life to fix the wiring.

A new high school had opened in Miraflores, out on the western slope, where the lawyers and doctors and other fortunates lived. It was called the Hugo Davila School. Basketball courts graced its front yard, welcoming students to its perch on the crest of a hill. The architect, smitten by the Bauhaus masters he had met in Germany before the war, had designed a building resembling a child's pile of building blocks, sharp angles and concrete and balconies and levels so confusing that one's height from ground floor was usually a mystery.

It bothered Escalante and his friends that those high school students had so much space. Something had to be done! El Piquete discussed this informally, then met with other concerned students of the Normal. Within three days they found themselves at the head of a mob of future Bolivian teachers, caretakers of the nation's moral fiber, which dashed through the red steel gate of the Hugo Davila School and occupied all its front classrooms.

The Education Ministry officials secretly rejoiced. This kind of thing had happened before. Someone had again been kind enough to make their decisions for them. They endorsed the negotiations between the Normal invaders and the high school principal. The Hugo Davila classrooms were divided between the two schools. Escalante took over the basketball court most afternoons, but did not attend any more classes than he had in the old building.

Henry Gradillas's mother loved him. That was why she sent him to school wearing mustard plasters and several layers of sweaters. The bronchial form of asthma that weakened his lungs thrived on cold and wetness. He hated it. At Theodore Roosevelt High School in East Los Angeles in 1950, skinny boys in bulky sweaters did not win many admirers. Henry set out to change this.

He could not participate in the usual physical education courses, but he could join the Reserve Officers' Training Corps for high school students. Marching would not aggravate the asthma. It would not require him to shower in the middle of the day.

He had always liked uniforms and order and clearly defined authority. From childhood he often noticed when people were wasting time and activities were poorly organized. He never aspired to the highest positions of leadership, but he enjoyed managing a few people, like a squad or platoon.

At Roosevelt, someone put him in charge of the Red Cross overseas packages drive, and he found he was full of ideas. They had shipped only 100 boxes the year before. He thought it was because no one understood assembly lines. One of Gradillas's heroes was Henry Ford. He suggested that one girl do nothing but put the pack of needles and thread inside each box. Another girl just inserted the first-aid kits. They packed 1,000 boxes that way. The triumph led him to think more seriously about where he was going in life.

He had noticed that no one expected Roosevelt students to win top prizes in anything. It was a school of immigrants or the children of immigrants. The number of Latinos, always substantial, was about to become a majority. Yet people seemed to shrug when he talked about making the school number one in the ROTC competitions.

He knew he was not brilliant, but when he tried hard, good things happened. Before high school he fell in love with the Gilbert chemistry set an aunt had given him for Christmas. He struggled with it at first, because the instructions were difficult to understand. But gradually the secrets were revealed to him, and he delighted in each new discovery.

No one blew on this spark at school. Counselors and teachers in junior high concluded he was not very bright—he was a carpenter's son, wasn't he?—and placed him in the slower classes.

Because of his grades and his delicate health, Roosevelt High counselors also funneled him into industrial arts, wood shop, music, and basic mathematics. But they included a life science course, a biology program for slow learners. There he found something exciting.

Mr. Walcott's laboratory breathed wonders. The teacher displayed shells and myriad kinds of fish in an aquarium. He organized trips to the beach to explore the tide pools. Like Jaime Escalante at San Calixto, Henry Gradillas asked to serve as a laboratory assistant. He cleaned the Erlenmeyer flasks and beakers. He kept the chemical solutions in stock. He brought boxes of seashells back from the beach and classified each.

He had fallen hopelessly in love with science and wanted to take more chemistry and physics courses. But those were for students going to college, not industrial arts majors. He was a junior, and few people ever switched to a college preparatory course that late. The universities required too many courses that he had never taken. No one with his limited academic record could be expected to do it all in two years. They had put him in a cul-de-sac, and he wondered if he could get out.

"You know," Walcott said, "you've got to make up your mind pretty quickly. You either go on to college or you get out of school and stick with your group of friends and get a job. I thought you would be one who would go to college, but it's up to you."

Why did this decision have to come so late and be so difficult? What if someone had taken a little time and patience with him earlier? He realized that children in East Los Angeles often had more immediate problems that obscured the future. Parents lost jobs. Sickness forced absences. Sex and crime and ignorance all intruded. But if he had been pushed harder and earlier, what might have been the result?

He took a deep breath and decided to try to go to college. In his senior year he won a citywide ROTC award and a Sears scholarship offered to a few minority students. He was accepted at the University of California, Davis, one of the most distinguished agricultural schools in the country. No one he knew had ever heard of an East LA kid going to Davis.

He hauled his suitcase onto a bus leaving the teeming center of Los Angeles for a little valley town of 4,000 that smelled of cows and fresh alfalfa.

For a few days in April 1952 Escalante had one more excuse to skip classes at the Normal. There was a revolution on, perhaps the only one in the century to bring real change to Bolivia.

Víctor Paz Estenssoro's National Revolutionary Movement (MNR) took power after three days of mortar duels and rifle skirmishes. For a while the government held the heights of Miraflores, home of the Normal, but the rebels took Sopocachi. The thud of mortar shells and rattle of machine guns kept most people inside until the old regime disintegrated and Paz Estenssoro assumed control.

The MNR turned over vast tracts of the altiplano to the Indians, and nationalized the copper mines. The Escalantes suffered temporary food shortages and some long lines, but otherwise emerged unscathed. Escalante himself was not paying much attention anyway. He had his own little revolution.

His patron Bilbao had found another job for him—physics teacher at the National Bolívar school, a good public high school near the American Institute. Escalante had raised an objection: "I have no credential. I have no license to teach."

"Forget it," Bilbao said. "I'm the one who runs the show over here. I'm going to give you the job anyway. Jaime, you have to remember something. A lot of people you meet at the Normal know there isn't much else they can do but teach, and not very well at that. You don't have to teach, and it's hard to find people who don't have to teach because often they make the best teachers."

Mr. Pavón, the principal at National Bolívar, called him in. He ran a hand through his blond hair and looked hard at the young man he knew had no credential. "We've been watching you," he said. "You have a good system. You speak loudly and clearly. But you don't know how to use a blackboard."

Escalante became unusually quiet and attentive.

"It seems to me you prepare very well. You study. You prepare the lesson plan. But you don't emphasize the homework enough. You give them the exam, to be sure, but if they don't turn in the homework, you let them go."

"I do?"

"Yes. And then there's your entrance. When you go to class, make sure you are early. You wait for the students. Don't let the students wait for you. You have to be ready.

"Now last week, when I watched you take the roll, it seemed to drag on for thirty minutes." Escalante looked sheepish. "That's very bad. You should know all the students by heart." Escalante could not confess his terrible memory for names. He would have to concentrate on faces.

"Some of these things you should have learned at the Normal."

"Sir, maybe you forget. I'm only starting the third year. We haven't had that yet."

"Hmmm. Well, why don't you watch Gómez? He's an upper-division physics teacher. He has these techniques."

Escalante did, and was not impressed. The man worked his problems methodically on the board. He attempted no experiments. Escalante asked for another recommendation.

"How about that other science teacher, Tito Melcán?" Pavón said. After a few minutes watching the stout little man with the thatch of gray hair, Escalante was enthralled. Meleán had acquired a student nickname, Marshal Tito, but the Eastern European he most resembled was Count Vlad the Impaler. While lecturing, he roamed the class-room swinging a long, thick bone from the leg of some large mammal. The students believed it was human. He caressed it, bounced it off the palm of his left hand, swung it up and down as he watched a student squirm under the strain of a sudden lapse of memory.

"How many bones can you see in my face? Can't you count?"

The student froze, certain it was a trick.

"Twelve." The bone descended quickly toward the top of the boy's head. He flinched as it gave his skull a light tap.

"Fourteen, stupid! How many?"

"Fourteen."

"How many?"

"Fourteen."

If he mislaid the bone, he would carry a pointer, a very long one. "I'm talking to *you*, stupid!" The pointer would whip out, whisking past the dullard's head.

Flattered by Escalante's attention, he dispensed advice. "A teacher has to be up on every trick, Jaime. That's the only way to get the good results. Anything you produce, anything that works, stop and analyze it. If it works, use it. Save it. Study it. Analyze it. And you have to know how to tell dirty jokes to the seniors. Anything to get them to class."

At the Normal, Escalante finally had a course in teaching tech-nique. A mathematics teacher, a physics teacher, and a chemistry teacher sat in the back of a classroom and ordered Escalante to begin teaching the assigned lesson plan. After ten minutes he was ready to kill all three of them. They interrupted. They drank beer and traded jokes. They gave no sign they had even a small interest in his earnest explanations of Newton's laws until the very end. Then they shamed him.

"Escalante, we are sorry to say you cannot become a teacher."

He fought off panic. He realized he often used exaggeration himself to catch his students' attention. He smiled instead. "Why is that, sir?"

"First, the students cannot understand you the way you talk, the way you turn your back. Second, you cannot be a teacher because you show no sign of knowing how to motivate the students to learn the things you have just put on the board."

Escalante's temper began to simmer, but he knew he should re-spond only with polite questions, not bitter denials.

"You don't know how to use the board."

"You do not sit on the chair, ever. A teacher is always dynamic, moving from one place to another."

"Where did you learn to hold the book like that? No, no, in the crook of the arm. You have to do this properly, or the students will not learn."

Each day he strode off to try the new techniques, and work out his frustrations, on his own students. An unwitting teenager at National Bolívar decided, rashly, to risk a jocular response when Escalante asked him to get a new piece of chalk. "Why don't you go buy one?" the boy said. Escalante regarded him as if he were a particularly large and loathsome cockroach. "Next time I hear you say something like that, *llockalla*," Escalante said, "you'll find yourself going out and buying chalk for the whole class."

Escalante loved the word *llockalla*. He had heard it nearly every day of this life. His Grandfather José and Uncle Arturo both used it. It meant "boy" or "kid" in Aymara. If a father used it toward a favorite son, it took on a warm glow. If Escalante applied it to a pupil on his blacklist, it acquired a demeaning connotation without losing its special residue of affection. It had that taste of hope and redemption which lay at the bottom of the mounting demands Escalante began to make on his students.

Escalante's rumored dalliances with Pola Mardesich and Olga Carrafa had acquired near-legendary status. He had his favorite romantic spots—a *salteña* breakfast at the Potosí snack bar, a movie on the Prado, a Saturday picnic among the trees at Río Avajo. Strolling the markets revealed colorful expanses of beef hearts, llama fetuses, cheese wheels, tongue and liver hanging in bloody strips, tiny raisins, prunes, brown eggs in huge stacks, oranges, onions, *tuncas* (a tropical fruit), and, for medicinal purposes only, the numbing leaves of the coca plant.

When a misunderstanding or the Escalante temper or a feminine distaste for a man so absorbed in his work caused the romance with Pola to cool, Escalante would renew his friendship with Olga, and vice versa. For the first time in his life, he had money to spend and—with success at the Normal almost irrelevant—time to spend it. The college's insistence on 80 percent attendance only convinced him that he no longer needed to play by the old rules.

He might have vanished from the Normal campus altogether if he had not chanced upon Fabiola Tapia, a quiet, pretty girl with, Escalante learned, an iron backbone. A mutual friend introduced them. Cordero's new wife, Blanca, bored by Olga and Pola and sensing his interest, encouraged him. "Jaime, why do you waste time with these *chicas*? When you finish with one you start with the other one. That's no fun. Why don't you go out with this girl who is so nice and serious?"

Pola and Olga craved diversion, loud noise, and late nights. Fabiola stuck to her work. She was the eldest daughter of a family of devout evangelical Protestants, a rare and sometimes persecuted minority in Bolivia. Her father had inherited a potato farm in the valleys region east of the altiplano, but lost it to his Quechua tenants after the 1952 revolution. He had a degree from Biola, a small California Bible college, and worked as a schoolteacher while writing tracts on New Testament prophecy. No liquor was allowed in the Tapia household. With no Protestant church in the little town of Torotoro, they worshiped at the home of an uncle. Fabiola went to a La Paz high school on scholarship, but it was made clear to her she had to find an occupation that would support her. Teaching looked easy, so she enrolled at the Normal.

However strict her background, Fabiola Tapia was an extremely photogenic young woman with short dark hair and a keen appreciation of Escalante's sense of humor. Soon he was turning up regularly at the 11:00 A.M. class break—one of his rare appearances at the Normal—to bring her *salteñas*, stroll the Prado, and chat.

Fabiola found him following her around like a faithful llama of the altiplano. He was amusing, to be sure. She asked him to help her and a friend with some of their mathematics lessons. He borrowed a classroom and began to dance around in front of the blackboard, filling the empty black spaces with charts and diagrams and giving the subject a clarity she had never realized it had. This boy, she thought, had something.

He took her to the Potosí snack bar. They sampled the *salteñas* and talked about friends and family. He took her to meet the shoeshine boys at the Palacio Quemado, to applaud his best shots at the *frontón*, to meet his mother and sisters. Olimpia and Bertha were astonished that their ill-starred brother could attract such a quiet, sensible girl.

Escalante loved Fabiola. He also loved his classroom, the place where he could bring forty young minds to focus on a single point of time and space, where he could tell every joke he ever knew and dispense the insults and cuffs of a dictator who knows love is power.

One day he visited San Calixto. Someone had called at the last minute to ask him to give a final examination there. A young mathematics teacher, a fellow student he had known casually, took him aside. "Jaime, I'm supposed to see what you might think about teaching over here. We need someone in physics."

It was his dream, but it didn't seem possible. "I don't have my credential. I haven't completed the Normal."

"Yes. Well, the director told me to tell you that doesn't make any difference. We are a private school."

Escalante fulfilled his final requirement at the Normal—a mathematics course he never bothered to attend—a year after the rest of his class graduated. He did not care. It was 1954. He was only twenty-three and already teaching at San Calixto, considered along with La Salle, the German Institute, and the American Institute to be the best in La Paz. Escalante embarked on a schedule that would set his daily pattern for the rest of his life, and provide the seed of his unexpected triumphs when he moved to a country that, despite its problems, did much better providing teachers a living wage.

San Calixto began class each day at 8:30 A.M. and broke at noon. After a leisurely lunch, usually at home, students returned from 2:00 to 5:30 P.M. Other than the coat and tie required for Monday morning mass, there was no dress code. Students usually wore blue slacks or jeans, collared shirts open at the throat, tennis shoes—whatever the magazines and shop clerks said was fashionable in the United States and Europe. Escalante came to school in slacks, sports jacket, tie, and dark glasses, giving him a useful look of mystery and menace. On cold winter mornings in August he would add a sweater or sweater vest underneath the coat.

After mornings at San Calixto and afternoons at National Bolívar, he taught a late class at the Commercial High School, or saw tutees or instructed at a military academy night school. His reputation had spread so far that Cordero was able to get tutoring jobs posing as Escalante.

Escalante had become a minor legend, the teacher who was working at three different schools before he had even graduated from the Normal. San Calixto students had heard even more:

45

"Escalante will punch you out for one bad word."

"Did you see the size of his hands? He fought all the time when he was a student here."

"He had some trouble with the police when he was young. Nobody talks back to him."

Fear is a useful motivator, he knew, but he needed something more. It was not difficult for him to make physics or algebra clear to most of the students. He wanted a way to bring the slower, more cautious, more distracted along also. He would tell students considering a teaching career: "The most important thing is not knowing the subject. The important thing is transmitting the knowledge."

Something caught his attention. An engineering school, Major San Andreas, was sponsoring a competition in chemistry, physics, and mathematics for La Paz high school students. Escalante picked his seven best and sent them off. When none came close to winning, he was at first distressed, and then excited. The whole San Calixto curriculum, he concluded, was full of hidden weaknesses. He could use this incident to make demands and push people harder. He had a team and a game to prepare for.

Learn by doing—that seemed to work best. Each morning he wrote a problem on the board and required all students to solve it at their desks. The first to finish demonstrated his work on the board while seatmates corrected each other's papers. Escalante noted the number of incorrect answers and began the routine again with another problem. He might do several, checking the results each time, before the number of mistakes approached zero and he felt confident enough to proceed to the next lesson. If he was taking the class on an excursion to Copacabana, rather than preparing them for an examination, he would insist that they all ride the same bus, not separate taxis. All had to make the trip, or none.

Escalante assigned 50 to 100 problems a night. When Victor Bretel climbed over the school wall one morning and took a stroll up the ridge, he got 200 problems.

The teacher said many times, *"Lo mediocre no sirve.* [What is mediocre is useless.]" But if his students seemed about to break under the load, he became the genial older brother, getting up a handball game at recess, borrowing a cigarette, dispensing social advice. "I saw Abdo on the Prado Sunday," he announced. "I did not know Abdo had such bad taste in girls."

He could not remember student's real names, so he made up his own. The heaviest boy in class was always "Gordo." Jaime Delgadillo, a wiry boy with a quick temper, became "Chiuanco," a lean bird with a piercing screech. Héctor López, fated to be both fat *and* short, was "Corcho [The Cork]."

No one forgot Escalante's reputation as a street fighter. One thump of his fist into his palm usually stifled any dissent. He enjoyed pulling experimentally on a boy's cheek and suggesting loudly that the *llock-alla* needed a new head. Once a difficult student himself, he knew where the emotional fires burned and how to put them out. "You have entered San Calixto," he told wrongdoers, "but San Calixto has not entered you."

The Major San Andreas science and mathematics contest became his obsession. "You have to study, *llockalla*. I have picked you for the team and I never make a mistake. We are going to win." He heaped scorn on San Calixto's prestigious rival, La Salle: "The person who knows, knows. The person who doesn't know comes from La Salle." His team won the second year they tried. He never saw them lose again.

Fabiola, in long white gown, and Jaime, in black suit, married November 25, 1954, in Cochabamba, the largest city in the valleys. Fabiola's parents initially opposed her marrying a Roman Catholic, even a nominal one, but Escalante went to Cochabamba early and won over his future mother-in-law. He was charming, and he promised to accept baptism as an *Evangelista*, something, his wife noted three decades later, he never got around to. A hundred guests, mostly family of the bride, attended the service at the Calama Street Baptist Church. The couple spent a quiet three-day honeymoon in the drab altiplano city of Oruro before moving into their little rented house a half block from Escalante's mother.

Fabiola rejoiced at the birth of Jaime Jr. the next year, but other aspects of life with Jaime Sr. troubled her. Escalante had never let his few social vices interfere with his work, but the fact that he drank any alcohol at all pained Fabiola. He was an engaging personality with many friends and admirers. Party invitations rolled in—for a few beers and a game of *cacho* at the Corderos, for the Christmas party thrown by wealthy parents of his students, for drinks and *salteñas* with the San Calixto faculty. The dark glasses he usually wore around town sometimes hid the effects of a late party.

Fabiola permitted no alcohol in the house and did little entertaining there. The baby and her own strict moral code kept her from joining Escalante in his social whirl. Often she did not know where he was. She cried. They argued. His mother, living so near, heard of his absences and threatened to send Fabiola back to Cochabamba if he did not behave. He begged Fabiola's forgiveness, and promised to reform. Once she realized how soon he forgot such promises, she began to think seriously of moving to America. Her brothers, like their father before them, were going off to college in southern California. That seemed to her a way to separate Jaime from all this unholy congeniality.

Bolivian secondary school examinations usually were oral, a few questions from the visiting proctor to each student in turn while the others listened and prayed for mercy. Escalante loved the drama and the chance to expose the failings of rival institutions. "The Cat," as students called him, inspired terror. He was heard to say, after his questions bloodied a classroom full of physics students, that he should flunk the teacher. When he gave a written examination, he inspected each paper briefly as it was handed in and announced loudly, "Ooooo, *muerto, muerto.* [This one is dead, this one is dead.]"

Escalante's own brothers suffered under his regime. José graduated from Don Bosco before his elder brother joined the faculty there. But Felix, the nephew Sara raised as a son, and Raúl encountered him at National Bolívar. They shared Escalante's youthful preference for sports over homework. In one climactic week Escalante flunked both of them. Raúl failed a physics examination after he ignored brotherly warnings to study. Felix took an algebra test that ended when Escalante, disgusted at the boy's performance, persuaded the regular examiner to discard a tentative passing grade.

During one examination, Escalante made the rare mistake of stepping outside the room, giving a few desperate students a chance to compare answers. Suddenly, the Cat was at the door, leaping onto a desk and shouting, "Are you copying? *Are you copying?*" He snatched papers off desks and informed the occupants, with the hyperbole he had found so useful, that their academic careers were over. It was a moment he would remember much later.

In 1960 a small group of La Salle students demonstrated in front of Escalante's house in Sopocachi shortly after their examination. Two stones were thrown. That same year a boy visited Sara Escalante in tears and pleaded for her help in reversing a failing grade he had received from her son.

"He has no reason to complain, Mama," Escalante told his mother when she brought it up. "He's just a lazy guy."

"It didn't seem that way to me. In any case, I want you to rectify the situation."

"Mama, I can't do that."

"I'm sure you can do something. He told me he would not be able to graduate if that grade stands."

"Mama . . ."

"I'm asking you, Jaimito. This is *your mother* asking you to do this."

"Uh. . . . Yes, Mama. I see, Mama. But you've got to promise me, you won't let any more of these *llockallas* in here."

California in the mid-1950s had been U.S. territory for just over a century; its Spanish and Mexican heritage went much further back. But its American leaders treated its history as little more than pleasant decoration. Its remaining Latino residents represented only 11 percent of the population. The other 89 percent would not have dreamed of demographic history reversing itself in another generation and producing an influx of young Mexican Americans who would transform the state's social, cultural, and political atmosphere.

So, when Henry Gradillas, American son of a Mexican-born mother, arrived at the University of California, Davis, in 1953, he was greeted with the warmth and curiosity usually accorded a foreign exchange student. He enjoyed his special status. Professors took him home for dinner. The ROTC program eventually put him at the head of their small corps. He plunged into the intricacies of biology and agronomy in the happy knowledge that no longer would he be handled like a thin-shelled egg, an academically disadvantaged Mexican who might break if forced to work too hard.

When he made the top-ten academic list as a freshman, Anglos from wealthy Central Valley farm families began to drop by for private tutoring. Like Escalante at the Normal, Gradillas set up a little blackboard in his room and conducted informal classes for his most desperate classmates.

On weekends he picked walnuts and tomatoes, gaining 30 pounds in the process. His asthma and bronchitis disappeared, replaced eventually by a tendency to put on more weight than he really wanted. When the army offered him a regular commission upon graduation, he took it. He hopped a plane to Fort Benning, Georgia, to take the basic infantry officers' course and then undergo ranger and airborne training. He would compete with West Point graduates and the heirs of southern military families tracing their roots back to the Mexican War.

On the obstacle course, a drill instructor kicked a wad of foul-smelling muck into Gradillas's face as he crawled on his elbows and knees. The man laughed. "You fat spic. You must be loco to think you're ranger material. Why don't you go back to Mexico, you sniveling piece of garbage?" No one had ever spoken to him like that, but he knew if he stood and hit the man, he was out of the program. Self-control was the point of the exercise.

"Did you hear me, you little greaser? I bet your mama sucks marines in Tijuana." Enraged, Gradillas began to rise to one knee just as the instructor turned his attention to another trainee, a black lieutenant. "How about you, Thorneberry? You know that your mother is an old nanny? Aunt Jemima, right?" Gradillas saw the lieutenant open his eyes wide in anger and try to stand up. Gradillas grabbed the man's waist and pulled him back down into the mud.

"Let go of me, motherfucker."

"Come on, cool off. That's what he wants you to do. Did you hear what he said about me?"

"But this is my *mother*, man."

"Just cut it, just cut it." To himself, Gradillas added, I'm not going to do it. I'll get that sonofabitch some other day.

By 1961 the Escalante family had attained a living standard well above the poverty of the average rural or urban Bolivian. They had a new home in Sopocachi. It was a small, comfortable duplex of three rooms with a small kitchen Escalante had built himself. They had bought an old blue De Soto and hired a driver who used it as a taxi when he was not taking Jaimito to school.

Escalante took his six-year-old son on weekend trips to Lake Titicaca. They rode a small boat on the placid purplish waters, ate shrimp in a roadside stand, examined the faces of foreign tourists, and felt the breeze.

Could the good life last? Escalante's students won each year's important awards, and he had more requests for tutoring work than he had time for. But the government was as unstable as ever. The economy drifted and plummeted like the falcons above La Paz's western ridge. Many of the brightest college graduates left to pursue their professions elsewhere. Within five years Che Guevara would arrive to see if Bolivia might welcome a Cuban-style revolution.

Escalante listened to Fabiola's talk of emigration but said very little. Then he was asked to spend a year in Puerto Rico in a special program for Latin American industrial arts and science teachers under the new Kennedy administration's Alliance for Progress. He went and found the courses, particularly mathematics, very interesting.

A whirlwind State Department tour of the eastern United States followed. Escalante and the other teachers saw Niagara Falls, visited the White House, shook hands with President Kennedy, attended an international conference in Pittsburgh on education, and toured a Tennessee high school's gleaming physics laboratory. Escalante wondered what it would be like to teach at such a place, with its wide tiled hallways and acres of basketball courts.

He returned home. When Fabiola again raised the question of moving to California, he had an answer. "If we have any chance to go, we will go." He did not realize how ready she was for the faintest sign of assent.

He had complained, as did every teacher in La Paz, of his ridiculously low salary and the need to work three or four jobs at once. Cordero was so disheartened he was about to take a job in the customs service. Some of the National Bolívar teachers objected to Escalante teaching both there and at San Calixto. They said he was earning salary and seniority that should be spread around. Complaints continued about difficult Escalante examinations. The Copacabana scandal, in which he had saved more than thirty San Calixto seniors from expulsion, had drained his energies and left him at odds with the school's director.

Escalante took his brothers Felix and Raúl to dinner at the Casa de España. After a few drinks he unburdened himself. "I have to leave this country," he said, his eyes wet. "I cannot progress here. Fabiola is right. My friends always call me up, have me out for a drink. I'm drinking too much. . . . I am going to succeed. I am going down there to America and I'm going to start from zero."

Within months, Fabiola had acquired the necessary immigration

51

papers and arranged for her younger brother Samuel to be their official sponsor. They decided Jaime would go first to find work and a place to live and maybe enroll in some courses. She took Jaimito to live in Cochabamba with her relatives until Jaime sent for her. They sold everything—their furniture, the car, the land on which they had planned to build a house.

Escalante asked Olimpia to iron a shirt for him. He was headed for the airport and could not bear to say good-bye to his mother. He left a note, a half sheet of white paper with block letters in green ink. Sara kept it under her pillow the rest of her life:

Querida Viejita [My Dear Old Lady]: I don't want to give you any bad moments, but I can't leave without writing these words. . . . God grant that I may return home someday to live in peace. It is my destiny to elevate the name of my family and I am optimistic that I will succeed. Dear Sarita, don't worry about your son Jaime, who always has you in his thoughts. The lessons of yesterday will be good for tomorrow. . . . Good-bye to all of you.

He shared one last beer and *salteña* with a San Calixto friend, a physical education teacher and old drinking companion, before catching a taxi. He thought of asking the man to ride with him to the airport, but discarded the idea. "I have one piece of advice for you," Escalante said as he picked up his bag. "Don't drink so much."

He boarded a Pan American DC-4 and flew north.

‖ 5 ‖

Jaime Escalante arrived at Los Angeles International Airport on an overcast Christmas Eve. He had spent two days on the Pan American milk run up the spine of Latin America—Lima, Quito, Tegucigalpa, and Mexico City. He was tired and confused and uncharacteristically quiet. Sam Tapia respectfully escorted his brother-in-law to the baggage claim and helped drag Escalante's suitcase to his 1957 Mercury.

Escalante was one of the last of 728 Bolivians to enter the United States legally in 1963. A country with only 3 million people could never provide more than a trickle of immigrants to America. Legal immigration from all of South America reached only 22,919 in 1963. From Mexico it was 55,253.

United States Immigration and Naturalization Service agents apprehended 88,612 Latin Americans, mostly Mexicans, trying to cross the border in 1963. At least that many were thought to have reached America undetected. In ten years, such numbers would seem a golden era of border peace and quiet, a leaky faucet before a Niagara.

Within eighteen months of Escalante's arrival, the U.S. Congress, at the urging of President Lyndon B. Johnson, pried open borders that had been almost locked shut to certain kinds of immigrants for nearly a half century. The immigration reforms of 1965 created relatively generous annual quotas of 20,000 immigrants a year for most countries in the world. Relatives of U.S. residents received preference on the new waiting lists.

Since the turn of the century, Asians had had few opportunities to move legally to the United States, and Latin Americans had not come in very large numbers. Now, Californians of Asian descent had won the right to bring over planeloads of relatives. Simultaneously, Mexicans bothered by a deteriorating economy began to look northward for jobs.

Since World War II the American economy, particularly in the western states, had become the most rapidly growing labor market in human history. The defense needs of the Vietnam War, the community grants of the Great Society, the spread of new electronics, education, fast-food, and fashion industries required more workers than were available, even as the children of the postwar baby boom entered the job market. The legal immigrants found themselves sucked into the job market the minute they arrived, with no need for much English or any other proven skill. Illegal immigrants, impatient for American opportunities and encouraged by low border fences and understaffed guard posts, followed their compatriots across the border in the early dawn of every southwestern desert day.

America could soak up every ounce of available human energy, but usually the greatest demand was at the low end of the scale of education and experience. For Jaime Escalante, a thirty-three-year-old physics teacher with almost no English, there seemed far less opportunity than he had hoped.

For days he just sat. Sam had recently switched from a job in a machine shop to work as a topographic draftsman for a mapping company in Los Angeles. He had chosen to live in Pasadena, a smoggy northeastern Los Angeles suburb, because rents were cheap and the local junior college—Pasadena City College—was known for offering new immigrants the secrets of American success.

The large, beige stucco buildings of PCC stood on Colorado Boulevard, route of the Tournament of Roses parade, amid assorted camera stores, luncheonettes, movie theaters, car washes, fix-it shops, and jewelers. Its daytime classes attracted ambitious young black women from northwest Pasadena bent on teaching careers, sons of factory workers from Monrovia hoping to be accountants, and a scattering of recent graduates from heavily Hispanic Alhambra High School wanting to be insurance company secretaries.

As the first key step in his adjustment to American life, Escalante had spent $2,400 of the $3,000 he had brought with him on a light green, 1964 Volkswagen beetle. He had wanted to own such a car for a long time. He did not know what else he wanted to do. Fabiola had suggested he go to Sam's school, PCC. Why didn't he pursue that degree in electrical engineering he had always talked about?

He did not want to rush it. He watched television. He learned how to operate Sam's appliances, inspecting their innards when he had a chance. He strolled around the neighborhood. Whenever Sam was there to answer his questions, he asked about the weather, the availability of Bolivian food, and the job market.

Sam lived with another Tapia brother, David, a student at Pasadena High School, in a yellow wood-frame house on Wilson Avenue. The neighborhood had been welcoming recent immigrants since the early 1950s, but so far there were only a few Latin Americans. Escalante eventually tired of the house and began to look for work. Tapia took him to a few car washes and restaurants in Pasadena. When his brother-in-law was at work, Escalante continued the search on his own. He memorized enough English phrases to explain what he was after.

At a large blue-and-white Van de Kamp's restaurant across the street from PCC, Escalante found a gnarled, sour-tempered manager, Karl Polsky, who needed someone to clean up. He gave Escalante a mop and pointed to a corner of the dirty white linoleum. Escalante mopped. He swept. He scrubbed. At closing time, 7:00 P.M., he stacked all the chairs on the tables and gave everything one last hard mopping. "See you tomorrow, Jamie," Polsky said, pleased with his pupil's progress.

By the next morning Escalante could barely move. His back felt as if it were bristling with the knife of every high school senior he had ever flunked. He slid gingerly into a chair at the kitchen table and ate his breakfast toast with the slow grinding motion of a man three times his age.

Sam Tapia could not understand how such an educated man could stoop so low. Escalante was a graduate of the Normal. He was one of the most prominent Bolivian teachers of his generation.

Tapia took Escalante over to enroll at PCC. They found the instructor responsible for handling new night school students.

"My brother, he wants to take the test," Tapia said.

"Which one?" the instructor said wearily. "Math? Physics? Chemistry?"

Tapia had recommended a subject that required as little English as possible.

"Math, please."

"Okay, now listen," the instructor said, pulling the proper sheets from a pile and speaking as he would to a six-year-old. "This test will take two hours. If you have any questions, ask them now, because I can't help you once the test begins. I am going to go back in my office there. Under *no circumstances* are you to disturb me until you're through. Tell your brother he'll have to sit over there. You can sit here and wait for him, if you want."

Escalante smiled and took his seat. He hummed softly to himself as he opened the booklet and saw what awaited him. Twenty-five minutes passed. Then, looking uncertain, he stood up and walked slowly to the instructor's office door. He motioned to Tapia and knocked.

"Damn it," the man said. "It never fails. I told you, *no questions.* It's a *two-hour test.* Tell your brother he's just going to have to sweat it out on his own."

Escalante looked as if he had been slapped. "But . . . I finished," he said.

"Sir, he said he finished," Tapia said.

The man smiled knowingly. "Yeah, right. Okay, if that's the way you want it." He fished an answer sheet from the jumble on his desk and placed Escalante's sheet beside it. His red pencil poised, ready to strike. After a minute, his expression blank, he put it down.

"Okay, chum," he said, shaking his head. "You've done all right. Perfect score."

Fabiola and Jaimito arrived in May 1964, after a series of bumpy flights and a terrifying electrical storm above Mexico City. Escalante could not meet them at the airport. He had been promoted to cook at Van de Kamp's and could not be spared. He had reorganized the menu and redone the work schedule. Polsky spoke of turning over the whole operation to him.

Fabiola did not like the Van de Kamp's job. She also did not like Pasadena. The "smoge," as she called it, choked her lungs. The people were cold and unfriendly. But this had been her idea. There was no easy way to go back to Bolivia after they had sold all they owned. She did notice, without making a point of it, that her husband was now much too busy, and had far too few friends, to spend any time drinking at parties.

Eight-year-old Jaimito liked California. He was back with his father. There was much to see and new adventures, such as giving instructions from the backseat of the Volkswagen as his mother learned to drive. But he also was homesick and spent part of every day listening to Bolivian music on his uncle's phonograph.

Sam Tapia rented his small guesthouse—a tiny bedroom, kitchen, and sitting room—to the Escalantes. They remained welcome in his house. Jaimito did his fourth-grade homework at the table in the Tapia kitchen. He consulted his English book while his mother sat at his elbow, struggling along with him.

Escalante had his own routine: days at the restaurant, nights at PCC. He ignored Fabiola's complaints about his work at Van de Kamp's. It was not the wages that bothered her so much. He was actually making more than his $100-a-week teacher's salary back in La Paz. She disliked the taint of a blue-collar job for a man with a degree and a professional reputation. To her, this job sprang from her husband's old fondness for life among the unwashed—his friendships with the shoeshine boys outside the Palacio Quemado.

"Jaime, you could get a better job if you looked," she said.

"No, no problem. This is all temporary. I am learning English. I have some courses at PCC. Now I can write to the state, send them my credential and awards, and maybe they'll have a teacher's job for me. I will tell them I've been to the White House."

In August the California Department of Education responded to his letter and documents requesting a teacher's credential. It appeared to be a form letter, correct and curt. His Bolivian education and credential were not acceptable in California. The department was sorry, but he needed proof of mastery of an American college curriculum before he could even be considered.

He opened the letter at home, during his short evening break between work and school. Rarely in his life had he felt so disheartened. If he wished to teach in America, he would have to repeat his entire college education—four years of full-time study, plus another year of graduate school to earn a teaching credential. How long would that take, going just to night school? He could not support his family and carry a full academic load. It might take a decade. In his thirties and forties, his prime years, when many teachers did their best work, he would be barred from the classroom, the one place he was certain he had something to offer his new country.

Why bother to stay? Why not go back to Bolivia? It was a small pond, compared with this place, but at least he would not be wasting his time.

"Jaime, all this means is you have no need to go back to teaching," Fabiola said. "You can go into electronics instead. You've always been interested in that. Isn't that one reason why we came to America? So you could do something different, perhaps work for NASA?"

Neither of them mentioned it, but Jaimito's rapid adjustment to America and its schools made returning home that much more difficult. As bright as the boy was, the opportunities for him back in La Paz were limited. Perhaps it was too late for Jaime, but Jaimito had all the time he needed to learn whatever he wished to learn. What a festival of choices he had! Here knowledge was handed out for practically nothing, like cheese samples at the supermarket. These Americans did not seem to appreciate what they had. Look at all that time spent watching television! The Escalantes, no matter what the state education department said, were determined for now to make the most of it.

So, thought Gradillas, what the fuck were they doing now? He had caught two men with drugs. He had had them court-martialed and sent off for six months in the stockade. A general had reduced the sentence to ten days with good behavior. What kind of army was this?

His three years in Germany had gone swiftly. He was now a training officer at Fort Jackson, South Carolina. He thought of himself as old army. He had never seen a day of combat, but he felt much closer to the World War II and Korean War veterans among the enlisted men than the management-conscious lieutenants coming out of West Point and heading, before long, to Vietnam.

He had volunteered for Southeast Asia in 1961, when few Americans understood or cared what was happening there. We'll consider you, they said. You have a good record. Now tell us, Lieutenant, what do you do if you're over there working as an adviser and you get shot at?

I go after them, he said. We hit back real hard.

Not the way it works, Gradillas. We're going in as a police action.

Well then, he replied, you sure as hell don't need Henry Airborne Ranger Gradillas. Why send me in there if you don't want to do things properly?

He had learned a great deal in the army. He had discovered that the younger enlisted men would do their best work for the pure joy of competition, such as winning the brigade inspection award from Company B. He had learned that older men, wise in the value of time, shunned such games and only excelled if offered an extra day's pass to see their wives and girlfriends.

He was proud that he could grasp the soft part of a man's throat and pull out a jugular vein. He was confident the enemy could pull out his fingernails and he would still give them only his name, rank, and serial number. He was proudest of all of learning the secret of getting men to move, at precisely the moment and the speed that you wanted them to move. And you did not do that, he knew, by letting convicted drug dealers off easy or keeping homosexuals in the service or letting soldiers pursue any interest or distraction that might prevent them from moving when you said move.

He resigned in 1963, after nearly six years in the service. He had just made captain. His future in the army seemed bright. Regulations required that a general come around to find out why he was quitting. "Sir," Gradillas told him, "when I pushed my kids in training, the people over me said, 'Ease up, Gradillas. We're not in combat.' I said, 'But we will be.' It gets you in the gut, sir. It gets you to have been trained one way, and then told to work another way. I'd rather be a civilian."

He drove home, all the way across the country, in his old brown Mercury. He hugged his mother, shook hands with his father, and sat back to relax and collect some unemployment. Who wanted a twenty-eight-year-old agronomist who knew how to kill people? He stopped at some of the scenes of his youth, including Belvedere Junior High.

While strolling the school halls, he was recognized by a former teacher who had an intriguing idea for a job. Had he ever considered teaching?

This instructor taught life science and horticulture. The school board had once had a whimsical notion that growing things might engage young people who saw only concrete and telephone poles all day. The teacher was retiring. There was no one qualified to take his place. Gradillas needed only a year at Cal State to get his credential. He looked around. These kids were only slightly younger versions of the soldiers he had trained in the army, with many of the same needs and problems.

Why not?

When he returned to teach at Belvedere a year later, and felt the breeze from the first eraser whiz by his ear, he realized that the quieter days of 1940s discipline were over. He decided to re-create them, army style. He broke the critical mass of restless adolescent energy into more manageable squads and platoons. Each student had to turn in the homework or present an excuse to his or her squad sergeant. Those who misbehaved did push-ups and pull-ups, and Gradillas awarded prizes to those who did the most.

He was beginning to enjoy it when, in early 1967, he received an offer to manage a 1,000-acre ranch and peach orchard near Marysville. It was a UC Davis graduate's dream. He took the job, which included a share of the profits, and left teaching. Still, he could not resist having weekly chats with his farm worker crew in front of a blackboard. He would ask questions: What had gone wrong that week? How could it be done better? The farmhands, mostly men born in Mexico, began to call him *"el profesor."*

Production went up. He put down a threatened strike by promising never again to hire any disloyal sonofabitch who walked out on him. He enjoyed it, but when the ranch was purchased by new owners who did not want to give him a share of the profits, he saw a good excuse to go back to East Los Angeles.

He looked into teaching again. He had had his fun, but he thought he knew where he could do the most good.

The coal black mustache, the wide shoulders, the electric white smile and easy stroll were not there at the beginning. Benjamin Soto Jiménez, by the time he was thirty-six, would unconsciously draw glances from young females all over Garfield High School. But for most of his own adolescence he was chubby and withdrawn. All he shared with his older self was a confident hand with a pen, pencil, or chalk and a reluctance to raise his voice in any situation or to speak at all when speaking was not really necessary.

He grew up in Boyle Heights and went to Roosevelt, class of '69. He did not participate in after-school sports because his mother did not like the idea. He swept out a little grocery store for a dollar an hour on Saturdays. He helped his father, a tile kiln worker, with the chores. He had strong opinions on only one subject—he did not want to fight in the Vietnam War. So he stayed in school, studying just enough to slide through his high school courses near the middle of the pack.

He took algebra in the tenth grade, failed the course, and, appalled at the idea of summer school, took it again immediately. He found, once he was actually studying, that it was not so bad. His brief outburst of academic interest produced only a C−, but its effects lingered.

In the eleventh grade he took geometry, offered by a mountain of a mathematics teacher named Robert Drake. The man stood 6 feet 5 and weighed 280 pounds. He loved everyone, and his students returned his affection. Clumsy with his great size, he once fell out of his chair in front of Jiménez's class and landed with the ripping sound of a pants seam giving way. He laughed, groaned to his feet, and laughed again. At the beginning of the course, Jiménez was enjoying the show without much emotional commitment. He did no work. He was heading for another F. But he remembered what had happened in algebra and his continuing distaste for summer school. He had little ethnic consciousness then, but he began to wonder why the students of Asian descent did so much better than his fellow Hispanics. They couldn't be that much smarter.

He returned to the extraordinary device of his algebra year: He studied. At midsemester he began to collect A's on weekly quizzes. Drake saw the change and encouraged it with effusive praise and a huge hand enveloping the chubby youth's shoulder. In the end, he received a B, and felt he deserved an A. It was the first time he had really cared about such things. Mathematics became more than a subject in school. It was an interesting hobby, for somebody who had few personal pastimes. Some people noticed.

When Jiménez's college counselor at Roosevelt suggested that he might be eligible for some of the financial aid given to poor Latino families, he dutifully filled out the forms. He began to think he might enjoy college. At least he could see some of the world. San Francisco State, his first choice, rejected him, but Berkeley, USC, and San Diego State said yes. He chose San Diego.

The campus in the northeastern hills of that pleasant city appealed to him. He enjoyed the company of young Mexican Americans like himself from the barrios of San Diego and the Central Valley towns. But he felt homesick and under pressure. Very smart people were in his classes. Mathematics wizards, the sons of accountants and professors from places like Beverly Hills and San Marino. They spoke up in class, and spoke well. What was he doing there?

Fabiola had spoken often enough about the Van de Kamp's job to deliver the message to even Escalante's inattentive subconscious: He should find other work. He could speak English well enough, it seemed to her. People liked him. He was doing well at PCC. They could use more money. She had worked on the assembly line at the Burroughs Corp. plant in Pasadena since 1967. She saw plenty of technicians there who knew less than her husband did about electronics. The parts for the big business computers plopped off the line every day, often with little bugs that sometimes took their technicians weeks to fix. She had never seen any electronic or mechanical device that her husband could not repair. Why did he insist on being a cook?

Her campaign proceeded quietly and steadily. She enlisted Sam and Jaimito:

"You don't deal with people directly enough at Van de Kamp's, Jaime. Your English will never improve that way."

"Papa, doesn't the work at Burroughs apply more directly to what you're learning at PCC?"

"Probably more room for advancement at Burroughs, Jaime."

He acquiesced. He went to their personnel office. He filled out a form and took their placement test in mathematics and electronics. "We'll call you," a woman said. He smiled. He was off the hook. When Americans said "We'll call you," that meant "Forget about it." He had learned that English idiom very early.

As if to prove he still needed work on the language, they called the next morning. "Mr. Escalante, you got one hundred percent on our mathematics test. What do you do now?"

"I'm the head cook at Van de Kamp's."

"And what about school?"

"I'm about to get a double AA [two-year associate of arts degree] at PCC in math and physics."

"Well, we'd like to see you. We have an opening in the parts department." Counting the frequent overtime that often pushed his wages as a cook over $200 a week, Escalante would have to take a pay cut to work for Burroughs, but Fabiola now held the moral high ground. He took the job.

For a few weeks he sat in the supply room, answering orders from the line. "We need two more flying heads for the line, Jamie." "Jamie, where are those IDs?" But eventually he was touring much of the plant in his long white coat and white cap, advising the engineers on little trouble spots, suggesting new circuit designs.

If asked, as they often were, why they came to America, the Escalantes always had an answer, although not always the same one. Jaime wanted to be an engineer. Fabiola wanted to see her family. Jaime wanted to coach the Lakers.

Occasionally they gave the real answer—what kept them in California despite recurrent temptations to leave. They wanted Jaimito, and Fernando, born in 1969, to grow up in the United States because they considered it an incomparable educational supermarket.

By the time he was twelve, Jaimito was fascinated with electronics, a reflection of both his own interests and his love and respect for his father. Escalante spoke often about his work at Burroughs. He gave impromptu dinner table lectures about the circuits he brought home to experiment with.

Jaimito absorbed all this, and both his parents' excitement at the possibilities of their new life in electrified America. Jaimes Jr. and Sr. had intense discussions of oscilloscopes. The way his father described it, no work could be more wonderful or fulfilling. When Jaimito had to decide between physics or calculus his senior year of high school, Escalante examined the calculus text. "These are Mickey Mouse problems, Jaimito," he said. "I don't think you're going to get much out of this." He took physics, and went off to PCC to prepare for a career in electrical engineering.

Jaimito did well and transferred to California State Polytechnic University, Pomona, an engineering and agricultural school only 20 miles away. He lived at home, but needed little help from his father. When Jaimito took calculus, Escalante dusted off his old blackboard and showed his son a few tricks. Jaimito permitted family involvement in his senior project. Escalante examined his son's schematic and gave instructions to Fernando, age seven, who labeled each resistor with a crayon.

At Burroughs, Escalante memorized the circuit designs and pestered the engineers with questions about clumsy arrangements. He busied himself with extracurricular projects. He brooded over small inefficiencies. His supervisors liked him and praised him in the inter-office mail for his cost-cutting suggestions. In 1972 they offered him a supervisor's job in a new plant in Guadalajara, Mexico. He went down to look, then quickly came back. He did not want anything to interfere with the American education of his children. He also was about to complete his bachelor's degree at Cal State. Despite all Fabiola's dreams and plans, he was not sure he would stay with Burroughs much longer.

On an unusually chilly evening in January 1973, Escalante was buttoning his coat and picking up his books to drive home after a Thursday evening class at Cal State. He looked up to see the professor staring at him, a quizzical expression on his face.

"Could I ask you a question, Jaime?"

"Certainly, sir. I am the answer man. Ask away."

"What are you going to do with your degree?" He had been remarking on Escalante's skills in electronics. During a unit on inductions, Escalante had brought in some flying heads, the devices that funnel information from a floppy disk to the computer screen. "What do you really want to do with your math?"

"I'm gonna teach."

The teacher was surprised, and said so.

"I taught physics and I taught math back home," Escalante said. "I think I could do a better job teaching than at my job."

"But you could do a really good job in the industry. You have a real chance."

"I'm going to go teach," Escalante said, sounding as pleasant as he could. "That's what I'm going to do and I think I can do it."

Convinced, the teacher told Escalante about a National Science Foundation scholarship that might allow him to study for his credential full-time. He could be teaching in just a year!

It was time to face Fabiola.

"This is my chance," he told her. "They have to select someone. Why not me? The company isn't doing so well. There have been a lot of layoffs, you know that. They might lay me off."

Fabiola shared her husband's respect for the American educational system, but there were problems. "Jaime, you remember some of the things Jaimito used to see at Pasadena. The kids, they are not so well behaved here. You've seen things on TV, in the movies. The kids don't have any respect." She paused again, and looked at him hard. "The problems over here are not like you had in Bolivia, and you know

64

how you are, how you'd react to that. It would just mean a lot of trouble. If you try teaching, you're just going to complain a lot. You'll just make the situation worse."

Escalante strained to make himself understood. "Look, I enjoy teaching. I don't want to deal with papers anymore. That's all I do on my job. Papers, papers, more papers. Do you know what we talk about on the break? 'How is this IC?' 'Does that diagram work?' 'What about that one?' That's all we do. Our lunch break is only about thirty minutes, and the rest of the time I'm behind the computer and working and dealing with papers. That's very hard for me. I don't want to do it anymore."

She said nothing more. That was her way. They would avoid the subject. Even when she discovered his teaching would mean a pay cut, from $16,000 to $13,000 a year, she kept silent. His career was his domain. He would have his way, and Fabiola would bury her feelings. There had been sacrifices on both sides. It was too late to start adding up the columns.

To win the scholarship, he had to pass several tests. He welcomed the mathematics and physics exams like old friends. The second test, an oral examination of his views on teaching, also went well. For the third and final test, they brought in the heavy cannon—fifteen American college students placed in a classroom and told to act like unruly high school students. The five finalists were told to prepare a lesson plan in mathematics and then teach it, as well as they could, for thirty minutes.

When Escalante entered the Cal State classroom, two boys were staging a fistfight in a corner. Jaime greeted them with open arms. "You gentlemen want to fight? I think that's wonderful! Great exercise. I'm going to fight each of you after class. I was a good fighter in my country, you'll see." That was not the response they expected. They studied the robust man with the thick accent. One boy, his hair specially greased for the occasion, shouted a greeting from the back of the room: "Hey, man! What *is* your name? What *are* you going to talk about?" His accomplices tittered.

Escalante smiled. "I am Mr. Escalante. I am going to talk about math."

"Nah, that's *cold*, man. Let's talk about sex."

Escalante smiled warmly and put an equation on the board. "I'm going to talk about this," he said. He lowered his voice and winked at the boy. "We're going to talk about sex after this. After this we're going to have sex, too." Some members of the audience looked startled. "Don't worry about it. I'll take care of it. But of course you have to assign priorities. You want sex? Okay. But first we do my assignment. This is only going to take one minute."

He launched into a discussion of a shortcut to eliminate memorizing the times tables. His audience, intrigued, watched without complaint. He tried his number trick: "Take any five-digit number, subtract the sum of the digits, cross out a digit of the new number, and tell me the sum of the remaining digits. . . . What you get? You."

"Twelve," a boy said.

"Twelve? That means you crossed out a six."

The boy looked mildly astonished. "Yeah," he said, studying his paper. "That's right."

Some hands began to go up. "How did you get that?" someone asked. He led them into a discussion of the process of subtraction. Time was almost up. Escalante grinned and turned to his original interlocutor. "Now you said you wanted to talk about sex? Why not? Why don't you start? Tell us all you know on the subject." A supervisor stepped in. "Thank you, Mr. Escalante. Thanks, everyone."

A week later they told him he had the scholarship.

Ben Jiménez arrived on the sprawling campus of San Diego State University in the fall of 1969 with one strong emotion: relief. He was not going to have to dodge bullets in Vietnam, at least for four years. His Equal Opportunity Program scholarship paid many of his expenses. He planned to study mathematics and perhaps teach, like the jovial Mr. Drake. Except for a ruptured appendix that sent him crashing to the floor of his third-floor dormitory room one morning and almost took his life, the first year went well. The second year brought trouble.

By 1970, the insular, laconic mood of young Mexican Americans in East LA had shifted dramatically. Few young men spoke, as Gradillas's generation had, of accepting the cards dealt them. The civil rights movement of the 1960s set a new tone. Chicano students and teachers such as Sal Castro had staged a series of protests in the Los Angeles public schools in 1968. Many Hispanics realized that as the Mexican border turned to cheesecloth and their numbers increased, so did their political power. Latinos learned that organization brought news coverage on television and grants from foundations and the government. One of the most popular organizations for young, intellectual Hispanics was Movimiento Estudiantil Chicano de Aztlan (MECHA), the Southwest American Chicano Education Movement.

Jiménez, despite his shyness, made friends with several members of the MECHA chapter at San Diego State. He warmed to their message: Important parts of the society were judging them not as human beings and Americans, but as Mexicans. Maybe this had not hurt them individually too much. They were smart, and now attending a good school. But other Chicanos were not so fortunate.

Jiménez enjoyed feeling part of a group, this energetic, talkative MECHA bunch, even if their code of friendship seemed to include eating his food, borrowing his clothes, and driving his car on a moment's notice. But his new social life cut into his study time. By the end of his sophomore year he was in deep academic trouble, and did not know what to do about it.

That summer he worked at the tile kiln factory where his father had labored for twenty years. Young, strong, and in need of money, he put in sixteen hours a day, filling in on any understaffed shift—regular, swing, graveyard, he didn't care. He lifted and hauled and stacked and lifted some more. He learned what his father had had to do to keep his family housed and clothed and send him and his sister to college. He did not want to have to do anything like that ever again. Nor could he abide the thought of wasting the money his father earned through such physical strain.

When he returned to San Diego, a third-year student essentially repeating his second year, he found excuses to stop seeing his MECHA friends and did not return their calls. He began attending class again, and rediscovered his affection for the clean, logical progress of mathematical inquiry, where you were right or you were wrong, no matter what your ethnicity or who your friends were. He began weight lifting, played intramural soccer, and, after nearly drowning during some swimming pool horseplay, learned how to swim.

He began that third year with a 1.7 grade-point average in mathematics. By the time he graduated, in 1974, he had raised it to a 3.0 and decided that he wanted to teach.

For his student teaching, they assigned him to a San Diego junior high that was half black and half Latino. Fights broke out often, with particular bitterness when one race opposed the other. Sometimes as few as four or five students would appear for the basic mathematics class in which Jiménez assisted. Teachers issued only softcover work-books to their students; textbooks too often disappeared.

None of this discouraged him. He moved back to Los Angeles to enjoy his mother's hospitality and get his credential at Cal State, LA. He wanted to teach in East Los Angeles.

That was a place he now understood.

Gradillas was enjoying living off unemployment checks. He lay on his father's couch, watched baseball games, and savored his mother's cooking. But he could not resist stopping by Belvedere Junior High to see a few friends. That was all it took for someone to alert head-quarters. The school district's head of agricultural education tele-phoned.

"Henry? I'm just calling you on a long shot. We have a teacher who has not shown up. There's no one else there to teach the course. You seem to be right for it. It would just be temporary. You interested in going to work?"

Gradillas thought for two seconds. "Where is it?" he said.

"Washington High."

A high school, something new, he thought. "Sure thing. Let's do it."

Washington High School, a southcentral school of mostly black children, was a jaggling, noisy wreck. Controlling a classroom there required nerve and daring and physical courage. It was 1968, a year of assassinations, riots, politics, relevancy. What was his assignment? To teach horticulture. To children of the ghetto. He was also adviser to the Future Farmers of America.

He thought this was a good idea.

Still, he started badly. His students were difficult to control. He was supposed to feel sorry for these kids, right? They were black. Many were poor. Some things you had to overlook. Within two weeks his notion of himself as a gentle patron had worn very thin.

He thought about his own high school years. They had let him be free, just like these kids. He had been free to drift, to sit and not produce. If he received a C for doing nothing, so what? If he failed, who cared? So he was going to push. If he didn't, who would?

The natural advantages of teaching agriculture to city kids began to dawn on him as he watched the faces and reactions of the few students who had wandered into his course. They sought relaxation or novelty or, in some cases, actually contemplated a career in agriculture. He put the biggest boys, the potential discipline problems, to work on the Rototiller. Whoever tilled the most that week in the shortest time could paint his name on the plow.

He began to advertise. His class held big country barbecues on Fridays and invited a few football players and other social leaders to give the agriculture department a fashionable image. At the senior graduation breakfast, he presented student-made corsages to all the senior girls and flowers to their parents. He decorated other classrooms with lilies and chrysanthemums. A new French teacher from Michigan, a short, dark bundle of nervous energy named Stephanie Crum, saw this and wondered. She would later become Gradillas's wife, but at the time she thought his behavior very odd, if harmless.

Gradillas rarely left his classroom, for fear the spell its many flowers cast over his ghetto students might break. Rarely did he encounter vandalism or graffiti. He was treating young people the way he thought they ought to be treated, and it was working.

"Remember, these are the rules," he told them. "You mess up, you pay." A student who yelled at or cursed Henry Gradillas immediately found 210 pounds of pedagogical fury staring down his nose from an inch away. "Don't you *dare* raise your voice at me! I'm your teacher."

"Shit, this is the thing . . ."

"Wait a minute, I . . . *don't* . . . *want* . . . *to* . . . *hear* . . . *it*. You may talk like that to your mother or father, or somebody else, or some other teacher, but you're not going to say that to me. *Do you hear me?*"

"Hey, you're breathing on me, man. You know, get away. Dudes just don't like it. You got a lot to learn, man."

"Don't tell me about your troubles. I can tell you things about being a Chicano and the struggles. I don't want to hear it."

When they began to respond with homework assignments completed and chores done to the letter, he became fiercely protective. One day a campus security officer collared a student Gradillas had sent to open a gate. He dragged the boy back to Gradillas's room. Ignoring the teacher's explanation, he began to call the principal's office from the classroom telephone. Gradillas hesitated for a second, then ripped the instrument off the wall.

He was enjoying himself, but after four years at Washington he decided he wanted to pursue his old ambition to work in East LA.

He was still living at his mother's house, but a vacation in Mexico had convinced him and Stephanie, mother of a seven-year-old boy, that they wanted to marry and buy their own place.

He loved teaching. He thought he knew the secret. Why not use it on behalf of those Chicano kids whose troubled upbringing he had been claiming as his own?

He joined ROP, the Regional Occupational Program, one of an army of alphabetized programs that marched out of the 1960s and 1970s. This program provided money for after-hours training in special skills, such as computers or, in Gradillas's case, floriculture. He taught a class on Saturdays at Garfield High School to girls, and a few boys, interested in the flower shop business. The students, almost all Latino, seemed friendlier at the beginning than his Washington High kids had been. No one in East Los Angeles would accuse a man named Gradillas of being prejudiced.

But conditions were deteriorating. In one stairwell he was pleased to see a young artist studying a new wall mural glowing with yellows and oranges. But not far away he encountered a police officer holding a plastic bag with a few red pills and pushing two slim boys in handcuffs toward a squad car.

The police maintained a permanent outpost on campus, and as many as four or five officers were on duty at any time. Fifty percent of the student body eventually dropped out of school. Classes took ten minutes to begin, as wanderers strolled in from the halls. Dozens of radios carrying a carnival of sound blared in every corner of the campus.

He had come to school on a Friday evening in October 1971 to put a new supply of flowers in water for his Saturday morning class. He heard a band thumping loudly in the chill air, and his soldier's heart kept time with it. He was hungry. He could use a hot dog. He stood at the eastern end of the home team bleachers and watched Garfield's football team struggle with a much larger squad from a school to the west. He noticed the principal and introduced himself. It could not hurt to be recognized, if he needed a favor someday.

A noise, above and to his left, forced him to look into the stands. A gangly sixteen-year-old boy with his shirt open stood up and started yelling at someone sitting behind him. The boy took a swing at his tormentor, then hands reached for the boy and he turned and abruptly sat down.

70

Gradillas observed the scene with the professional interest of an inspector general at some other brigade's rifle drill. No one did anything, he noticed. That kid was likely to stand up again.

Within five minutes, his eye caught movement in the same spot. The boy had jumped up and taken off his jacket. He was gesturing wildly, challenging the people behind him to do something. Gradillas found himself sprinting up the bleacher steps, two at a time, past a wide-eyed principal and two teachers. He grabbed the boy, pulled him into the aisle in a hammerlock, and half-dragged the stumbling youth to ground level. A police officer was there. He had been watching the game. He gave Gradillas a look of mixed annoyance and bewilderment as the teacher brought over his captive.

"Officer, I want this kid out of here. And if he comes back, arrest him. Cuff him and arrest him. And I'll take care of him at the station. I'll call his parents."

"Uh, okay sir," the policeman said uncertainly, looking over toward the principal, who was watching quietly. The officer gripped the boy's elbow and escorted him to his squad car on the other side of the fence, then released him and told him to go home.

That summer, 1972, the principal invited Gradillas to come teach biology. Stephanie and he moved to Alhambra, five miles north of the school. Seeing Garfield every day, he began to wonder if the place did not need more than just one airborne ranger.

One student had died on campus the year before. Someone had hit him with a sharpened concrete reinforcing rod. It pierced his neck and he bled to death.

But Garfield, Gradillas thought, was not really a violent place. Most of his students were gentler than any he had ever encountered. They were no more interested in fighting than they were in anything they learned in the classroom.

The faculty, grown accustomed to their students' cheerful indolence, lived from one small victory to the next. One student managed to get into Berkeley. Another won a contest for oil paintings. Teacher morale was low, but undemanding students left a residue of energy for other things in life. Some teachers had flourishing off-campus careers in real estate and insurance. The faculty baseball and bowling leagues attracted many participants.

Some teachers still promoted the fading intellectual ferment of the 1960s. Their students did poorly on standardized tests, but there were jobs for them. What they needed most, some faculty argued, was more of a feel for their history and a pride in their heritage. How about a course in barrio politics? Chicano history? Get them interested, then they'll achieve.

Something about this train of thought bothered Gradillas. When he had attended high school at Roosevelt, he had always felt he was swimming in a flat, becalmed sea, with no wind or current to move him along. He saw what he wanted off on the horizon—science courses, college scholarships, awards, recognition—but no one seemed interested in helping him get there.

At UC Davis, and in the army, he felt like the Gulf Stream had suddenly picked him up and given his feeble strokes new power. People there expected him to perform. His roommate was as ambitious as he was.

Perhaps Garfield students could not relate to all their courses, but it had not been the curriculum that had held him back at Roosevelt. It had been the general attitude and expectations, the lack of things as insubstantial as hope and inspiration.

In his second year at Garfield, noticing only modest progress in many of his students, Gradillas decided to experiment. He did it quietly, certain he would be severely reprimanded if anyone found out. He had two basic biology classes, period 2 and period 3. Period 2 became his pet. Period 3 became his scapegoat.

He gave period 2 an initial test and, without bothering to look at the results, told them the next day: "You guys are good. I just gave you an exam and on the face of it it shows you've had some background, a little training." The Good Gradillas spread his hands grandly and grinned. "I think you're going to do a good job. You're college material. Don't worry, I'm going to work with you."

Period 3 suffered under the Bad Gradillas, a pessimist from the start. "You know, I've checked that test, and all I can conclude is that you are all very lazy, not worth a hill of beans. You're all a bunch of Latinos, and it shows. Some of those grades were the worst ever. I don't think there is any hope."

In period 2, he gave difficult tests and heavy homework. He investigated all absences and called parents when work was not turned in. Period 3 received little attention and less praise. They were told they were getting the baby course in biology, the absolute minimum, all that he could expect of them.

By the end of the first marking period, period 2 was flying high, heading toward a triumphant semester finale in which they would score high on a college-level biology test Gradillas prepared. Period 3 produced 30 percent D's and F's in the first grading period, and only one A. Both convinced and depressed by the results, Gradillas buried his negative alter ego and did his best to salvage the rest of the semester for period 3. But they were never quite the same.

It was a cruel experiment, he admitted to himself, and then he looked around and saw small versions of period 3 in many Garfield classrooms. Unlike Gradillas, these teachers had no idea of the negative impact they were having on their students.

He began to brood about the treatises on human intelligence he used to read at Davis. In the 1950s, when such research was still fashionable, anthropologists argued openly that the brains of blacks, Indians, and Latin Americans were biologically underdeveloped and that it would be centuries before they had the Anglo-Saxon's capacity to learn and create. He remembered his readings of *Mein Kampf*, loaned him by a fellow army officer.

It was all wrong, and yet the nicest people he knew acted as if they believed it. Late at night, talking to Stephanie, or with close friends, the thought would thicken his throat and make his eyes water. When you see a living kid, a human being, and somebody is going to damn him for the rest of his life because he's Latino, that sucks. That's hard. That is not the way.

You've got to say to them, Look, I know you have a problem. I know you come from someplace where education is not held in the greatest esteem. I know you come from a home that has eight or nine or ten kids. I know that your mother and father were immigrants to this country, that they live in the most poverty-stricken conditions. I know you don't have the books. I know you don't have a quiet place to study.

That's not going to mean a hill of beans to me. I'm an educator, and I should be prepared to give you those things.

Why can't we tell teachers this: We know your students have problems, but why add to those problems by not insisting that they do their homework, by not helping them, by not pushing education onto them, by not taking the role of the father and the mother and doing what the community can't do? You have children of your own. Your children know that you care. You can provide for them. They don't need this kind of push from the schools. But our kids do. It's a shame, but they do.

They're down at the 20th percentile. They cannot even breathe down there. So you have to push these kids. They do not have inferior brains. They've just lost a lot of time, and they have to be pushed.

He remembered his mother, Sara Rascón Gradillas. She never spoke English. She never had to. She could pick up a telephone and get a bilingual operator. The tax man, the meter reader, the repairman all spoke Spanish. She was never pushed. And she never became part of American society.

So Gradillas began to push.

He brought out the microscopes. In the past, students had been distributed among the biology classes based on their grades and reputations. The bottom tier, gang members, laggards, and poor English speakers, were clumped together and kept as far away as possible from expensive laboratory equipment. Gradillas brought the microscopes back into those classes, and tried some of the competitive tricks that had worked in the army. He held a contest to see who could cut the thinnest onion slice for microscope viewing. He threw out their textbook; it read like a sixth-grade health primer and did little to inspire interest in the subject. He opened a course in zoology, and looked around for more to do.

Ed Martin's parents saw nothing wrong with a career in commerce. That was how they had succeeded in America. They had come from Russia, and Martin's father had worked in the fur trade, later moving to Chicago, where he prospered with his own general store.

His small, energetic son took a degree in business at the University of Illinois and went west to Los Angeles in search of his fortune. A clothing company hired him as a manufacturer's representative. He had a company car. He had a generous expense account. He traveled to Phoenix and Las Vegas and San Francisco and met a lot of other salesmen who seemed to him caricatures of a person he did not want to be. So he quit and enrolled at Cal State, LA, to get a teaching credential.

He found he liked not having money. A trip to the movies became very special, because it took so much of his disposable income. He also loved, as he thought he would, his trial run as a student teacher. He found the students at Lincoln High School, the East LA campus where he began, warm and funny and appreciative of his needling wit and interest in all their secrets.

When a reorganization forced him to transfer to Garfield in 1970, he discovered many of the same delights. A vice principal, noting Martin's unusual involvement in student activities and student lives, suggested he try counseling. It fit him. A salesman could read a child's eyes and make a good guess as to why he was missing class, why she resisted taking a tougher course, whether he was telling the truth. A good salesman would search his mind for just the proper tone, just the right argument to steer a bright boy with immigrant parents into a series of courses that might yield a college scholarship, rather than the job in the sheet metal factory his father thought was best for him.

But even as nimble a diplomat and as persuasive a salesman as Martin could not avoid Garfield's growing difficulties. Downtown, as school district headquarters were called, was eager for a Hispanic principal at the nearly all-Hispanic school and had sent the thoughtful, vigorous principal of Belvedere Junior High, Alex Avilez. He found a faculty full of Anglo teachers with long tenures and little patience with experiments.

Avilez loved experiments. His own views on education had been forged during a decade of intense debate over the need to give Latinos, and other minorities, more pride and a sense of their importance to the community. In 1968, during the East Los Angeles "Blowouts," students and some faculty had demonstrated for more attention to the Latino heritage in every school. It was an era of concern for self-determination and respect for *La Raza*. Avilez was a part of it, and to show his good faith he even granted youth gangs special rights on campus.

That was enough to turn at least half of his faculty against him. Even more joined the opposition when, to weaken his opponents, he tried to cripple several powerful department heads by creating a new level of administration above them. Every little problem, like the "Chino, Chino" announcement, became a crisis.

The school bulletin item, a bit of crude Spanish doggerel, was intended to appeal for yearbook sales: "*Chino, Chino, Japonés*. Buy a yearbook *y no me des*. [Chinaman, Chinaman, Japanese. Buy a yearbook, and don't give me any trouble.]" Jo Ann Shiroishi, a Garfield counselor, saw it and felt slightly queasy. Ed Martin heard his friend Steve Yoshizaki grumbling at lunch over the appalling display of ignorance. They felt whoever did it would have to be disciplined.

But Avilez balked. The item was harmless, he said. It had nothing to do with the real atmosphere at the school. And so it became worse, a cause célèbre in a school heading toward a nervous breakdown, just as Jaime Escalante prepared to take his place in what he had always considered the wonderful, affluent, open-ended, tolerant American system of education.

6

By 1974, after a decade-long deluge of immigrants unlike anything since the early part of the century, scholars began to worry that a twenty-first-century American society might split apart at the seams.

In the 1950s, 59 percent of U.S. immigrants had been of European origin, compared with 22 percent Hispanic and 6 percent Asian. In the 1970s the little stream of immigrants from Latin America and East Asia surged to flood level, and the percentages reversed: Only 18 percent of 1970s immigrants were European, while 41 percent were Hispanic and 36 percent Asian.

Educators joined demographers in noting potential trouble. In 1973 Latinos had become the largest minority group in the Los Angeles public schools, edging past blacks 25.6 to 25.3 percent. In another ten years they would constitute more than half the total city school population, with all the attendant problems of cultural differences and limited skills in English. Less than 5 percent of the district's teachers in 1974 were Hispanic, and that proportion had only increased to about 10 percent when Latino children became the majority.

The Latino students were dropping out in large numbers, at a rate of up to 70 percent for those born in Latin America. Few Hispanic youths were going to college. Many universities, including the huge California state systems, made strenuous efforts to recruit Latino high school students in the early 1970s, but they remained a largely blue-collar, low-income population. The 1980 census would show that Latinos composed only 6.4 percent of all Californians aged twenty-five or older who had college degrees, a percentage less than any other major ethnic group. Unskilled work in manufacturing, one of the few sources of decent wages for Latinos without college degrees, would shrink to only 12.6 percent of the job market by the year 2000, the U.S. Bureau of Labor Statistics predicted, and be replaced by work requiring more training and academic skills.

As demographers and social critics watched hundreds of thousands of undocumented Mexicans slip across the border each year, as they saw the maternity ward of Los Angeles County General Hospital overflow with the babies of illegal immigrant mothers, they visualized an unsettling future.

The American baby boom of the 1950s and early 1960s had left a population bulge that would swell the number of retirees in the opening decades of the next century. But that same baby boom generation had been almost all Anglo and black. The younger working population of the early twenty-first century, the people whose taxes would support the swollen Social Security and Medicare rolls, would have a far higher percentage of Latinos and Asians. By the year 2030 in California they would be the majority of the working, voting population.

How would they feel, sociologists began to ask, about propping up an elderly population with which they had so little in common? Wouldn't the smallest economic mishap, a recession, a painful federal budget deficit, create desire among younger Latino taxpayers to trim benefits going to older Anglo and black retirees? What social and political conflict could result? How could a working population of young Latinos who had failed to get through college, or even high school, expect to earn enough to keep federal and private retirement and health systems intact?

First in private chats and seminars, and then in conference papers and op-ed page pieces, the social scientists and futurologists trained to sift the complex census data sketched a stark image—a twenty-first-century editorial cartoon depicting a young, slim man with black hair and brown skin, wearing jeans and workshirt, carried an elderly white woman in tennis clothes on his back.

Jaime Escalante realized from the very beginning of his job interview with the Los Angeles Unified School District that he did not know what was going on. In the rambling hillside headquarters overlooking the Hollywood Freeway they did things differently than in Bolivia.

"Where do you want to teach, Mr. Escalante?" the interviewer, a seemingly pleasant man, asked him.

"Well, . . . uh, in a school, sir, if that is all right."

"No, I mean, *exactly* where would you like to work?"

Escalante wondered if this was a trick question, one more unexpected hurdle. He threw up his hands. "Really, *any* school."

"I don't think you understand the question."

"I am sorry, sir. You are right."

The man silently pulled a map out of his desk drawer and unfolded it in front of his pupil. All Escalante saw was a hopelessly contorted maze of red, green, and yellow lines.

"What I'm asking you, Mr. Escalante. This is the Oriental community [he pointed to small enclaves dotted around the downtown area], this is the black community [a vast flat expanse of the city's southern center], this is the Anglo community [hills and valleys in the west and northwest], and this is the Chicano community [a large splotch east of downtown and some patches in the northwest]. I'm asking you, where would you like to work? You understand?"

Escalante nodded. "The Chicano, I think." He had always wanted to teach the Mexican Americans. He knew the language. He was an immigrant too. And this area was closest to Monrovia, where he lived.

The man seemed satisfied, but he had a question. "Tell me, what would you do to eliminate the graffiti over there?"

Another trick? He was an American citizen now, but many words were still a puzzle. "Can you tell me what that means, sir?"

The man explained about words and slogans spray-painted, chalked, inked, dabbed, penciled, or carved over assorted walls and items of school property.

Escalante was appalled. "I don't think I'd be able to eliminate that, sir. Because the only way to eliminate that is if you get together with the community, you get somebody to help you out, like the PTA or someone. I'm not going to be able to do that myself. I didn't know you had these things over here. I don't think that's gonna be my assignment."

The interviewer seemed as pleased with Escalante's bewilderment as with his faith in the community. "I like your idea, Mr. Escalante. I think that will do it. We'll call you. Have a nice day."

They called almost immediately. He had three schools to choose from, a junior high, Belvedere, or two senior high schools, Roosevelt and Garfield, all in East Los Angeles, all overwhelmingly Hispanic.

He visited Garfield first. He parked in front and took the concrete walkway past the worn grass littered with bright lavender petals from the towering jacaranda trees. It seemed like a nice place. Upstairs in the main building, he met the short, slim, dapper principal, Alex Avilez. Escalante found him to be a man full of enthusiasm for adolescents, the potentialities of humankind, and the need for love, kindness, and understanding. Avilez welcomed the balding teacher with the thick accent as the answer to his fondest dream.

"I see you have a lot of experience with computers," he said, leafing through Escalante's papers.

"Yessir."

"Well, I think we're going to make you a computer teacher."

Escalante asked him to repeat it, afraid that his uncertain English had deceived him.

"Computer teacher, that's right," Avilez said. "We have a new program here."

"*Wonderful.* Oh, thank you, sir. That is exactly what I want."

Escalante could not wait to put a dime in the office's pay telephone and tell Fabiola. He canceled his appointments at the other two schools and quickly drove home. There was equipment at home he could bring to demonstrate the wonders of the computer age, state of the art, as told by that phenomenal new teacher fresh from the industry, Jaime Escalante.

Whatever Escalante's hopes, the prospect of a technological revolution at James A. Garfield High School was not nearly as good as Avilez had indicated. After a half century of faithful service to a growing community of immigrants, Garfield High had worn itself down to the breaking point. A distracted collection of American teenagers, their usual adolescent resentments exacerbated by a thriving gang system, sparred with a disheartened group of teachers. Together they produced something that often resembled street theater more than education.

When Escalante returned in September 1974, he noted the graffiti that covered school walls with crude pink, brown, green, and blue gang mottoes, symbols, and musings about life. He saw debris plastered against the Cyclone fences or wedged into the hard angle where asphalt walkways hit the concrete bases of each building.

He had been called to a meeting with other mathematics teachers. At the principal's office, a dean handed him his class schedule. "Excuse me, sir. This says I teach five periods of high school math. What is that, please?"

"That's the basic math course, Mr. Escalante. Most of our new teachers start with it."

"Excuse me again, but Mr. Avilez said I would be teaching computers."

"Oh, I'm sorry. They didn't tell you? We haven't been able to get that program expanded yet. You're a math major, aren't you? So it's good you're teaching math."

Escalante frowned and walked slowly to his meeting in an adjoining building, wondering what he was going to tell Fabiola. In a large conference room he encountered a dozen teachers. A slim man with bushy hair and long sideburns was speaking. He was Michael Litvak, a renaissance man—musician, political activist, mathematics teacher. He filled his afternoons with assorted extra duties and now headed the mathematics section of Garfield's Title I program for remedial secondary education.

Known in later years as the Chapter 1 program, the Great Society legislation was the largest federal effort in support of elementary and secondary education. By 1987, in the midst of a federal budget squeeze, it would still be spending $3.9 billion in about 14,000 school districts on nearly 5 million children, most of them from low-income families. To Garfield, it meant nearly $1 million a year in federal grants.

Litvak wanted the mathematics department to introduce a new series of games and exercises designed to engage the interest of teenagers who resisted formal approaches. After a struggle, he had won over the skeptics. While Escalante watched with a puzzled expression, Litvak demonstrated how each student would cut out and measure pictures of household objects in a book. Several teachers, at his signal, began trying the puzzles themselves, while Escalante studied the high school math textbook someone had just given him.

This was high school? In Bolivia, they would have finished these problems in the fifth grade. Litvak interrupted his thoughts.

"You must be the new teacher. Mr. Escalante?"

"Yessir. At your service."

"Mr. Escalante, if you are going to learn how to use these materials, you better get going. Everybody is ahead of you."

One teacher told him that students in this school carried the multiplication tables on laminated cards for easy reference. He noticed that some of the teachers' roll books had graffiti on them.

He started home, wondering if Burroughs would take him back.

The next day the students arrived. Many of the boys pulled back their long, black hair with bandannas around their foreheads, a colorful finishing touch to a costume that usually included clean white sleeveless undershirts and tapered jeans. One youth, huskier than most, frowned severely when Escalante pulled into an empty parking spot along one school building.

"*Hey*, not there," the boy shouted. "Over here." The indicated space, between two other cars, left virtually no room for Escalante to get out of his Volkswagen once it had slithered into the spot.

"Any problem, sir?" said a young man emerging from a nearby building. He looked too old and too well dressed to be a student.

"Uh, . . . no, where is the counselors' office?" Escalante asked.

"Through those doors and upstairs," the man said.

"Thank you, sir," Escalante said. "You a teacher?"

The man produced a small, strained smile. "In a way," he said. A bottle thrown into a garbage can nearby distracted him. He turned sharply and Escalante caught a glimpse of the pistol under his coat. Now, Escalante thought, I know what you teach.

The new teacher sat bewildered in the main office for an hour before the head counselor could tell him where to find his first class. By then it was too late, so he went in search of his second-period room. A counselor would have to find him later to give him instructions for periods 3 through 6. After his initial brush with his second-period students, he wondered if there was any point in staying that long.

They had taken over Room 801. The desks had been pushed into a semicircle, and the room rattled with talk and minor scuffles. He hated to see desks rearranged without his permission, and he had never heard language like that from sixteen-year-olds in any European or Indian tongue.

He wrote his name on the board and listened, with a mixture of annoyance and despair, to his first question from a student at Garfield High School: "Hey, sir. What class is this?"

"*Sex!*" said a girl in the front row. She smiled as the class tittered. Escalante frowned, pulled out his roster, and checked off names. He was going to have to call the company and say he wanted his job back. But if he did that, Fabiola would smile and say she'd told him so. Maybe he would quit the second semester.

He tried to explain a few class rules and sketch a problem on the board. The whispers and chatter made it impossible to concentrate.

"So, sir, what is the assignment?" The question dripped with sarcasm.

Escalante scowled hard. "The assignment is sex," he said.

Two weeks into the semester, Escalante told Avilez he planned to leave by the end of the year. "No, no, no," Avilez said. "You've got to give it a chance. You're gonna love these kids."

Escalante had been the faculty vagabond, moving to another classroom every period. To pacify him, Avilez moved Anthony Critelli and his small special education class out of Room 801, a bungalow in the school's northeast corner, and moved Escalante in.

Escalante immediately invited every able-bodied student he could trust with a can of paint to come by Saturday and help bring the room up to his standards. He scraped the graffiti off the desks. He put up posters of his beloved Los Angeles Lakers on the wall.

Avilez walked in and gushed with delight. "The district is doing a good job over here," he said.

"Excuse me, sir," said Escalante. "I'm the one who painted. I'm the one who did it. Now you probably want to change the room, right?"

"No, no, no, this is nice. This is gonna be a demonstration room." Avilez stopped by several more times as Escalante added posters and painted slogans. The vice principal visited. Several teachers looked in. It's too bad, Escalante thought. I'm not going to be here next year to enjoy it.

Determined to use the time he had, he tried explaining many of his lessons in the language of sports and small business, two items of interest in East LA. He created a penny time clock—a lesson in multiplication, fractions, and the demands of the American workplace. All the students filled out time cards each day they arrived, clocked out when they left, and figured from that—at a penny an hour, time and a half for after-school work—how much he owed them.

He found that these students, like the ones he'd known in Bolivia, relished a challenge, if it was properly proposed. "I'll play you handball," he told one campus athlete. "You can choose, I use left hand or right hand. I'll give you points. You beat me, you get an A. If you don't beat me, you do this homework." The contestants and observers met at the Griffith Junior High handball court on Saturday morning, and many Saturdays after. Escalante always won, creating that much more interest in the next game.

His own challenge was to invigorate his most listless and discouraged students. He could rarely remember names, so he often called boys just "Johnny" and tried to use their backgrounds to his advantage. "The Mayans were way ahead of everybody on the concept of zero, Johnny," he said. "You *burros* have math in your blood!"

He tried to pick fights with them over dress, or tardiness, or anything that might engage their anger, and then their interest. One girl complained bitterly after a month in basic math: "I hate you and I'm going to drop the school. You bother me too much. The school's no longer fun, and you're the only teacher that bothers me."

Escalante smiled. "I see, señorita. You certainly are using a lot of makeup today. You have a contract with Dracula?"

His own choice of working clothes celebrated dullness. He always wore a long-sleeved shirt, unbuttoned at the collar with no tie. It usually came in dark gray, sometimes brown, with small monotonous geometric patterns. He wore dark slacks, usually gray or black, with a crease and a belt. He wore dark loafers and socks and left it at that. The ensemble had two purposes: require the absolute minimum of his attention and never distract his easily distracted students.

In the front row of one of his basic math classes sat María, a slim beauty with hair piled half a foot above her scalp. When in the mood, she wore nearly transparent blouses, hitched up in front to the navel. This did not help class concentration. Escalante called her to his desk. "María," he said, "you want me to bring up your grade? You know, I just look at you, the way you dress, and the most I can give you is a C."

"Sir! How can you? That's it?"

"It just makes a bad impression here."

"I'm gonna see the dean."

"Okay. That's fine. I hope you do."

The dean told her what she wanted to hear. The teacher was wrong. She was well within the student dress code. She rushed back to tell Escalante.

"Oh, certainly, he is very right. You can dress any way you like, just so it is not in my class."

Escalante resorted to bluster when he sensed defeat, but he tried to turn the dean around. "Sir, you don't understand. If I go to class and I wear a yellow tie with a white shirt, the kids going to pay attention to the things I'm wearing and not to the things I'm doing."

The dean smiled tolerantly. "I'm sorry, Mr. Escalante. I don't see it that way."

When wit and persistence did not suffice, Escalante handled the most incorrigible malcontents as he would have in Bolivia—he sent them to the principal's office. Often that produced only a note from the dean saying he had spoken to the miscreant. The note was usually delivered by the student himself, smiling angelically.

So Escalante gave up on higher-ups, with only a few exceptions. Administrators as well as teachers usually avoided him anyway. He had an almost incomprehensible accent: *math* became "moth," *kid* became "keed." He enjoyed his own brand of American idiom. "Have a nice day" seemed in his experience to mean "get the hell out of here," and he used it that way.

No one quite knew how to deal with him. Most did not try. When he approached the mathematics department chairman with a proposal for new, somewhat more challenging basic mathematics textbooks, the response was polite but quick: "I don't think these kids are going to be up to it, Jaime. It's all I can do to get my kids to sit still and add a column of figures. You've seen last year's test scores?"

"No, sir. But if we just pushed a little bit, I think we would get the big plus. Some kids will just come and watch the girls, others could do it. We would help some, sir."

"I don't think so, Jaime. Besides, there isn't really any money for more books."

"Thank you, sir. I appreciate your time."

Fabiola was right. It was time for him to fly.

Hundreds of Garfield students dropped out every year. Teachers, supervisors, and police officers assigned to campus broke up dozens of fights, often between rival gang members. Avilez wanted to give these young people a stronger feeling of attachment to the school, a confidence in him, and a willingness to put their differences aside. What he needed to do, he concluded, was make a gesture of peace, something that said he understood their point of view and would treat them as the adults they were about to become.

So he put up the *placas*, the signboards that would forever become the symbol of his short, tragically unsuccessful administration. The word in Spanish means "insignia," the official seal or logo of a specific group. At Garfield they were boards he ordered erected at various outdoor locations so that each of the major gangs could have their insignia displayed, and their own gathering point defined. All gangs were offered the privilege of registration with the school. A total of eighteen declared their official presence.

When gangs divided up sections of the cafeteria and the stairways among themselves, he acquiesced. At one point, to demonstrate his good faith in one of his endless negotiations with gang leaders over decorum and violence, Avilez gave a boy the keys to his office. He wanted all at Garfield to love each other and there to be peace. He got almost exactly the opposite.

The cafeteria, tacitly declared gang turf, became a zoo. Gang members entertained themselves by taking the tiny pads of margarine distributed with their rolls and flicking them onto the walls. They liked to see which pads would stick and which would not. Students who were not gang members avoided the cafeteria, as well as the stairways, where gangs would sit and chat. Even teachers made long detours. The *placas*, which included vivid drawings of smoking machine guns and knives dripping with blood, became not only popular gathering points but lightning rods for provocateurs from rival gangs.

At a meeting with a few other administrators in 1974, Gradillas heard a shouting match begin outside. Raucous Spanish obscenities, usually the prelude to a fight, penetrated the conference room soundproofing. "Let's go break it up," Gradillas said.

"Awww, wait a minute," one administrator suggested. "It will quiet down."

"Yeah, security will take care of it."

Gradillas moved to a window, opened it, and roared: *"Hey, . . . knock . . . it . . . off!"*

He studied his colleagues. "Doesn't this bother you? Doesn't anybody really give a damn? I mean, these kids should be in the classroom, learning. They shouldn't be out there yelling and disturbing us. I mean, they're Latinos just like you guys. This bothers the hell out of me."

"Who the hell do you think you are, Henry? These are our kids. We care every damn bit as much as you do."

"Yes, but we're allowing this decadence to go on. We're allowing the destruction of these kids."

"Well, Henry," said one man, with unmistakable sarcasm, "someday when you're principal maybe you can change things."

As the new chairman of the biology department, Gradillas had declared the 300 Building, home of most of the school's laboratories and science classes, off-limits to loiterers. He and other teachers patrolled the halls during their conference periods. They locked the doors during lunch and snack break and thirty minutes after school to limit the opportunities for mischief. Students complained of being kept from their lockers and being forced to detour around the science building in their lunchtime travels. Gradillas and company ignored them.

Other buildings still had trouble—particularly the 600 Building, off in its southeast corner, far from normal surveillance. Gradillas made the place his personal project. One day, before he could shut down for lunchtime, he heard a crash of glass on linoleum. Five boys were moving through the building with a baseball bat, carefully smashing every light fixture. Turning a corner quickly, he surprised them, grabbed the bat, and roughly ejected the group from the premises.

This, the youngsters and their parents concluded, did not fit with Principal Avilez's views on the proper handling of errant teenagers. They summoned Avilez to a meeting in the auditorium and demanded he fire Gradillas, who was, they thought, demonstrably unbalanced. Avilez asked Gradillas to come and see him.

"I'm sorry, Alex," Gradillas said, declining the offer to take a seat. "I don't want to discuss it. Whenever a band of kids is allowed to go through a building and purposely break every light they can reach, and you say nothing to them, and consider removing *me*, well, that's something I won't discuss. That's wanton destruction. It's punishable *by state code*!"

"Henry, they're kids and I'll work with them. Besides, that can be repaired. A *life* can never be repaired."

"I'm not killing them. I'm just trying to stop them."

The advisory council, a group of parents and community leaders created under Title I, complained about Gradillas's behavior, but his views had strong support among the faculty, and he was not disciplined.

Avilez, despite his differences with Gradillas, had always had a good eye for administrative talent and saw that the biology teacher had a commanding presence. He put Gradillas in charge of the counseling department for the English as a Second Language (ESL) program and the new bilingual program, the twenty-one teachers responsible for ushering a steady stream of Mexican, and sometimes Chinese and Vietnamese, immigrant children into the English-speaking world.

Gradillas agreed to take night classes at Cal State to get an administrative credential, so that no one could say Avilez was promoting unqualified Hispanics to these higher-paying jobs. The classes introduced him to the sort of people he might have to compete with for administrative plums, the principalships, the supervisory jobs, more money and power. After a week, he did not worry too much about his ability to keep up with his class. These guys, he thought, did not know the first thing about putting out a fire.

Whenever the occasion permitted, Gradillas enjoyed lobbing hypothetical hand grenades into the midst of this group of intelligent, friendly, hopelessly out-of-touch theorists.

"What would you do if a kid gave you the finger in the middle of the class?"

"Well, uh . . ."

"What would you do if a snake got loose?"

"Well, I'd ring the fire alarm bell. I'd evacuate the building."

"Then you'll be doing that every five minutes."

A visiting professor from Michigan said the best approach to a student found in the halls during class was a mild inquiry about his purpose there and an invitation to take a walk. Gradillas raised his hand. "Sir, I think the standard response to that would be, 'Hey, muthafucka, I *ain't gonna take no walk with you*. That's sumbitch, muthafucka. I'm gonna walk with you? What the hell's *wrong* with you?'"

It took two years of night school to get the credential and master's degree. Gradillas loved every second of it. He had always been good at expressing himself. He enjoyed teasing civilians, which is how he thought of these nice people from nice families and nice schools. He would never have to pay a psychiatrist if he could just continue these weekly explorations of modern educational theory, in which he could yell and pontificate and laugh and explode.

He was developing a personal theory of motivation and discipline. It had ancient origins and many names: the distraction principle, the Tom Sawyer theorem, the Shakey's corollary.

PROBLEM: Restless student Ramírez, looking for attention and diversion, loudly tapped his pencil in biology class.

WRONG SOLUTION: "Hey, Ramírez. Stop it this minute. Nobody can think straight."

RESULT: Ramírez diverted everyone's attention to himself and disrupted the educational process. He would strike again.

RIGHT SOLUTION: "Hey, Ramírez. You turned in a paper I don't believe. You got a C+ on that exam. You've never done that well. Ramírez is finally studying, he's gonna pass a few of you guys up. He keeps this up and he'll be able to come after school to clean the aquariums."

RESULT: Ramírez becomes the one distracted. He is pleased, but so confused about this development that he drops the pencil.

FOOTNOTE: In Gradillas's biology class, aquarium cleaning became a status symbol of some importance. The few earnest souls who first volunteered to help with this grimy chore discovered they were treated to a pizza at the Shakey's on Brooklyn Avenue. Word spread quickly. Aquarium cleaning became premier duty, worth reading a chapter for.

When an accreditation team from the Western Association of Schools and Colleges visited Garfield in the spring of 1975, Avilez's enemies on the faculty provided them with a vivid picture of confusion and decay. They did not speak to Escalante, who finished his first year only mildly encouraged by the reaction to his room decorations and the progress of a few of his students.

He spent the summer working at two electronics plants. He told them that he planned to be with them indefinitely, but he knew as the summer progressed that he would go back to Garfield for one last try.

He returned a day early. He set to putting his desks in their proper positions after weeks of unauthorized movement by summer classes and janitors. He considered some new posters. He sketched out a few more attention-getting class openers. Then Anthony Critelli, the special education teacher, came by for their exchange of friendly insults. This time Critelli seemed unusually quiet and distracted.

"You gone up to introduce yourself, Jaime?"

"Introduce myself to what?"

"The new principal, the new deans," he said, then saw Escalante's blank look. It was a triumphant moment. He would have the fun of delivering the news. "Jaime, where have you been? They fired *everybody*."

7

This was like Bolivia, Escalante thought. The behavior of the big shots never ceased to surprise him. Was it a revolution? Or just a purge?

Critelli explained to Escalante that Downtown had become so distressed by the unfavorable report from the accreditation team that it had transferred Avilez and every other Garfield administrator to other schools. The assistant principal, the head counselor, the deans, all were gone.

Perhaps, Escalante thought, events would proceed just as they did back home—a few promises, a headline or two, and then everything back to normal, that is, bad. Of course, he reminded himself, we *norte americanos* do some things differently.

Paul Possemato, a rail-thin native of Waterbury, Connecticut, had been installed as the new principal. He had a reputation as a troubleshooter. Downtown liked him. Unlike many of the men and women drifting through the school system's enormous bureaucracy, he always seemed to know what he wanted to do and how to do it. He sketched his ideas on legal pads and oozed self-confidence. He spoke softly and always sought out others' opinions before risking his own.

James Taylor, the deputy superintendent assigned to solve the Garfield problem, explained the situation to Possemato in late June 1975. They were walking around the collection of school office buildings on a hillside north of the Civic Center.

If Garfield did not change to the examiners' satisfaction in a year, it would become the first school in the district's history to lose its accreditation. They might even have to close it.

Possemato was annoyed. He had been about to take over Fremont High, a predominantly black school. He wanted to demonstrate the advantages of integrating administrators—a white principal for a black school, and vice versa—just as a task force of his had recommended. He was tired of cleaning up other people's messes.

Taylor emphasized that the district could not risk losing Garfield. "You've got two years," he said. "The accreditation people come back in one year to make a decision, and then if they clear you, they'll come and visit another year. Two years, and we'll make you a regional superintendent."

So Possemato went to Garfield. It would prove to be the beginning of what was probably not a revolution, as Escalante jokingly described it, but at least a change in attitude with revolutionary consequences, particularly for Jaime Escalante and his students.

One look at the campus, and Possemato knew where he had to start. The place was filthy. For two successive Saturdays he and his twelve-year-old daughter, Carla, his only child, cleaned the school rest rooms. They scoured away the paint and graffiti and other unpleasant stains.

"Why am I doing this, Daddy?" she asked.

"Because Daddy says so," he replied.

He could not be so peremptory with the rest of the Garfield community. He spent the summer listening to teachers, counselors, parents, students, community spokespersons. He said very little. It was all very depressing. He loved challenges, but everything spelled disaster. Everyone had a different villain, a different solution.

By the time Escalante discovered what was going on, Possemato had a plan, but it was going to take a good deal of improvisation. He wanted an administrative team as fresh and as free of preconceptions and previous experience as possible. He had wasted a lot of valuable time in his life trying to reeducate other administrators in the right way—his way—to do things. So he installed teachers in the key slots, people he knew or had heard of who liked action and could accept direction.

One was Henry Gradillas. Possemato had heard of Gradillas's heroics in the defense of the 600 Building. The teacher had done some administrative chores, though not enough to be caught in the great purge. Possemato needed every good Latino he could get. His file said this guy had been in the army six years. He had an eye-popping intensity, a squirt of seltzer water to make the mixture fizz. Gradillas would be dean of discipline.

Possemato brought in painters and janitors to remove the *placas* and obliterate any trace of graffiti or gang insignia. He closed the campus, locked the doors, dispatched all students to their assigned classes, and then inventoried the hordes of people who remained in the halls, on the lawn, and in the bleachers—a total of 250 nonstudents, mostly aged nineteen to twenty-five. Garfield had become their gathering point, a friendly, sunny place to meet the opposite sex, convene a gang parley, and reminisce about their own brief high school careers. All were personally escorted out and told they would be arrested if they came back. Some tested the rule, were arrested, and went off to find a café or parking lot that might serve as a new gathering place.

Doors and gates at every entrance were locked. Administrators patrolled the grounds from 7:30 A.M. to 4:00 P.M. Possemato refused to meet with gang leaders, but spread the word that he would not harass gang members if they behaved themselves. As long as they went to class, students were assured that school was a refuge, a neutral zone oblivious to neighborhood alliances. Girls were no longer allowed to sit on the front lawn. "You are the honey, girls," Possemato told them. "You only attract boys, driving by, and that means fights. We move the honey inside."

Possemato organized academic award banquets. He insisted on faculty curriculum councils to provide a clean progression of courses. He embraced any public relations device that had the slightest chance of changing the school image. He asked community artists to paint murals, with the theme of "creation," on the once graffiti-covered walls in the main building stairwells.

Skeptical teachers began to call him Saint Paul and ask if he'd spoken to the pope lately. That was fine with Possemato. Humor blunted the hard edge of power he was forced to apply to meet his deadline. He told himself, over and over: Be available, be vulnerable. He called an afternoon faculty meeting in the auditorium and for two hours absorbed bitter denunciations and complaints. One persistent comment was "You're gonna leave soon, just like all the rest."

The small cadre of teachers who had tried to start Advanced Placement and honors courses were encouraged to expand them. Honors and AP had suffered for years from a widespread belief that they were too difficult for most Latino youths. Why risk a B or C or worse, many students and parents argued, if a regular course will yield an A and catch the eye of college admissions officers?

John Bennett, who taught a small Advanced Placement American history class, and Ed Martin, now assigned to be gifted student counselor, organized field trips to the movies for their students—*Apocalypse Now* or *Zoot Suit* or Kurosawa's *Seven Samurai*. Admissions officers from local universities came to tell students that they gave extra weight to an honors course grade—even a B or C.

Possemato had heard other administrators praise Escalante for his touch with hard-to-motivate students. He had seen the spectacular decorations in Room 801. He moved Escalante to a new room, 233, in a less remote part of the campus, and coaxed him to sign a permanent contract, something Escalante had put off.

"I guarantee you are going to be here doing the job, a job that will make a difference," Possemato said. "We're impressed with you. You are really a teacher. What would you like to do?"

"I would like to teach math."

Possemato wrinkled his brow. "Isn't that what you are doing?"

"No, sir," Escalante said. "That is only high school math."

Possemato promised to give him some algebra classes. Escalante liked the idea. He had let the difficulties of making headway at Garfield become so central to his life that he was willing to bury his doubts for the moment and sign the contract. He could still leave if he wanted to.

When the principal was not available, Escalante took his problems to Gradillas, the new dean of discipline. Escalante thought Gradillas had the right instincts. All he needed was more experience.

Gradillas encountered a steady trickle of Escalante students, two or three a week, filing into his office with angry notes from their teacher. They had defaced their books. They had marked their desks. He wanted them transferred immediately, the farther away their new school was, the better.

Escalante began to patrol the halls of the 200 Building, enlisting any other teachers or teaching assistants willing to give up a break or lunch period. He chased one student who defaced a book to another classroom, then received Gradillas's permission to go in and pull him out.

Gradillas thought Escalante had the right instincts. All he needed was more perspective.

"Jaime," Gradillas said, "I just don't have time to deal with a kid that got a pencil and marked on your wall. Erase it and I'll deal with him, I'll talk to him, but how can I suspend him when I've suspended thirty-two for narcotics, marijuana, the bennies, the pills, the uppers, the downers?" He could see Escalante's deep frown. "I'm being looked at as a bad guy already for suspending so many kids in one day. Can you imagine me adding another ten or fifteen because of some writing or graffiti or because some other guy didn't bring his book? I mean, *everybody's* writing things in books."

"Not everybody, sir."

"Well, the majority of the kids are doing their *placa* things. If I can have just one less fight a day, one less kid smoking a joint, if I can have that, that to me is progress."

Gradillas had a point, Escalante acknowledged, but it would do no good to tell him that. Proctors and principals and deans, and every other supervisor he had ever encountered, moved more swiftly to help the complaining employee than the satisfied one.

He was not doing that well himself. Too many of his students were not listening and were failing. They came and went like dummies. Those few who did their homework and answered questions in class heard strange sucking noises and whispers of "*lambe*" (roughly, "boot licker") from the back of the room. He had to do something to make this material attractive, and change their attitude about learning.

For a basic mathematics class discussing fractions, he appeared in the chef's hat and white apron he had saved from Van de Kamp's. Girls giggled. A boy shouted from the back: "Lunchtime! Early lunch!" He lined several apples up on a cutting board on his desk. With a meat cleaver in his thick right hand, he pulverized one bright red fruit in a few seconds, bringing laughs and rapt attention. Then, he deftly carved the other apples into thirds, halves, fourths, and fifths.

"What you got there, Johnny?" he asked one boy, after distributing his handiwork. He received a blank look.

He tried a girl in the front row. "How much have you eaten now, Sonia?"

"A fourth, sir."

"And how much is left?"

"Three-fourths, sir."

He smiled. He pointed to another customer. "How much, Johnny?"

The boy paused and inspected his piece of fruit. "Two . . . thirds left," he said. But Escalante had already snatched and bitten into the remaining apple. "Too slow, Johnny," he said, pausing to swallow. "It is only one-half left."

Ben Jiménez, having survived his academic roller coaster ride at San Diego State, came back home to earn his teaching credential at Cal State, LA, and student teach at Lincoln, another East Los Angeles high school. The San Diego junior high where he had worked while in college wanted him back full-time, but home looked better. He applied to Roosevelt, Garfield, and some nearby junior highs. They'll call you, the lady from Downtown said.

Jiménez had grown weary of taking things as they came. Wasn't that what had lost him a year at San Diego State? He went to each school and introduced himself to the principal. Possemato thought this was an outrageous violation of protocol. He hired Jiménez, age twenty-four, immediately.

Then the new teacher met the mathematics faculty and wondered if this had been such a good idea. The mathematics department chairman showed him the books and exercises used in basic mathematics. Jiménez was appalled. The material would not have challenged a sixth grader. And no one seemed concerned.

He had his students sign a contract promising to complete all of the assigned first semester basic mathematics lessons. Within five or six weeks, some students were already finished. What was he supposed to do with them the remaining three months? He borrowed a successful basic mathematics lesson plan from a friend at Lincoln High, but received only polite evasions when he suggested Garfield try it out. That was not, in any case, his worst problem.

From his first day, Garfield students had been taking deep psychic bites out of him. He could not control his classes. Hecklers ruled. The bored, the frustrated, the otherwise disturbed gravitated, or were pushed into, the basic mathematics courses. They walked in late. They said they forgot their homework. They told jokes while Jiménez worked problems on the board. That last was the worst, for he loathed being interrupted.

With a sickening twist of his stomach, he realized all that he had

95

learned in college, plus the lectures and student teaching at Cal State, had failed to prepare him for this. As a student teacher at Lincoln, he'd had everything done for him. His supervising teacher stood by him, threatening malcontents with harsh punishment and keeping order with subtle signals that taught Jiménez nothing at all about discipline.

He had walked into a madhouse. He did not want to teach at Garfield anymore. There must be something better than this. John Howard, one of Possemato's more perceptive administrators, sensed Jiménez's unhappiness and guessed the cause. "Go talk to Escalante," he said.

What struck Jiménez when he stepped into Room 233 was how quiet it was. Students were so absorbed in their work that all he could hear was the scratch of No. 2 lead pencils and a few winter coughs. Escalante welcomed him, and they talked quietly in a corner of the room.

"Everything is so quiet here. You could hear a pin drop. I wish I could do this with my own classes."

Escalante beamed. This young man had said the magic words. "Ben," he said, "let's switch classes for the next couple of days. You take my classes over, and I'll go to your classes."

Somewhat puzzled, Jiménez agreed. When he walked into 233 the next day, it was as quiet as before. Escalante had given him the general lesson plan. He had to do very little. He handed out a quiz at the beginning of the hour, answered questions afterward, and briefly sketched a new principle on the board. He noted the homework assignment pasted into their books and went on to the next hour.

In his classroom, he learned later, life had suddenly become much more exciting.

"Mr. Jiménez asked me to come over and talk to you *burros*," Escalante announced. He stalked the aisles and paced in front of the blackboard, eyes ablaze, a stocky, balding thespian with ham-thick hands playing a mad King Lear. "I am now the boss. *Are you listening?*" He dashed down an aisle to snatch away a car magazine one student had been studying. "You are going to do what I say. If you *don't* do what I say, you gonna fly. We got all kinds of places we can send you. You won't like them. Any questions?"

The lesson proceeded, with the usual giggles and private conversations. After three guilty parties were ejected, the noise level began to subside. "So where do I go?" asked one ejectee.

"I don't care [he pronounced it "I dun care"]. Just go, fly, I don't worry about things like that. We here to learn math." He proceeded with a lesson. He assigned homework and promised a quiz the next morning.

The next day, he gleefully distributed a fistful of D's and F's on the quiz, and indicated strongly that they were lucky to have Mr. Jiménez as a teacher. "I would flunk all you *bandidos*. You're wasting my time. You're wasting Mr. Jiménez's time. He might give you one more chance. I doubt it."

When Jiménez returned, both refreshed and somewhat bored by two days within the humming Escalante machine, he found a chastened group of students. "Uh, Mr. Jiménez," said one girl, politely raising her hand. "Mr. Escalante said you were unhappy with us, and a lot of us are sorry. We were kind of rude, you know." A boy yelled from the back of the room, "Never again, sir." Nervous laughter followed.

"Thank you," said Jiménez, "I think I learned something too."

The class, he knew, would soon fall off this wagon of attentiveness and respect, but he had an idea now what to do about it.

He began to consult regularly with Escalante. He found the man engaging and entertaining, even if he did have a very high opinion of himself. There was much, of course, to back that up. When the subject of handball came up, and some students claimed Escalante was very good, Jiménez refused to believe it. The man was nearly fifty and developing a potbelly. Their match at the PCC courts ended very quickly, with shots whizzing past Jiménez's ankles like small streaks of blue smoke. Jiménez managed to get only a point or two, but Escalante was gracious about it, and the bond between them grew.

They were two American adults—Escalante seemed less Bolivian every year—with very similar opinions about the need to push American teenagers beyond their self-imposed limits. The key to Escalante's quiet classroom, as far as Jiménez could tell, was quick, harsh action at the first sign of trouble. You could wait until something happened that crossed some imaginary threshold of awfulness. That moment would come. But then it would be twice as difficult to repair the damage.

Keep them busy, Escalante said. In Bolivia, he had begun every class period with a question on the board. Everyone wrote an answer at his or her desk, and if there were not enough right answers to suit him, another question would follow. Here in this marvelous country that had invented the copying machine, a short, punchy six- or seven-question quiz on a half sheet of paper could be ready every morning. Before they had plopped their backpacks on the floor, before they could settle into their usual introductory conversations, they would have work to do.

The quiz caught their attention—this was for their *grade* after all—and gave a focus to everything else that followed in that hour. How did I miss that one on the quiz? Would you do it please, Mr. Jiménez? Having satisfied that bit of curiosity, he stayed at the board to take them an extra step. They kept their eyes on the action, knowing all too well now that *this* would be on a quiz the next day.

Jiménez realized what had happened. He had been diverted by the cares and feelings of the East LA boy who had made good, gotten a college degree, and felt sorry for these young people, so much like himself. If they told him they had not done their homework, he tried to understand. He knew these kids. They had no fathers at home. Or they had no desk. They had to work at the restaurant at night.

He also remembered when he was sixteen and watched his friends put new teachers to the test at Roosevelt. An East LA boy lived by his wits. You could always snow some teachers. He resolved not to be one of them.

Escalante thought of his students as murderers. They killed time. He saw them do it every day. They were lazy. They were also poor, ill educated, discriminated against, harassed by the Immigration and Naturalization Service (known as *La Migra* in East Los Angeles), and sometimes abused.

But first and foremost, he thought, they were lazy. He was going to do something about it. He would have to befriend them and frighten them at the same time.

He knew as much about the gangs as anyone did. Like aging movie stars or lobbyists for the oil industry, the gangs lived as much on reputation as on execution. They were, in reality, small groups of teenage boys with loose ties of friendship or acquaintance to a wider circle of youths who dressed like them, and admired them, but rarely engaged in any organized combat or crime. They lent a bit of romance to flatlands and low hills covered by gas stations and telephone poles

and little wood-frame houses with Cyclone fences. They were interesting because so few really knew what they did. Mystery had its
uses, Escalante knew. It worked more ways than one.

Al Santoyo, a counselor he had known since his student teaching
days at Stevenson Junior High School, provided a list of the known
East Los Angeles gangs. Escalante learned their names and locations:
Lobos Madres there, Stoners over there, Del Oyos back there. When
one of his students, a junior dressed in the basic uniform of white T-
shirt, tight jeans, and bandanna, was found marking his textbook,
Escalante brought him to a corner of the room. He pulled the list out
of a drawer. "Could you please tell me," he said in a low, conspiratorial tone, "which group you are in?"

The boy, interested but apprehensive, ran his eye down the list,
then said nothing. Everyone in East LA knew you didn't answer such
questions.

"You're not in any of them?"

"No. Uh, no."

"I'm only asking you cause I was in Cyclone myself. This one over
here."

The boy's eyes widened slightly. He was startled enough to speak:
"Why you asking me that?"

"Look, I know the kids are writing in the books, there are graffiti
in lots of books here. Now, I was Cyclone. I used to do this. But
please, I don't want you to do this. Don't mess me up with the books.
I know you're in one of these groups. I'm not going to say anything."

Santoyo provided Escalante the gang nicknames of a few students.
Escalante had never been able to remember even their real names, but
he worked hard on memorizing these. They might have some impact
if properly exploited.

When calling roll, he let a name slip. "Let's see . . . Jesse . . . Mosca
[The Fly] . . . oh . . . no, no, where did I get that? My apologies . . ."

"Here," the boy said, with a sullen nod. The word spread.

If some of his students were teetering on the edge of the law, he
could use that. With each textbook he handed the student a small
white card and asked for a signature. On the back of each card he
wrote "$25."

"What's that for?" one boy asked.

"That's how much the book cost. That's how much you pay if
you mess me up, put in the graffiti."

"Whatdya mean?"

Escalante ignored the question. He pulled an inked stamp pad from his desk. "Now, please, if we could take your thumbprint."

"Why?"

"I have to check with the police, Johnny. Maybe you mess me up with the book. What am I gonna do?"

"No, no, no. Come on, you know me."

"I know you, but just in case. Everybody doing this, don't worry about it."

Bribery might work as well as fear. To stimulate attendance on days he planned tests, he began to distribute small hard candies. "Make your life sweet," he whispered seductively in a nervous sophomore's ear. "Don't be afraid of the test." He walked down the aisle like a balding Easter Bunny, patting shoulders and leaving the little red treats. "Don't be afraid. . . . Should be sweet. . . . Don't worry about it." When he ran short, a chant went up: "Candy, candy, candy." He dispatched a teaching assistant to the store for chocolates. He handed them out as the class exited cheering "Candy, candy, candy."

Despite support from Possemato and Gradillas, Escalante could not count on administrators to preserve his gains. One dean, for instance, became so overwhelmed with the morning flood of students needing absent slips that he passed them out like Escalante dispensed candy, no questions asked.

Escalante saw this and wondered: Was this the way they controlled attendance? None of these students' teachers would ever learn why they were absent. No consistent class cutters would be uncovered.

"Listen," he told his class. "I know some of you ditch, or sick, or something. You go to the office and they throw out absent slips like potato chips. I don't want you to go through that. It's a waste of time. So be honest with me. If you need an absent slip, I have some here. I'll give one to you anytime. Just come tell me." He ordered several slips from a printing shop, then waited for customers.

"Hey, Mr. Escalante, can I ask a favor?" The boy was at least 6 feet tall and weighed 200 pounds. He wore jeans, a plaid flannel shirt that seemed too small for him, and a blue knit cap of the sort favored by farm workers in the San Joaquin Valley. His voice seemed a few octaves too low.

"Yup," said Escalante, studying a paper on his desk.

"I need an absent slip. I did not come the last two days."

Escalante registered annoyance. "What? Hey, don't ask me such questions. I let you know later."

"But I . . ."

"Okay, okay. Here's one. Fill in your name. Thank you. That will be ten cents."

The student bent over slightly to study the man's face. "Come on, I can't owe you anything."

"You're right. That's very unprofessional of me. Instead, why don't you just tell me why you didn't come to school the last two days, and I no charge you anything."

If mild extortion did not work, he exploited the spirit of athletic competition that seemed to pervade every aspect of life in American high schools. His friends the special education teachers, Ted Davis and Anthony Critelli, had solicited his help with the varsity soccer team. In a game against Venice High a Garfield midfielder, a goal behind and enraged by a dubious offside call, punched the referee in the mouth. A riot began, and did not stop until the police arrived.

When Escalante fended off Possemato's attempts to identify the offending student, Davis nodded approval. "If you see somebody doing something like that, just keep it to yourself. No trouble that way."

That might be true, Escalante thought, but there ought to be a way to get something out of it.

In class one day he tried out a short sermon, something serious to leaven the jokes and insults. "Look, I know. When we have these kinds of gangs and so on, it's good to be there, you socialize, you have friends and this and that and so on, but it would be better if we get an education too." They were listening. This was new. "When you associate in a club or anything and you do anything good for some people, they going to realize. They going to recognize you. They going to remember you if you do something positive. And that's what I'm trying to do, something positive."

A puzzled silence followed, but a slim girl, a shy one with long brown hair, approached him after the bell. "I know you're trying hard, Mr. Escalante," she said. "But we're learning. Sometimes we don't know we are, but we're learning, sir, we're learning."

Escalante beamed. "That's it. That's the main thing." He had to take this one step further. "One day you going to be using, and if you're using math, remember you learned it over here. But don't remember me, remember Garfield. You have to remember the school, and remember math is fun. And that you were part of the team."

As dean of discipline, Gradillas felt as if he was back in the army, exploring the mysteries of the human soul under pressure. He had believed for a long time that every child in the world knew the difference between right and wrong, no matter how poor they were, no matter how badly they had been treated. He resolved never to give in to a youth's temporary veneer of amorality because he felt sorry for him.

He had seen many young men tell lies in the army; he thought he could spot a lie now. If he approached from the proper angle, with the proper force and speed, he could bring out things the student did not know were there.

Some money disappeared from a teacher's desk. Gradillas brought the prime suspect and his mother into his office. "I didn't take it, sir. You can search me and everything."

"Well, you were the only one there."

The mother spoke up. "My boy didn't do it. You calling my boy a liar?"

Gradillas straightened up in his chair, then leaned toward the mother. "Listen, we could sit here all day long going and talking about this. There is no one in this room except you know who who knows exactly what happened. I wasn't there, you weren't there. The teacher wasn't there. The person who is accused of this is your son."

He turned toward the boy. "Now you search your heart because in your heart you know who did it. You know what's involved. *Damn it,* I'm not going to kill you. I'm not going to throw you to the cops. But I think you're man enough in front of your mother to admit the truth, because in your heart you know exactly what happened.

"Now, tell your mother right now, in front of me, *in front of your heart that you didn't do it. LOOK AT HER IN HER EYES AND TELL YOUR MOTHER YOU DIDN'T DO IT.*" The boy continued to look straight ahead. The mother sat quietly, not saying a word when Gradillas said there would be a brief suspension.

He had to use basic instincts to show them who they were and what they were worth. He asked young males if they had the *courage* to cast off a lie. "You're a man and you're worth something, and you don't lie, not for some stupid thing like this."

And there was a father whose son had destroyed a piece of laboratory equipment. The father backed the son's denials completely. Gradillas threw up his hands. "Okay, your kid can come back to school. I'm just very, very sorry and tremendously disappointed. He's your son and if he can sit there and really, really tell me that he didn't do this and have *no knowledge of it*, and he had no involvement with it, then that's your son, and I pity you as a father. He's not only making a fool out of you, he's destroying himself forever. It shows how little respect he has for you and it shows how little you know about your son and the way you brought him up."

The boy's eyes blazed and he shook his fist at Gradillas. That was what Gradillas had been hoping for. "That's all right. You can come at me. You can hit me, and I won't hit you back. I'll give you one hit, but you try to hit me a second time and I'm going to throw both of you out.

"Your son is a coward. *Es un cobarde.* You know what that is? And that's exactly what you are and you going to throw me right through that goddamned window but you're lying, and you know it. *And your mother knows it and the Holy Ghost knows it and the Father knows it and I hope you never take confession for the rest of your life.*" He lowered his voice. " 'Cause it's going to choke in your throat, *cabrón.*

"Tell your dad right now, you tell him right now that you knew nothing of this. Just for the record. That you knew nothing of this, that you were not involved in this, that you're clean, and you swear that on the Holy Virgin Mother, you right now, 'cause I know you're Catholic. *SAY IT TO YOUR DAD!* Tell me, *did you do it?*"

"Yes."

"Louder, so I can hear it."

The boy looked relieved. "*Yeah.*"

Gradillas's secretary appeared at the doorway. "Is there some trouble?" she asked. Gradillas waved her back. The boy had caught fire. "*Yes!*" he shouted. "Is that what you want to hear? *Yes. Yes.*"

He stood and faced his father. "Yes. Fuckin' A, yes. And I hate your guts 'cause of the way you treated my mother."

Escalante liked the idea of teacher evaluations. He wanted to display his skills, and he had seen enough to know that some of his colleagues needed serious evaluating. But when his first evaluator, a new dean with a clipboard, resisted his suggestion that she come into the classroom rather than peer in the door, he gave up. They were not evaluating. They were checking boxes on the form, guessing on a multiple-choice test.

Who set the standards? At Burroughs each employee punched the time clock and went to work. At the end of the day, they all knew how they had done. There was an accounting. Escalante remembered the routine: How many magnetic heads did you do today? Standard is twenty-one and you did only twenty, so that's going to go on your review.

His third year, a student came to see him at lunch. "You teach Algebra 2, sir?" she said.

"Yes, *señorita*."

"Is that also gifted?"

"I don't understand anything gifted. This is a regular class."

"I'm gifted, sir."

"Great. If you're gifted, welcome."

She had a question on a problem. He smiled. "I'm going to ask one of my students to do that who is *not* gifted." He summoned a protégé who quickly worked it out on the board.

"If you're gifted," Escalante said, "you should be doing a better problem than this one. This is for Boy Scouts. You never going to go too long with that."

The girl reported this amazing statement to her Algebra 2 teacher, who soon confronted Escalante. He looked her in the eye. "I did not say anything about you, I said it about your student. Naturally, it reflects on you."

"Mr. Escalante, I have been teaching here fifteen years."

"I know, I know. I had seniority too. Bad luck they didn't recognize over here the years I working in another country. I hate seniority. The only problem is you not teaching the right stuff."

A vice principal, hearing of this, warned him to avoid friction with other teachers. "There is no friction over here," Escalante said. "The only thing is a misunderstanding. She is teaching the wrong stuff. She's teaching the basic math instead of Algebra 2."

There was a basic mathematics teacher down the hall whom Escalante referred to as "a Ph.D. in fractions without denominators." He used his two teaching assistants, paid for by the school's federally funded Title I program, to hand out puzzles and games each morning while he sat in the back reading the *Los Angeles Times*. Another teacher had a real estate franchise sticker on his car's rear bumper. He spent much of the school day consulting with a fellow part-time realtor in the music department or pitching deals to other teachers.

No matter how much Escalante complained about what he saw and heard, there always seemed to be other things of higher priority for Garfield administrators.

The leadership was changing again. After two years, Downtown found another job for Possemato. Gradillas would also be leaving soon. Having decided he liked administration, he would now match his skills against the hormonal rages of the newly pubescent, as assistant principal of nearby Belvedere Junior High School.

In the fall of 1977 Garfield would receive its first female principal, a slim, soft-spoken woman named Jessie Franco, who had been principal at Belvedere. She was a very nice lady, Escalante concluded, but if he was going to get something big done, he had to do it himself.

In the summer of 1976, Escalante took Fabiola and the two boys for a summer holiday in Bolivia. His mother was ill and in the hospital, although the doctors felt she would recover. He had not been home in twelve years. He wondered if he had made any progress at all, given his high hopes when he first left La Paz.

Cordero met them at the airport and drove him to the hospital where his mother was convalescing. Bertha waited in the lobby. She saw her elder brother walking very slowly up the hospital steps, fighting the high-altitude oxygen deprivation that would render the rest of his family light-headed for days.

Escalante was losing his hair. He weighed more. Bertha felt a shock of recognition—he looked just like Uncle Arturo! The mischievous little boy had grown into the image of the jovial uncle who had pulled him out of so much trouble.

They hugged and celebrated Sara's recovery. But when the talk turned to his work, he became preoccupied. When things were going well, Escalante could talk all night. Now he was quiet, until the conversation moved away from Garfield.

The vacation was a joyful whirl of dinners and folk music *peñas* and markets and *salteñas* and trip to Cochabamba and Copacabana and Lake Titicaca. The farewell party was an agony for Bertha. She could not believe Jaime was leaving them again. She guessed there had to be something very special back there that he still wanted.

Escalante returned to Room 233. There were satisfactions at Garfield, but he wanted more, some feedback, something.

A few weeks after his return, he received a small taste of it from an unexpected source.

A fat, dark-skinned student with a scar on his cheek materialized in front of Escalante's desk. The boy wore the standard uniform, white T-shirt and tight jeans. He was in the basic mathematics class and getting by, which was more than Escalante had hoped for.

"Hey," the boy said, in guttural tones.

"*Sí, señor.*"

"I don't like your name, Mr. Escalante. You need a real name."

"Thank you, but I like Escalante."

"No way, man. I got one. *Kemo Sabe*. Like the Lone Ranger. You got it?" It was the boy's favorite show, a Saturday morning ritual, even if many of the episodes had been produced before he was born. He liked the flavor of the name: friendly, with the Spanish connotation of knowledge and competence. He and the other students chose to spell it Kimo.

The teacher did not know what to say. He paused, and then tried a polite demurrer: "I prefer Escalante."

The boy ignored him. "Kimo. You are Kimo."

‖ 8 ‖

Around the turn of the century, the deans of Harvard College discovered that many young gentlemen admitted in their freshman year had already acquired a solid grip on some introductory college material in preparatory school. Why not give them a special test in that subject, someone suggested, and allow them to skip the college course?

To make what would eventually be called the Advanced Placement examination convenient, three test sites were provided the summer before matriculation: Cambridge, Massachusetts, the university's home; Quincy, Massachusetts, an exclusive Boston suburb; and Paris, France, for those spending their fathers' money on the Grand Tour.

A few other private colleges began similar programs, but the idea did not go far. After World War I, American educators focused on creating a standard high school curriculum for every youth, rich or poor. They had little time for elitist notions like Advanced Placement.

During World War II, many college administrators noticed remarkable results achieved by wartime crash courses for young men and women who needed to absorb detailed technical data and languages in a very short time. After the war, as scientific learning expanded at the speed of light and left the standard high school and college curricula far behind, a large number of educators began to wonder if they were missing something.

Harlan P. "Harpo" Hanson, later head of the College Board's Advanced Placement program, was an assistant dean at Harvard in the mid-1950s. He and others at similar colleges noticed that many of their apparently strongest preparatory school graduates seemed to lose momentum in their freshman year at college, despite the deliberately advanced and challenging courses they had taken in their schools. Research showed that when college-level courses were offered in secondary schools, the need to repeat the same material under college graduation rules led to boredom and surprisingly poor grades for otherwise accomplished students.

So a few colleges and secondary schools decided to revive and extend Advanced Placement. From its infancy, the program held a silver pencil in its hand. It was a device to relieve the boredom of a few bright high school seniors in extremely wealthy or unusually competitive schools. A few secondary schools would offer college-level courses to a few students. The colleges, with the help of panels of experts, would create special examinations to prove the students did not need to repeat the same material. If they passed, they would receive college credit.

The 104 secondary schools who participated in the first Advanced Placement examinations sponsored by the College Board in May 1956 included Andover, Exeter, Groton, Deerfield, the Bronx High School of Science, New Trier, Bethesda–Chevy Chase, and Cranbrook.

The College Board, originally known as the College Entrance Examination Board, had been set up by a few select colleges in 1900 to provide a way to test college applicants before deciding whom to admit. It created the Scholastic Aptitude Test (SAT), and in 1947, with the American Council on Education and the Carnegie Foundation for the Advancement of Teaching, set up the Educational Testing Service (ETS) to administer the SAT and a growing number of other tests.

At the advent of the AP program in 1956, the College Board, aware that its membership had grown far beyond the Ivy League, agreed that any AP test would be open to any student who wanted to take it.

Some educators accepted this decision reluctantly. Certainly, they acknowledged, the AP program should not be just for schools with brick walls, dark green doors, and withered ivy. But no one expected it to move far beyond that privileged domain. One Harvard admissions officer guessed that 120 high schools might eventually participate. Feeling optimistic, Hanson wagered the maximum would be 220.

Escalante had been at Garfield more than a year before he even learned of the existence of Advanced Placement. Jaimito had not encountered it at Pasadena High School. Occasional efforts at Garfield to teach AP mathematics—essentially a course in calculus—had died in infancy. In the most recent effort, the calculus students had become known for dropping books out of their second-floor window to test the echoes in the courtyard below. Few passed the test. Ralph Heiland tried to teach AP physics, but few of his students took the test at all.

Escalante was so disheartened by these stories that he declined an initial invitation to take over AP calculus. Then he reconsidered. His students needed a goal, something more inspirational than a handball game or a piece of hard candy. The AP examination, Escalante thought, imposed a valid standard, some outside measure of how well he was doing, like a proctor at a Bolivian high school examination.

When Escalante became interested in AP he found a natural, though wary, ally in John Bennett, the history and government teacher with a soft voice and slender build. Bennett had come to Garfield in 1968 to escape the draft. He had studied in college to be a diplomat, and gravitated to the history department. Beginning in 1973, a year before Escalante arrived, he taught the school's first AP history course. He never had more than twelve students, and only half dared take the examination. His was the only successful AP course outside the Spanish department, where Garfield students enjoyed a rare academic advantage, even if many struggled with complex grammar. So he agreed to coordinate the school's entire AP program, what there was of it.

Despite the improvements of the Possemato era, Garfield was still considered an academic sinkhole. Bennett winced inwardly at the thought of the principal over at Lane Elementary School, who did all she could to have her brightest students, her little darlings, promoted to junior highs in the distant, predominantly Anglo, San Fernando Valley. In return for long bus trips, they received enriched instruction and guaranteed admission to a Valley high school, escaping exposure to Garfield and its unsavory reputation.

From the beginning of their discussion of AP calculus, Bennett sensed Escalante's own intensity. Bennett was surprised to find an immigrant, particularly one with such a thick accent, so sure of himself, and with such good reason. Escalante definitely knew his mathematics. Escalante liked Bennett but feared what the mathematics department might do to any Advanced Placement program.

In 1978, Escalante lost patience with the textbook used in most basic mathematics classes. It had a winning title, *Consumer Math*, and a series of entertaining illustrations but made no pretense of teaching any of the algebraic or geometric concepts required on the mathematics skills tests that had come into vogue. Nonetheless, his pleas for a new book were rejected.

Jessie Franco, the new principal, had begun sending letters to every teacher each June praising the school's accomplishments and appending a handwritten note of thanks for that individual's personal contribution. She commended Escalante for his "excellent classroom organization and lesson plans." He confronted her with the letter in his hand.

"Mrs. Franco, instead of having these beautiful words, can we exchange this for three thousand dollars for the books?" She told him it was out of her hands. The money was not there.

"Well, then, Mrs. Franco, here are my transfer papers. Could you sign, please? I'll transfer to another school, and when you have money for the books, I'll be back."

Franco called in another administrator to ask about money. A parents' group had some and the teachers' union had some more. He could have his books, she said. He thanked her. Now that they were going to have AP, he needed to pull everyone up to a higher level, and this would help.

For his first AP class Escalante collected a few members of the previous year's mathematical analysis course and one or two students who claimed to have taken the prerequisite course at East Los Angeles College. He had fourteen enrolled in the first-period class by the fall of 1978, but many, including Escalante, felt like babes lost in the woods.

Heiland brought him a copy of an old calculus AP free-response test, the problems requiring written answers that make up the latter half of the three-hour examination. Escalante fingered the green paper gingerly. It had seven questions. He knew this group could not come close to answering any of them. He wondered how far he could take them in just eight months.

He assumed his sharpest look and addressed the class: "You going to be able to do this class, but you need to brush up your Algebra 2, your math analysis, your trigonometry. You don't know anything in this class. Okay, you get credit for high school calculus, but that's not enough. We have to pass the test.

"First period start at eight o'clock. We open the doors here at seven. We start at seven-thirty. Then from eight to nine we have regular class. I'd like to change this textbook, but no way. I got to

110

be honest, I don't understand myself this book. So we going to have to give you a lot of handouts and you have to take a lot of notes and keep a folder. Every morning we have a five-minute quiz. [Now several students began to exchange looks.] And a test on Friday."

He began the routine. To his surprise, in two weeks he was down to seven students.

He went to see one of the school's counselors. "Why these kids dropping?" he asked.

She regarded him calmly, sympathetically. "It's too hard, Mr. Escalante. They are not going to be able to do it. Calculus here used to mean just a few problems."

Escalante flopped into a chair, defeat and annoyance in his voice. "This is a class at the college level," he said.

"That's not the point," she said.

"Okay, you just drop the kid." He was disgusted. That day two more boys approached him defiantly.

"We gonna drop, Mr. Escalante." They watched closely for his reaction.

"But you gotta *try*," he said.

"Nah," the taller boy said. "I don't want to come at seven o'clock. Why should I?"

The second boy said, "I'm going to be in the marching band. I prefer just to play my flute. Period. I don't want this class."

Escalante had convinced himself he could teach rope climbing to sea lions, but only if they appeared in class. How could he arrange that with so little power and so little time?

The Los Angeles school system had determined long before that its high schools would have just three grades: tenth, eleventh, and twelfth. Sociologists, psychologists, and economists disagreed on what system worked best—the three-year or the four-year high school. If Escalante had gotten his hands on a class of ninth graders, with four years ahead of them, he might not have needed accelerated classes, summer training, or—most important—extra money. But because of psychological worries about making pubescent ninth graders the lowest class in a high school and because of the unwieldiness of four-year high schools, Escalante had only three years to work with.

Time is a teacher's most precious asset. In Bolivia Escalante had grown accustomed to working twelve to fourteen hours a day to support his family. He taught at San Calixto in the morning, National Bolívar in the afternoon, and tutored or taught night school after dinner. His first decade in America had followed a similar routine: work all day, go to school at night, do homework on the weekends. Fabiola had stopped working when Fernando was born. With a starting salary at Garfield of only $13,000 a year, Escalante had to continue working at night, teaching elementary mathematics to recent immigrants and repentant dropouts.

He treasured time. He could not bear to see it wasted. He hated summer, at least the three-month vacation as celebrated by American educators and their students. He wanted to wipe it out. Since he had to work during the summer anyway, he saw a chance to end the months of summertime idleness that sucked precious memories from his students' brains. But that took space and money.

Los Angeles school supervisors used summer school largely to pull the more academically troubled teenagers back into step with their classmates. Students took required courses they had failed in the regular school term. Escalante wanted to create a summer course in trigonometry and analytic geometry. The subjects were prerequisites for calculus but absolutely unnecessary for high school graduation. Since he could not show a great remedial need, no one wanted to help him.

Escalante had, unknowingly, picked the worst possible time since World War II to seek funds for a special school enrichment program.

In June 1978, just as he began to consider the need for a summer program, the voters of the state of California passed by a 65 to 35 percent margin a ballot initiative called Proposition 13. The measure sharply reduced the real estate taxes of longtime homeowners. Public schools had depended on those taxes more than on any other source of revenue. Summer school courses were dropped to prevent massive layoffs and other financial horrors in the regular school year.

Adding a new summer course was unthinkable. Escalante had been tentatively scheduled to teach a summer trigonometry course at Garfield to help prepare more students for calculus. When it was dropped, he became depressed and angry.

He decided his only alternative was to lobby the local colleges. They all said they wanted better Latino applicants; this was the way to produce them.

The Cal State, LA, mathematics department chairman, a man Escalante had never met, received him politely. "Perhaps you don't know too much about my school," Escalante said. Garfield was only three miles away, but he wanted to play it safe. "It's in the heart of East LA. It doesn't have a good reputation, and it's probably not going to sound good to you, but we could have really good kids in mathematics, which could open the door in any field, engineering, computers, and so on. And I'd like to keep the continuity in the program. I've only got maybe seven kids to start. I'd need the money to pay one teacher and maybe a bus to get them over here."

The man offered an understanding smile, then spread his hands in a gesture Escalante had seen many times, mostly from mathematics department chairmen. "You know about Proposition Thirteen, Mr. Escalante. Our budget is just a mess. But it seems to me you have a wonderful idea. If we could help in a way that wouldn't cost so much money, we would certainly consider it." Escalante thanked him and left.

He tried the University of Southern California. Located at the edge of the vast flat plain of southcentral Los Angeles, a mixing bowl of black, Hispanic, and Asian minorities, USC frequently announced its commitment to improving the education of the disadvantaged. But the official he spoke to seemed interested only if the summer session could become a psychosociological experiment. A university psychologist—probably armed with a National Science Foundation grant—would check on the level of stress in allegedly happy-go-lucky Latino kids wrestling with cotangents.

Proposition 13, Garfield's reputation, his accent—for some reason Escalante was not getting across. He called a friendly administrator Downtown. "You're not going to get anything from the district, Jaime," the man said. "All they'll give you is a lot of paperwork. Forget it."

He had one more chance—East Los Angeles College, often called ELAC (pronounced "*ee*-lack"). Its assortment of buildings and low trees spread over a small rise six blocks from Garfield, in Monterey Park, just north of the Pomona Freeway. It was a two-year college, part of a large network of state-supported schools that had given California its unusual reputation as one of the most productive university systems in the world. For a modest fee, any graduate of a state high school could enroll at a nearby community college—the old term *junior college* had lost favor. The student earned a two-year associate of arts degree in a trade, such as dental hygiene or electrical mechanics. If the student discovered a spark of academic talent and interest, he or she transferred to a four-year college for a bachelor's degree.

Among the state's more than one hundred community colleges, ELAC had one of the neediest student bodies and creakiest physical plants. The school still used twenty-two refurbished World War II temporary barracks, along with some newer structures. By 1978, most of its 12,000 students were Latino, many of them Garfield graduates looking for something better than a job serving hamburgers on Atlantic Boulevard or sewing swimsuits on South Hill Street. The school's mathematics department was small and weak and dealt mostly with business arithmetic.

Ignorant of all this, Escalante parked his VW on Brooklyn Avenue and wandered around the campus until a student finally pointed him toward the president's office. A secretary suggested he see Paul Powers, a thin, gray-haired administrator specializing in programs for minorities. Then he met George Madrid, a round-faced man with mustache and curly dark hair who had grown up in East Los Angeles and had already heard of Escalante.

Madrid's assignment then was to shepherd about one hundred East LA kids each summer through the federally funded Upward Bound program. It needed a good mathematics teacher. Upward Bound attempted to prepare ordinary students for college with enriched courses in several fields on Saturdays and in the summer. Escalante already taught in an Upward Bound summer program at Occidental College for mostly black students from southcentral Los Angeles. Madrid's Upward Bound students from Garfield had spoken of a hard-nosed mathematics teacher with a flair for the dramatic. Madrid had passed this intelligence on to Powers. "This is a guy who kicks ass," Madrid said. "We could use him."

Madrid asked Escalante if he would switch to the Upward Bound program at ELAC, but the teacher wanted his own show. Mere summer enrichment, putting a little skin on the bones of the regular school year, was not what he had in mind.

Madrid was an ex-marine, a Vietnam veteran with a frenetic self-confidence. He thought, All right, I'll find another way to get Escalante. It was just a matter of time.

Only five students in Escalante's calculus class—three girls and two boys—lasted through the spring. It was a test not only of their patience but of the district's and the principal's. Administrators were not supposed to sanction such tiny classes.

Escalante still insisted the students see him before and after school, but he had to treat them more gently now. He assured them repeatedly they could handle AP questions. He gave them what sample questions he could find from past examinations.

First systematized by Isaac Newton and Gottfried Wilhelm Leibniz in the seventeenth century, the calculus (modern writers eventually dropped the *the*) provided the means to calculate the slope of a curved line and the area of a region it bounded. Its inventors sought a way to determine the motion of planets, but as the discipline grew it provided ways of understanding nearly every natural—and some unnatural—system of change.

Differential calculus tracks satellites, blood flow, and international investments. Mathematician Ronald G. Douglas has noted that most large-scale scientific computing has become essentially the solution of complex calculus problems. Integral calculus led to the theory of transforms, now the basis for the CAT scan and other tools of medical diagnosis. Calculus revealed the uses of approximation—the secret of the hand-held calculator. Einstein used the calculus for curved spaces to develop the theory of relativity.

Calculus solves problems in modern engineering, physics, astronomy, biology, chemistry, and even some social sciences such as economics, but its intricacies have intimidated generations of college students and frightened all but a few high school students from trying it at all.

From the beginning Escalante knew he had to soften calculus's granite-hard image. His principal devices were humor, nonchalance, and an appeal to the team spirit. The class motto appeared in a huge poster on his wall: CALCULUS NEED NOT BE MADE EASY; IT IS EASY ALREADY.

In May 1979 all five Escalante students sat down in the English classroom just inside the main door of the school and took the AP calculus examination. They came back looking bleak and shell-shocked. One girl, Leticia Arambula, could barely speak. She was mortified. She had panicked and answered only a handful of multiple-choice questions. By the time she opened the free-response booklet, her mind had gone blank.

Escalante knew how quick East LA youths were to wallow in self-doubt. He comforted her. She had not been his best student and was slow in finding her answers to daily quiz questions. But she worked hard and did her homework.

The counseling office called him in July with the results. The Educational Testing Service scored the examination on a five-point scale. A 5 was best, a 1 was worst. A 3 or better meant the student could be said to have passed a college-level calculus course and would receive credit for one at most major universities. In Escalante's class, the grading report said, there were two 4s and two 2s. Leticia Arambula had received a 1.

Escalante resolved to do better.

He combed the algebra classes for talent, acting like a scout seeking pitchers for the Dodgers.

He persuaded the department chairman to assign an Algebra 2 class to Jiménez, whose self-confidence was rising since Escalante's lesson in discipline. The younger teacher had discovered that simply remaining in his classroom at noon and after school brought enormous benefits. Even his laziest and most disruptive students were more willing to try if he was available and showed he cared.

Jiménez borrowed some Escalante materials and subjected his Algebra 2 students to the same daily quizzes and spiraling homework assignments that had worked in Algebra 1. But mostly it was his own methodical approach. Unlike Escalante, he did not curse boys' long hair and threaten to yank it out. He did not test concepts he had not recently reviewed. He did not threaten to transfer laggards to some very distant high school. His Algebra 2 students turned out well all the same. Escalante himself said they were well prepared for trigonometry.

Jiménez felt much better. He did not have to mimic every Escalante mannerism to succeed. He did not have to become another Bolivian showman.

In the fall of 1979 Escalante raised the number of students in his AP calculus class to nine. He had heard suggestions, particularly from Tom Woessner in the history department, that he not force every AP student to take the examination. If we did that, Escalante thought, why not just change the title of the course to Senior Calculus? If this is AP, they take the test.

In May 1980 the calculus class scored one 4, five 3s, and two 2s. One of the students who received a 4 on the 1979 calculus AB examination, an eccentric, wispy boy named Alex Barkaloff, became the first Garfield student ever to take the Calculus BC examination. Calculus BC was reserved for students with more than a year of preparation or an unusually accelerated yearlong course. Barkaloff received a 3, a passing score.

In May 1981 the results were even better. Fifteen students took the AB examination—one 5, four 4s, nine 3s, and one 2. The 5, Garfield's first in AP calculus, had gone to a tall, slender, sardonic young woman named Raquel Soto, later to serve as Escalante's assistant and goad. The import of the scoring was clear: fourteen of fifteen students from East LA families could *pass and receive credit* for college calculus.

Escalante sensed he was moving toward something good. But every day was an improvisation, as hard to predict as the *peña* musicales he used to love in La Paz.

Chicano students needed something extra from him to accelerate their understanding. Andreda Pruitt, the new head counselor and a former mathematics teacher herself, sat transfixed as Escalante turned a seemingly irrelevant discussion of the relative heights of Laker guard Norm Nixon and center Kareem Abdul-Jabbar into an unforgettable lecture on inequalities.

Several of the trigonometric concepts carried difficult names. Could he change them? The *burros* in basic mathematics seemed to appreciate some visual presentation—a little show like his apple-cutting routine. Would that work in algebra and calculus?

When his students faced a complex polynomial, they panicked. They needed to remember to factor. He wondered how to associate factoring with something pleasant. What do these kids enjoy? What do they like to see?

There was, he remembered, a very popular motif for student body campaign posters, dance announcements, and football banners. Charlie Brown. Everybody liked Charlie Brown. He borrowed a drawing from a cartoon book Jaimito had discarded and fashioned a two-dimensional cardboard Charlie Brown with jaws that mouthed Escalante's words, "Factoring, factoring."

It seemed like a non sequitur, but it worked. His students had never seen anyone try to bring mathematics down to this level. The quicker students thought it was silly. The slower thought it was odd. But they remembered.

From that small beginning, Escalante collected assorted props, which he kept in a special cabinet. A windup toy consisting of two walking shoes became the symbol for a careful, step-by-step approach to all algebraic functions. A plastic monkey climbed up and down a small pole to illustrate the inverse function, exchanging x for y. A picture of a clown symbolized a popular fast-food chain. "You don't do your homework," he told them, "you gonna be working the rest of your life at Jack-in-the-Box."

Movement and repetition were critical, as in his introduction of absolute value the fourth week of Algebra 2.

"You guys play basketball? You know the give and go?" He bounced an imaginary ball in front of him. Next year, he thought, I'll have to get a real one. "Give and go, give and go. Can you explain what is this give and go?" He crouched with his back to an imaginary basket, passing the ball to an imaginary guard crossing on his right. He repeated the routine, this time passing to the left.

"The absolute value function is the give and go. I have two possibilities. If this fellow on this side is open, it is going to be from the left." He wrote $x < 0$ on the board. "If it is from the right, then $x > 0$.

"So my little ball is going to be the absolute value. I don't know which ball I'm going to use. This guy has two options, come from the left, he's gonna make it, or come from the right. *Every time* you see a number between two bars"—he wrote $|x|$ on the board—"you have to, you have to, you have to say, well, all right, it's coming from the left or from the right. You have to break it down into two parts. I can do that."

He wrote:

$$|a| = a \text{ if } a > 0$$
$$|a| = -a \text{ if } a < 0$$

"But you must take into consideration three positions, I call, the three-second violation. Now, I don't really understand what is the three-second violation. Can somebody explain me?"

"Yeah, Kimo. You can't keep the ball three seconds in the key, when you're on offense."

"But how they know? How they count that?"

"They just do, Kimo. They have a clock."

"Well, okay, but I use the three-second violation my own way. The three-second violation is, this is one ball: $|x| < a$; this is the second ball: $|x| = a$; and the third ball: $|x| > a$. That right?"

"Yeah, right."

"How many you see?"

"Three."

"You know, you gonna be in *bad* shape if you don't know how to solve these three things." He thumped the board next to each expression. "When the *absolute value* is greater than a, when the *absolute value* is equal to it, when the *absolute value* is less than a. You have to *know* this three-second violation. Look."

He wrote, with sweeping gestures, the meaning of each expression in turn:

$$-a < x < a \qquad \begin{array}{c} x = a \\ x = -a \end{array} \qquad x < -a \text{ or } x > a$$

"As soon as you see that, absolute value of x is more than a, be able to say, immediately, minus a is more than x, or x is more than a."

He assigned homework to underscore the point. Absolute value would be vital to understanding calculus. They had to get it down now. He had glossed over some mathematical niceties, but it was important first to help his audience find the theater before he directed them to their seats.

The next day he closed the classroom before the period began and kept everyone outside.

"Line up! Line up!" he commanded the puzzled throng. He stood in the doorway and confronted the first boy. "Absolute value of x greater than a," he said.

"What about it?" the boy replied.

"Okay, you stay out there for ten minutes. Maybe you read your book, you remember what we talk about."

"Hey, man, you didn't say you gonna . . ."

Escalante snapped his large, thick fingers. "I don't care. Next?" He eyed a tall girl. "Absolute value of x less than a."

"Uh, . . . oh, . . . well, . . . oh God."

"Where your book? Ten minutes."

"Next? Absolute value of x equal to a."

"Three-second violation?"

"Nah, that's to help you remember, but you gotta give me the solution. Next?"

When the end of the line began to profit from intelligence relayed from the front, he switched to numbers. "Absolute value of x equal to four. No? Next!"

After twenty minutes, he had only three who could not produce a satisfactory answer. He sat them in front of the room. "Look, I want you to sit close to the door, 'cause you're gonna fly. You're just going to have to sit there today, then you're gonna have to go to another school because the situation is, you walk into Garfield, but Garfield hasn't gotten into you."

He tried them again the next day, with better results. Then, riding on their sense of accomplishment, he announced a quiz on everything they had learned in the first four weeks. "If you have any question, come after three o'clock." Many came, convinced that he meant business.

Everything had to be part of a system. Escalante abhorred disorder; that was one reason why he liked mathematics. Every student could expect a five-minute quiz at the beginning of every class. He created files holding quizzes and tests for an entire year, four different courses, each labeled with approximate date and numbered so a teaching assistant could pull the proper paper, photocopy it for the class, and leave Escalante free to conceive his next toy town visual aid.

When Alex Barkaloff, the eccentric genius of the class of 1980, nearly missed graduating for failing to attend an art class, Escalante conceived his contract system. All students who joined the calculus team, or its underclass farm clubs, would have to sign, along with their parents, a paper promising attention, homework, good attendance, and consistent effort in all their classes. He would in turn promise to teach them what they needed to know.

He passed out homework as if it were vitamin C. The more he gave, he thought, the better off they would be. But that created other problems.

Students coaxed into any of his classes—Algebra 2, Trigonometry, Calculus—discovered they were going to have to work very hard to survive. Escalante said little about the work load to students who had yet to enroll. He wanted them safely inside the classroom; then he could confront their fears. Some counselors, with his encouragement, put students in his class without warning them of the consequences. After their first look at the homework, many tried to bolt.

"I don't like this class," a surly sixteen-year-old said after he had received his first assignment in Algebra 2.

Escalante eyed the student with calculated disdain. "So?"

"So I wanta drop it. You got to sign this for my counselor."

"Oh, I'm sorry, I cannot do that," Escalante said. It was a half-truth. The boy had the right to drop the course, but Escalante had persuaded some of the counselors to keep this quiet.

When the boy returned the next day, bewildered and upset, Escalante softened him up.

"Look, in this class all you have to do is sit up here in front, and I will give you an A without doing anything. You want an A, or not?"

"Yeah."

"So you can correct these papers for me, but before you do that, you'll need a little practice, so do these exercises first." The boy sat down and began to work.

With some counselors, particularly Ed Martin, the drama could take particularly subtle forms. Some students who stepped over Escalante's invisible line—failed to produce homework or disappeared for more than a day—saw Escalante the friendly clown suddenly change to something out of a drive-in horror movie.

"Could I speak to you, Johnny?" Escalante motioned to a student who had not done his homework. It was a polite request, and the boy followed him out the door, expecting a mild lecture. Escalante turned, looked at him for a moment, then jerked a thumb toward the stairs. "Get out of here," he said.

"Sir?"

"Take off. It's time to fly. I don't want you in my class."

The boy stood for a moment, stunned, then tried to collect himself. "Uh, . . . sir, . . . don't I need a hall pass?"

"I don't care what you need. Go."

The student walked down the hall, turned into the stairway, and looked back to see Escalante glowering at him. He walked through two buildings to Martin's tiny office. Martin, in his usual short-sleeved sports shirt, smiled at the boy and invited him in. He knew the student, and he knew who his teacher was that period. Escalante and he had performed this rite before.

"Look, what did you do?"

The boy looked at him with a mixture of fear and defiance. "I didn't do the homework."

"So," Martin said, gazing at his ceiling to let the word linger awhile, "*why* didn't you do the homework?"

"Well, . . . I had other work."

Martin leaned forward. "Look, this is an advanced course. This is like college. You're going to have to allot your time so you get everything done. It's unfortunate, but in college each teacher is going to give you *x* amount of work and you're going to have to do it. That's the name of the game."

The boy nodded. He rubbed his hands together. He looked worried.

"Look," Martin said, softening his tone. "I'm gonna try to get you back in the class, but you got to promise me you will do the homework, because I'm going down and I'm putting my heart on the line here . . . and . . . [Martin suppressed a smile] . . . and I'm begging him to take you back."

He escorted the boy back through the two buildings to Room 233, just as the bell rang. Martin waited for the class to spill out, then pulled the boy inside. Escalante frowned at them. Martin had his cue. "Mr. Escalante, look, I just had a long talk with him and can we get him back? Let's give him another . . ."

"Noooo, I don't think so. Send him to Jordan. I don't care."

"Come on, let's give him a break. I *guarantee* he will do the work. I'll take it upon myself."

Escalante appeared moved by this personal gesture. "Uh, . . . well, I may have to talk to his parents."

"Fine, fine," Martin said. "Let's just give it another try." And so the boy returned, not sure what had hit him.

Escalante hoped Jessie Franco would be his guardian angel. He liked her very much, but there were times when she seemed to have other things on her mind. He heard of teachers leaving a day early to catch a long weekend. He encountered a counselor who would not cooperate in his intimidating little playlets. When he suggested that errant faculty be transferred or fired, she told him that was her concern, not his. When he wondered loudly why she took no action, she lectured him on the iron rules of seniority, which protected even the incompetent from immediate discipline.

When blocked, Escalante often threatened to resign. Burroughs would take him back in a minute. And there were other schools.

In 1980, after a particularly tense conversation with Franco, he sent his résumé—with sample lessons from his calculus class—off to Monrovia High School, just two miles from the ranch house on a small lot he and Fabiola had bought in 1977. A Monrovia school official asked him to come in for an interview.

He was intrigued. He told Fabiola, "If I can get a job in the senior high, or even the junior high, I really don't give a damn, but then I could really show what I can do." He retreated to his den and typed up a detailed outline of a program to give Monrovia the best Advanced Placement mathematics program in the San Gabriel Valley. He donned a coat and tie—a signal of his serious intent—and went to see the principal of the junior high and the district's teacher recruiter.

They asked questions about his disciplinary methods, his handling of ill-prepared students, his background in Bolivia. Monrovia was a small suburb with more than the usual number of lower-income Anglos and blacks. Coiled like a spring, Escalante pulled out his outline and began to preach. "If you prepare the kids in the junior high and high school, and you build a really good background, these kids when they graduate and they go to college or university, that's going to be a piece of cake for them."

His listeners smiled at his evident enthusiasm. He plunged on: "Okay, this is my outline. You have a really good chance because you start the high school in the ninth grade, the kids be with me for four years, and by my second year here, I might be able to get at least thirty students in the Advanced Placement, then much more by my fourth year." He tacked on an old dream. "Plus, I would like to teach physics at the same time. I'm qualified, see? Here are my papers, here's what I did back in Bolivia."

The smiles were bigger now. He was certain he had them convinced. Once they saw the outline, appreciated the force of continuity, regular school immediately followed by afternoon and vacation sessions, they would welcome him. He drove home lighthearted, fulfilled.

A week passed with no call from Monrovia. He waited ten more days, then called their office. After some difficulty, he reached a man who identified himself as the district superintendent. The man seemed busy. "I'm sorry we haven't gotten back to you. There didn't seem much point. We went over your papers. We just don't think it's going to work. We wish you success in East LA, but our kids come from better homes. You know, you live here. They don't have the problems you have over there. Sorry."

Escalante hung up the phone and sat down. He felt like he was twelve again, and had lost a fistfight in Sopocachi Park. "Jaime?" Fabiola asked. She always worried when he was quiet. "What is the matter?"

"Monrovia High. They give me a shot in the rump. Maybe it was my British accent. I could have done something there. The parents of those kids care, not like Garfield. I could have done twice as much there."

They had closed the door.

He would go back to Garfield, and try to salvage something.

9

Some observers suspected the other faculty members in the Garfield High School mathematics department elected Escalante chairman in 1981 as fitting payment for his years of abuse. It was not a popular job. The administrative details and meetings were tiresome. The extra $500 a semester did not begin to make up for the trouble. Perhaps, some suggested, the job would wear him down so much he would stay out of their lives.

Keenly aware of the problem, Escalante immediately announced he would not attend meetings, or call any himself unless absolutely necessary. The discussions at those gatherings, he thought, were either trivial or turned into a monologue by him about his teaching methods. He wished to be polite when people asked questions. But if they wanted to know how he taught, they could come over and watch. Anytime. Don't worry about it.

When Jessie Franco scolded him for missing a department heads' meeting, he tried to explain: "Mrs. Franco, I had some students after school and then some parents I had to call."

"Mr. Escalante," she said patiently, "one of the things an administrator does is attend such meetings."

"I understand perfectly," he said. "I'm not coming to any more meetings."

She understood the personality she was dealing with. She said nothing. Having learned how American bureaucrats seize such opportunities, Escalante quickly repeated his policy in a written memo. She did not reject it. His meeting days, he thought, were over.

He discovered something about the chairmanship that he had not considered before. He now controlled, to a certain degree, the department schedule. He could assign high-level courses to teachers he liked. He could give basic mathematics classes to those he disliked. The job had all sorts of possibilities, and he wanted to see what he could do with them.

Gradillas had enjoyed his two years as assistant principal at Belvedere. The principal, Tommy Ikeda, let him roam the halls and apply his usual disciplinary regime.

To boost scores on the standardized tests, a Downtown obsession, Gradillas encouraged teachers to give careful instruction in testsmanship, just like they did for Anglo kids in the Valley—how to make a proper erasure, how to make a reasonable guess. He sponsored competitions. Could Room 15 beat Room 13 on the California Basic Skills Test? The winning class would get a pizza party.

In early 1980, friends suggested Gradillas take the principals' examination. He thought the idea presumptuous. There were people he respected who had been assistant principals for fifteen years without a chance to run a school. People still pressed him. William Anton, the district's highest-ranking Latino, said they needed good Hispanic principals.

Someone who knew Gradillas very well realized the most persuasive argument would be a list of the assistant principals who *were* taking the examination. Gradillas looked at the list, blinked, and shook his head. They were nice people, most of them, but many knew nothing about motivation or discipline.

He signed up.

About 350 other people joined him. Of those, 120 including Gradillas survived the first cut. A panel of seven administrators conducted the oral examination. He reminded himself not to ramble. Keep to the point. When it ended, he felt fine.

The following autumn he did not return to Belvedere but remained where he had spent the summer, the campus of Brigham Young University in Provo, Utah. His friends joked about a Mexican Catholic among the Mormons, but he loved it. They had invited him to join the doctoral program. If he kept at it he could earn a Ph.D. within a year. The BYU professors said they liked his thesis topic—"Characteristics of Capable Teachers in Mexican American Junior High Schools of Los Angeles."

Provo was as clean and orderly as a well-run army barracks. Gradillas saw no graffiti. When they played "The Star-Spangled Banner" at a football game, everybody stood up, and *sang*, and even the popcorn machine stopped running. It was a spiritual experience, his kind of town.

The telephone calls began coming from California in November.

"Congratulations on your exam, Henry."

"Who'd you pay, Henry?"

He had placed sixth on the examination. He was a cinch to be a principal, and very soon. But Gradillas loved Provo, and when the area superintendent called in December with a job offer, he was not certain what to do.

They wanted him to take over Jackson High School, a tough, experimental school catering to students with discipline problems. Gradillas did not want to be known only as a bad-boy principal, the ex–airborne ranger with muscles.

His friends cautioned him: Even if you don't like it, take it. Many assignments do not last long. You will learn something and build up valuable seniority.

He took the job. As his friends had anticipated, Jackson was turned into an elementary school six months later. The area superintendent called again. Jessie Franco wanted a sabbatical to spend time with her small daughters. Would Gradillas like to take over Garfield High?

It was like asking if he loved his country. He took the job eagerly, providing the last essential ingredient for a mix of personalities and talents which would, unexpectedly, coalesce into an academic marvel.

Escalante had finally put aside all thoughts of leaving Garfield. He still ached with frustration at the sloth and ignorance all around him. That was part of his nature. But now he resolved to focus all that outrage on a program that would change the school.

Jiménez had finished his first five years of teaching with at least as much enthusiasm as when he started, a rare feat. He began to sense Escalante and he had a chance to do something unusual. In their two small classrooms, they could seriously undercut the persistent notion that Americans were dividing into two distinct groups, the rich and the poor, the well-educated Anglo and the dropout minority, with no chance of a merging.

All they needed was a little help from their new principal, the continued patience of their wives, and perhaps, if they were lucky, some galvanizing event.

10

By 1981, Escalante could see the calculus program making substantial progress. That only made it worse when unexpected problems nipped at his ankles.

A month before his first AP examination he was informed that each of his students had to pay a testing fee. Even at the reduced rate of twenty-one dollars for economically disadvantaged students, it was a heavy burden for most East Los Angeles families. He was forced to launch the first of what would be a series of candied apple sales and car washes.

He threw up his hands in disgust when a joint working group of college faculty from both the University of California and California State University recommended diagnostic tests for anyone contemplating calculus. How was he ever going to find any students, he said, if these experts tried to erect such barriers?

The homemade obstacles were enough, particularly among the eighteen students preparing for the 1982 AP calculus examination. The ten boys and eight girls would provide some of the most harrowing, and satisfying, moments of Escalante's life. But even getting them into the course was a struggle.

Jiménez encountered the most difficult case, a quiet, thin, trigger-tempered junior named Leticia Rodríguez, in the spring of 1981. She was in his trigonometry class and due to be on the calculus team the following year. She absorbed the subtleties of mathematics with little apparent effort, but something was eating at her. She told Jiménez she saw no point in all that work. She wanted to drop the course.

Rodríguez was the third of seven children of a couple who had met in their native Mexico and came to America to work as cooks, before starting their own small restaurant, El Farolito (The Lantern), west of downtown Los Angeles. She did not learn English until the second grade. Despite a quick mind, she was not in the gifted program. A grade school teacher failed to send in her test results. She could not persuade anyone at Garfield to wedge her into the better courses until she reached the eleventh grade. By then she was almost too tired and too frazzled to care.

Her father demanded she work at least three school nights each week at the restaurant. His waitresses regularly stole from petty cash. He needed someone he could trust, someone quick with figures, to operate the cash register and catch discrepancies.

At home Rodríguez shared a bedroom in a little house on Herbert Street with an older brother and two younger sisters. She studied, when she had time, in her parents' bedroom. On the days she worked, she had to catch a bus that chugged here and there through downtown Los Angeles for ninety minutes before reaching the restaurant on Pico Boulevard. All this, she thought, and she had to fight to get into the gifted program? She was, she told everyone, pissed off.

She liked mathematics and was good at it. Lydia Trujillo, one of the department's best teachers, gave her an A in Algebra 2, but then took maternity leave, so Rodríguez had Escalante for the second half of the course. She began to fall behind. The restaurant duties frustrated her, and sometimes, she said, she could not understand Escalante's accent. He gave her a C, mostly for effort.

In Jiménez's trigonometry class the following year she did well for a while, then, tired and frustrated, stopped turning in homework. Another student who knew her told Jiménez what was happening. He called her in. Tearfully, she told him her parents wanted her to drop out.

"How about if I went to talk to them?" he asked. She answered with a smile, and a nod. Jiménez collected Escalante, who had more experience with difficult parents, and drove out to the restaurant one evening after school.

Escalante thought the place looked more like a bar than a restaurant. It was dark and oppressive, with men nursing beers at booths and tables. But the place was also clean and well-kept, in sharp contrast to other establishments on that rundown block.

A small woman came up to take their orders. "A glass of milk?" Escalante asked. She frowned. "Okay, just a glass of water. Are you

Mrs. Rodríguez?" She looked surprised. "We are teachers at Garfield High. This is Mr. Jiménez, Leticia's trigonometry professor. I am Escalante, the department chairman. We have to talk to you about her."

"What is it, Mr. Escalante?" she said, wiping her hands on a towel.

"Look, this is the situation. She could be an engineer, she could be a physicist, she could be a teacher. You should look to the future. This kid could be taking chemistry. If she does well this year we're gonna have her in calculus next year, but she needs to study. She can't be working here all the time."

The woman listened quietly. She seemed sympathetic, but Escalante sensed the decision was not hers. He recalls asking to speak to her husband. He had spotted the man replacing a beer keg in the back. Escalante remembers approaching Rodríguez's father, identifying himself and beginning a speech praising her academic talents.

The man listened quietly for a while, then raised a hand. "I think you have the wrong picture," he said. "Women are just here to get married and have kids and that's all. She has to work."

Escalante had kept his temper in low gear. Now, purposely, he shifted up a notch. "I think *you* have the wrong picture, sir. Number one, this kid is not eighteen years old. They have laws about children working in this country. Number two, you cannot force that on her. I just may have to tell the authorities. We have someone at school for that." He had no notion if the law applied at all, or if anyone at the school cared about any of this.

The father shrugged and waved them away. Escalante's shoulders slumped. He moved toward the door. The mother stopped them before they left. "What is it she has to do?" she asked.

"She has to do the assignment and the homework," Escalante said. "She has to have time to do that."

They left. "I think we're gonna lose this kid," Jiménez said. Escalante shook his head. "We gotta keep trying. Maybe we can call somebody."

The next day, Leticia Rodríguez appeared in trigonometry with a rare smile. "I guess I have to thank you," she told Jiménez. "I heard what you did. My Dad told me: Only two days a week at the restaurant." Her parents planned to buy her a desk—something she had never had before. She paused, frowned the usual Rodríguez frown, then looked up at him. "I have *so* much work to do," she said.

Luis Cervantes considered that sort of attitude unsophisticated. Homework was fine, as long as you did not talk about it or let it interfere with work on your automobile. On cool evenings he raced his 1965 Chevy Impala on the dusty, usually empty streets of the Commerce warehouse district, near Union and Pacific. He liked to feel the wind ripple his shoulder-length hair.

He wore a Judas Priest T-shirt, Levi's, and Levi's jacket and hoped no one knew he was an A student. He loved the car. He had had it since the ninth grade. He had worked several hours a week as a night clerk at a local hospital to pay for it. He was going to take calculus the following year, and be in the marching band too, no matter what Escalante said about it.

Martín Olvera was with his friend Cervantes all the way. Olvera was quick and bright, with eclectic tastes in music, clothing, and acquaintances. He lived in a small wood-frame house throbbing with television sets on too loud, emotions left unchecked. His parents did not get on well. His brothers were rough. He blocked it all out and sampled the Garfield social scene. He tried the rockers one year, wearing a T-shirt advertising a heavy metal band. Then he tried disco, the guys with the flowing hair, and even made friends with the computer nerds, who had their own special loneliness. But he liked Luis, straight, clearheaded, thrill-seeking Luis. And they both loved mathematics and thought they would be brilliant, rich doctors someday.

Aili Tapio expected trouble pushing her way into Cervantes's little marching band clique, but not that much trouble. Everybody knew she was smart. Her father, dead of a liver ailment when she was seven, had been a Finnish immigrant, a machinist who married an East Los Angeles grocer's daughter whom he met at the Hollywood Palladium.

Tapio was slim and pretty, with small delicate features and brown hair. She was very stubborn, but no one saw that in such a private girl. She only got A's. When she joined the marching band, and announced she wanted to be a drummer, the boys—led by Cervantes—teased her badly. They could be very cruel. She cried once. But one of them, René Gardea, a boy as quiet as she was, felt sorry for her. That feeling soon turned to something deeper, and that helped.

Margaret Zamarripa was in the drill team, the next best thing to the band. By her junior year in high school she was living virtually on her own. Her father tended his various properties, scattered among the flatlands stretching east of Los Angeles. He let her, and an elder sister and brother, stay in his house in El Monte, while he and Margaret's mother stayed in Los Angeles. Father and daughter argued often. She had his temper and his independent streak. She drove his black Cadillac to school and thought about graduating into a business career. She wanted to make her own money. She liked numbers, and calculus sounded interesting.

If she hadn't been a good friend of one of Jiménez's better seniors, a teaching assistant in trigonometry that year, Jiménez probably would not have accused her of cheating on an examination. It seemed out of character for this girl with the bright red lipstick and the dark flowing hair, the long aristocratic neck and aquiline nose, suddenly to score a solid A on a test. Jiménez told her he was giving her an F instead. He was certain she had taken the answers from her friend. She was livid. She had not liked Jiménez anyway. This was the end. She complained to Escalante, and something was worked out. But she did not forget it.

Elsa Bolado also had a long memory for slights. She did not remember her own youthful excesses, such as in the second grade when she called Leticia Rodríguez, struggling to learn English, a wetback. Bolado called lots of people lots of things. She played a saxophone in the band; no one dared make fun of that. She played softball and volleyball and ran the 400- and 800-meter dashes, usually making the city finals. Boys followed her movements with loving eyes, but usually she ignored them. She had things to do. She was attractive, with dark hair. An unmistakable strength showed through, and some fire. She hated mathematics, but she was going to take calculus and get a good grade because she wanted to go to college. God help the student, the teacher, or any mortal, who stood in her way.

Gradillas would encounter an enraged Bolado much later. For now he returned to Garfield to find Escalante joyous in praise of his latest calculus team. "Next year, we will have eighteen, sir. *Eighteen!* We

132

get the big plus, sir. All we need is a few more books. You come and talk to them. They going to do well on the exam."

Gradillas studied the previous year's class chart and noticed that Escalante seemed unwilling to trust many other teachers with the prerequisite courses for calculus. He used Jiménez, and gave some promising Algebra 2 students to Lydia Trujillo. But he took most of the higher-level courses himself, including calculus. That, Gradillas felt, was not good.

A few years before, John Bennett had enlisted Tom Woessner to team-teach an expanded Advance Placement American history course. Bennett never had more than fifteen in the course, but to justify two teachers, they coaxed the number up to twenty-five, and allowed a third of the class to skip the AP test itself.

The expanded course worked fine. Bennett was quick-witted and imaginative. Woessner, a short, genial man with a gray-streaked beard, enveloped his students in love and concern. He remembered the pain he had suffered in his own youth when he could do nothing right in class. Bennett and Woessner worked well together, and increasingly viewed Escalante, in his little empire atop the 200 Building, as a wild Bolivian autocrat who wanted results at any cost. Gradillas also thought Escalante was working too hard, particularly with his load of night courses.

Gradillas appreciated what his little squad of AP teachers was accomplishing, but he recognized that they affected a mere handful of teenagers. Advanced Placement did little for the vast majority of Garfield's 3,000 students. Standardized test scores, in math as in everything else, were low and had not moved much in the four years Gradillas was away.

Escalante complained weekly about the thin crust of prepared students he had to choose from. The junior highs did not encourage much mathematics. Most Garfield students took no more than one basic math course for graduation. He had to show what could be done with these Chicano kids. He could not do what he wanted to do if he had to scour Martin's list of gifted students each year for the few that had not written school off as a waste of time.

Gradillas, for all his hesitancy about Escalante's raw enthusiasms, admitted to himself that the teacher had a point. He had to push the standard higher. That meant less basic mathematics, more algebra, more real mathematics teachers. Downtown might not be ready for it.

‖ 11 ‖

Jaimito Escalante heard his father several times that night in March 1982. The man's feet hit the carpet with a leaden sound as he went into the kitchen, poured a glass of water, walked back to his bedroom, returned to the kitchen again, poured a glass of milk, all in a seemingly endless cycle. The next morning the elder Escalante was pale and unusually quiet.

Jaimito was twenty-six and an engineer at Teledyne. He had long felt that his father childishly avoided inconvenient facts of life and had to be reminded he was no longer a San Calixto schoolboy.

"Dad, I don't think you should go to school today. I know you didn't sleep well."

Escalante arranged his features into a look of surprise. "No, no," he said. "I feel lovely."

He did not want to recount his stomach-churning thoughts about the Medfly Lady and that counselor, Big Mama. The Medfly Lady was one of his algebra teachers. He had so named her because she was an admirer of then California Governor Edmund G. (Jerry) Brown, Jr., whom many had blamed for a recent outbreak of the Mediterranean fruit fly. For months Escalante had complained about her determination to bring her algebra lessons down to a level she thought her students could handle, rather than challenge the *burros* and throw out those who failed to measure up. Big Mama, so dubbed by the students for her warmth and malleability, had let seven students drop his Algebra 2 class without telling him, or putting up a fight.

How was he going to build the program with such people? That must be what was keeping him up, he thought. He did feel a little woozy, but it was probably something he ate. He had eighteen calculus students. It was just two months before the AP test, and he had no time to get sick.

About eleven in the morning at school he felt a twinge on his left side. He had been erasing the board with an annoyingly tiny eraser. He had asked for a big one, a chamois attached to a long board, but it took the district a year to come up with such things. When the pain became worse, he carefully walked to his desk and sat down. He asked one of his problem students, the one he purposely placed in a desk next to his own, to erase the board.

The boy gave the teacher a close look. Escalante made many demands on him, but this was the first time he had ever been asked to erase the board. "Kimo, you not feeling well?"

"No, no, no. Everything's all right." Escalante flashed a confident smile. "I just lost my control because I didn't know how to solve the problem."

"I think you're not feeling well, Kimo. Don't worry, we gonna behave. We not gonna do anything."

Escalante realized he was not going to be able to stand again without severe pain. He called for attention and, still sitting, assigned six problems from the textbook for the rest of the hour. He sent a student to get a cup of water. When the lunch bell rang, he sent them on their way and asked the last one to close the door.

"Kimo," said the boy, "you been drinking?" Escalante's door was never closed, particularly during lunch.

"Yeah," Escalante said. "I'd appreciate it if you do this for me."

"Some kids will want to get in."

"Well, like you say, I've been drinking."

Locked away from the world, he put his head on his desk and focused on the pain in his intestine. Had he ever felt something like this before? He would skip lunch and take it easy the rest of the day. When fifth period arrived, he managed to write two problems on the board, assign a few more from the book, and then sit and meditate. "You look a little yellow, Mr. Escalante," a student said.

The calculus team arrived for its afternoon drills at 2:00 P.M. He pointed to the proper exercises and sat still. They drifted away after a couple of hours. At 6:00 P.M. he greeted his night school class. It was only basic mathematics, but he liked the students, immigrants like him, and it kept him busy.

At 8:00 P.M., while sketching a problem on the board, he felt a knife-edged blow to his left side, passing over to his right. Without a word, he walked slowly out the door and down the hall to the stairs. There was a drinking fountain on the next floor.

Halfway down the steps, he began to wonder if this had been such a good idea. His eyes refused to focus. His grip on the handrail weakened. He slipped, slid, and then tumbled down the rest of the stairs, landing unconscious on the linoleum floor below.

His students had their assignment; no one came to check. Five minutes later he woke up. He staggered to the water fountain and felt the cool liquid bathe his face. The mirror in the boys' lavatory revealed a cut over his eye and his face caked with blood. He tried to clean himself with paper towels and wipe the blood off the floor.

It was a slow evening in Jiménez's night school class. He was at his desk examining some homework when Escalante appeared at the door. "Come on in, Jaime," he said. "Don't be shy."

The voice from the door was barely audible: "I can't make it. I got to go home."

Jiménez rushed out and inspected the crusted gash in his friend's forehead. "It's nothing," Escalante said. "But can you do me a favor? Tell the principal I'm going home and please watch my class for the rest of the period. And, uh, . . . my desk's open, please lock it."

"You should let me drive you home. I don't think you're going to make it. You're almost entirely out of it."

"No, no, no," Escalante said, heading down the hall. "I'm going to leave. I'm going to leave."

He steered the VW onto the Pomona Freeway and fought to keep the pain inside until he was home. He pulled into his driveway, safe, and then discovered he did not have the strength to get out of the car. He listened to his heartbeat for a few minutes, then managed to stagger in, breathing heavily.

Jaimito met him in the kitchen and immediately saw the cut. "Holy smokes, Dad, what happened to you?"

"I fell. It's nothing. Don't worry about it. Just get me a cup of coffee." His eyes were moving in odd directions as he said it.

"No, Dad. We're going to the hospital."

Escalante hated hospitals. He distrusted doctors. He had felt something like this pain in his side before. At Fabiola's insistence, he had seen a doctor and been told he had gallstones. He'd ignored the diagnosis and returned to school.

Now, in the emergency room, a young resident was poking and

prodding and telling him he needed stitches for that cut. Several times he tried to get up and leave, but Jaimito and the doctor formed an unbreakable wall. When Escalante became particularly troublesome, the doctor gave him a sedative, and he dropped into a deep sleep, the first he had had in some time.

In the morning, he pestered the nurse until she let him call the school. He reached Elsa Bolado. He had had an accident, a fall, he said. "Are you all studying?"

"Yes, sir, don't worry about a thing."

A substitute, a little man with round glasses, came to his classroom and did his best to fill in. It was not the same.

The resident told Escalante he had had a heart attack. That, Escalante thought, confirmed the idiocy of doctors.

"Mr. Escalante, you couldn't move your arms when you came in here."

"Ah, that because I used to play handball. That probably what it is. If you'll excuse me, I have to go back to school. I'm feeling well."

At Garfield, the first substitute had given way to a second. This one, a thinner, younger man, attempted a solution on the board, then stepped back and asked for questions. "Sir?" said Bolado, raising her hand.

"Yes?"

"Sir, just how far did you go in math at school?"

The hospital staff became so weary of Escalante's demands and escape attempts that the resident offered a deal. If Escalante promised to go home and rest, they would let him out. "Two weeks' rest, minimum," the doctor said.

Fabiola drove him home. She watched without surprise as he dropped her off, moved over to the driver's seat, and headed for Garfield.

Four or five hours into the school day, as Escalante basked in the glory of near martyrdom, Gradillas came by to make his own examination. Escalante wore a large bandage over one eye. "I'm not going to accept you back in class," Gradillas said, "unless I get something from the doctor."

"Certainly, sir! No problem. Don't worry about it."

No doctor's note ever appeared. When the attacks resumed in November, he submitted to a weekend at an Arcadia hospital to remove his gallbladder. In the meantime, the episode added to his mystique. Every member of the 1982 calculus class thought he had had a heart attack and just shook it off.

Cervantes pondered this one night as he sat exhausted at his desk, his homework still undone. If Kimo can do it, we can do it. If he wants to teach us that bad, we can learn.

For days after his return, Escalante chanted his new mantra. "You see! You see! You *burros* give me a heart attack. But I come back! I'm still the champ."

If it had not been for teenage sloth and counselors with limp spines, Escalante thought, he might have had thirty students in calculus in 1982. But eighteen was, still, the best ever, and as he learned more about each one, he discovered they had some unusual qualities.

Fernando Bocanegra adored animals and numbers and displayed uncommon talent with both since he was a child. But no one considered him especially bright. He had had to force himself into Algebra 2 in the tenth grade. He was not on the gifted list—a primary source for counselors seeking good mathematics students—and was told there was no room for him. A youthful uncle of his, just a grade ahead at Garfield, told him to appeal to Escalante. The teacher grunted and said he had room.

Bocanegra always fought nervousness in difficult classes, but Escalante was different. His accent was ridiculous, his classroom manner intriguingly casual. When Bocanegra moved on to Jiménez's trigonometry and math analysis, he found he also enjoyed the younger man's straightforward approach. Back with Escalante in his senior year, he felt the pieces fall into place. Some thought Bocanegra might be the best mathematics student in the class, and Bocanegra did not disagree.

The gifted list had also missed Josie Richkarday, but she was too outgoing to let that bother her. She was beautiful—a perfect figure and long, light brown hair. She had been a cheerleader for as long as she could remember. When she appeared in class one game day, glowing in her white, red, and blue uniform, Escalante broke into a clumsy parody of one of her cheers. She studied him for a moment, then said calmly, "That's not the way to do it, sir."

Her smile lifted spirits, and her laugh raised male goose bumps. But she churned inside. Her father had left the family when she was nine months old. Her mother supported five children on her wages at a local spring factory. When Richkarday was fifteen, she began to work twenty hours a week making keys at Sears. She wanted to teach, then go into business and make enough money for a life-style she had only seen from a distance. The pressure of work and study would help give her an ulcer by age seventeen, but no one who watched her smile and laugh could ever tell that.

Raúl Haro's father, like some other fathers of Garfield students, had been forced to leave grade school in Mexico to help support his family. Most Garfield parents who came north shrugged off their lack of education. Haro's father never did. He told his children of his love for working mathematics problems and word games and all the academic pursuits he missed. His son was very dark and slim and quiet. He, too, never made the gifted list. But from the time he was ten he could play the flute with enough skill to win the tutelage of a local university professor.

At Garfield, the irresistible lure of the marching band moved him to switch to a more muscular instrument, the trumpet. He also liked mathematics, and he thought of becoming an engineer. Escalante wrote him off in Algebra 2 as a hopeless musician, and seemed astonished when he took a summer trigonometry course, under the federally funded MESA program, and appeared in calculus his senior year.

Escalante teased Haro and the other band and drill members— Bolado, Tapio, Cervantes, and Zamarripa. "All you do is follow the leader," he said. In his senior year, Haro became band president, in Escalante's eyes a cut below king of the gypsies.

Although all of Escalante's 1982 calculus students traced at least part of their ancestry to Mexico, María Jiménez was one of the few actually born there. When she was two, her parents left Aguascalientes for California. They sneaked across the border with María and her two older brothers. Her father found work in a Los Angeles fish-packing plant, and they settled into a tidy four-bedroom house on Arizona Street. María studied hard for college and was put on the gifted list.

Her parents discouraged dating, as did the parents of her friend Sandra López, another calculus student. Escalante saw her ability and took her into one of his basic mathematics classes to give her special instruction in Algebra 2 when a scheduling mistake put her into geometry instead.

Jesse López had the short, thick arms and muscular torso of a boxer, along with the wide smile of a ringside announcer. He liked parties and other forms of teenage recreation, but he came from a family unusually serious about education. His parents had come from Mexico, but his mother, tall and attractive, had the unusual distinction of a high school diploma. His father worked at a metal-plating factory and lectured his children on the need to do well in school and escape a life of hard labor, like his. In the third grade, López was sent to a parochial school and encountered the motivating power of a certain Sister Nicholas, until the distance from home forced his parents to return him to the local public school.

López did not like Escalante when he first had him in Algebra 2. He asked a question and the teacher snapped at him: "Didn't you pay attention?" At the beginning of his calculus year, López walked into Room 233 two minutes late. Escalante folded his arms and stared at the boy. "We're not going to start class until you leave," he said. "You have to be on time. You can't be late." López did not move. Escalante disgorged his five-minute lecture on the unredeemable shortcomings of American teenagers, particularly high school seniors. Then he resumed the lesson. After class he took López aside. "Look, I'm only trying to discipline you guys for your own good. You have to discipline yourselves to be on time. Everything counts." The boy liked that approach. He resolved never to be late again.

All of the 1981–82 calculus students adopted, to various degrees, the Escalante work ethic. Some, like the quartet of Bocanegra, Jesse López, Roy Márquez, and Alex Guerrero, arrived at school when the library opened at 7:00 A.M. to finish their calculus homework, or other homework delayed by calculus. At 11:22 A.M. they would begin Escalante's hour-long class in 233, then stay there through lunch.

Escalante had insisted that each student, and parents, sign a contract promising the student would return at 2:00 P.M., when most seniors were leaving for the day, and remain for more lecture and exercises until 5:00 P.M. That was to remind the parents as much as their children of the seriousness of the venture. Many adults living in East Los Angeles had never even attended a high school, much less taken a college-level course in one. They had to be persuaded the time might not be better spent in chores at home.

Escalante treated his calculus students like a well-drilled team looking forward to the big game. It had been an exciting year for Garfield sports. The football team had beaten archrival Roosevelt and won its first city 2-A Division championship with a 3–0, last-second field goal victory over Jordan High. Escalante wanted that same kind of excitement in Room 233.

He liked to mix the routine—drills and jokes and a quiz and lecture and more jokes and drills and card tricks and a bit of volleyball and more drills. He became the coach, also a big brother, an uncle, in some cases a father, and used that relationship to lay heavy guilt on all who did not do their homework.

After Escalante and Jiménez rescued her from the worst of her restaurant duties, Leticia Rodríguez took on an aching load of new courses. She took chemistry in the afternoon at Cal State, which kept her from some of Escalante's after-school calculus classes. Sometimes she did not finish her homework.

In December, after she missed an assignment, he exploded: "Go to your *stupid* counselor and tell him you're dropping this course. I don't want to see you in this class."

Hurt and enraged, refusing to cry in the classroom, she walked out the door and stomped downstairs to the rest room. She did not see Martin, but simply returned the next day.

Within a week it happened again. "You're going to have to drop the chemistry course or you're out of here," Escalante said. She flushed beet red as he continued, "I don't know why Mr. Jiménez always said you were his top student. Look at how bad you're doing over here." She thought she could hear people giggling in the corners of the room.

"I'm leaving," she said.

"Nah, you can't leave."

"I'm leaving!"

Her shoes hit the linoleum with an audible slap as she headed for Jiménez's room. She told him she was dropping calculus. After all that trouble with her father, with the restaurant work she still had to do, this just wasn't worth it.

"Just calm down," Jiménez said. He had seen the Escalante technique. He had, very occasionally, used it himself. She would finish the chemistry course by January, Jiménez explained to Escalante.

So she stayed in calculus, but she did not forgive. It had been very embarrassing, and Escalante had sounded just like her father.

No romances blossomed within the class. They were all too close, perhaps, or too competitive. Some of the boys teased Rodríguez, the quickest to anger and, next to Tapio, seemingly the brightest of the girls. "Ah, Letty, you'll just end up barefoot and pregnant in the kitchen," one said, and waited to see the steam rising from her ears.

As the examination day approached, even the smallest spark could ignite an emotional explosion. Someone brought a precious supply of McDonald's provisions to one after-school study session. When Bolado returned from the rest room to find her french fries gone, she began to weep uncontrollably. Richkarday, her friend and the culprit, was too embarrassed to confess. Only when Escalante offered his own fries did Bolado stop to sniffle and chew.

Too much was happening at once. In the last three weeks before the AP examination, most of Escalante's students had to decide on a college. In Beverly Hills, offers of admission from large eastern campuses were quickly and eagerly accepted by high school seniors as their parents quivered with pride and relief. In East Los Angeles the same offers produced a very different reaction.

Like most recent immigrants, Latino families stuck together. In many cases both parents and children in East Los Angeles agreed that an East Coast education put too much distance, geographic and cultural, between the family's central core and one of its members. The family might be fractured for survival, such as sending a brother or son from the barren farms of Sonora to the job-rich cities of the United States. But it made no sense to travel so far for just the upward mobility of an Ivy League degree. The journey from Mexico was traumatic enough.

Even when offered huge scholarships to distant universities, Garfield students sensed they would be uncomfortable and homesick at such places. Their parents disliked the distance and the cost. Even if the money was not coming out of their pocket, it still made them wary. If the student was a girl, her parents often objected to any arrangement that meant living away from home before she was safely married.

Rodríguez might have been expected to yearn for a break from her family, but she agonized over her offer from Princeton. Fernando Bocanegra and Alex Guerrero took some time before they agreed to go to Columbia. Tapio, who would be the class valedictorian, turned down Harvard in favor of USC. An astonished visitor, unfamiliar with East LA values, accepted at face value her explanation that she did not want to pass up a chance to play her drum in the Trojan band.

Bolado could not make up her mind between the University of California, Los Angeles, and Pomona College. She skipped calculus to see the Pomona campus, her last chance before the deadline. When she returned to class the next day she found Escalante, his expression stormy, waiting at the door.

"Go to your counselor," he said. "You're kicked out. You're not going to take the test."

She broke into sobs, huddled against the wall for a moment, and then headed downstairs to find Martin. The counselor knew she had gone to Pomona, but never guessed Escalante would use their old routine on Bolado. Anyone but Elsa, he thought. "I'll talk to him for you," he said.

The night before the May 19 AP examination, Josie Richkarday tried to doze off early on the dining room floor, just as she had been doing every night. It did not work. By 11:00 P.M. she was awake and she was crying. She prayed to a statue of the Madonna on a living room shelf. I'm certainly a devout Catholic this week, she thought. She lay back and sobbed until sleep finally came.

Escalante had advised peace, quiet, a good dinner, and early bed. Socially precocious, often offended by adolescent behavior, Margaret Zamarripa considered that excellent advice. She would not have crammed even if ordered to. You either knew it, she thought, or you didn't. At seven-thirty the next morning, when the Cadillac ran out of gas on the Pomona Freeway, some of her adult composure evaporated, and she wondered if she could find anyone to rescue her in time. Her father appeared promptly with a can of fuel, and she was off with minutes to spare.

In 233, the assembled calculus team fought nervousness by creating a locker-room atmosphere. It was the big game, they told themselves, and they had it sewn up. Several had slept poorly, some had cried, but adolescent hormones had wiped away most traces of the difficult night. Cervantes had arrived in denim shorts, a symbol of his disdain for the test and a concession to the late spring heat. Bolado tried to pull the shorts down in back. When she failed, she spent several minutes chasing him around the room, pleading for another chance.

Andreda Pruitt, Garfield's head counselor, looked forward to May and the AP calculus examination. The College Board required schools to provide their own proctors; she always volunteered. She had been a mathematics major at Alabama State College. She enjoyed taking an extra free-response section off to her office afterward and trying the problems herself.

As the calculus students strolled into Room 411 on the ground floor of the main building, Pruitt pointed them to scattered seats. She began the test and watched with pride as they attacked the multiple-choice section, grinding down on their No. 2 pencils with wide-eyed intensity. She enjoyed the happy, confident talk at the break. When the free-response part of the test began, she felt sure the overall result would be very good.

Although each of the seven questions required more thought than any of the forty-five multiple-choice problems, most of the students went through them quickly with few mishaps. Question 6 proved to be the toughest. It said:

> A tank with a rectangular base and rectangular sides is to be open at the top. It is to be constructed so that its width is 4 meters and its volume is 36 cubic meters. If building the tank costs $10 per square meter for the base and $5 per square meter for the sides, what is the cost of the least expensive tank?

Escalante loved problems with an engineering twist, but the formula to unlock this particular riddle had come up at the time of his gallbladder attack. It was an element that often made AP more difficult than a college final: AP questions could easily diverge from the material a student had been taught, whereas few college professors would test a concept not included in their lectures.

Escalante's substitute during his absence had proposed a solution for volume problems that some in the class vaguely remembered. They tried to work it in as best they could. Others took only a swipe at question 6 before going back to check their other work. They could get a 3, the minimum score for college credit, with good answers on only three of the seven questions or partial credit on six or seven questions.

For most of the class, the examination had gone well to this point, but question 6 remained a puzzle. They had only a few minutes left to wrap up two to three years of intense effort.

It may never be entirely clear what happened in Room 411 near the end of the examination. Years later two students would say that they and others copied from a suggested solution to question 6 surreptitiously passed around by another classmate when Pruitt was not looking. Pruitt and the other students would vehemently deny this, and the original two would then deny or back off from their statements, leaving the circumstances cloudier than before, with only a few pieces of test paper, a pile of statistical analyses, and differing notions of chance and human nature left as guides to the truth. Time and emotion are an explosive mix, as the next several weeks would prove.

John Bennett collected the eighteen calculus examinations from Pruitt and slipped them into the special AP mailing envelope for return to the College Board.

He felt good. Garfield students had taken a total of sixty-nine AP examinations, a school record. Besides the usual glut of Spanish language examinations, thirty that year, and the surging calculus program, he and Woessner had persuaded six students to take AP American history and Dennis Campagna had fifteen who took English composition and literature.

No screwups this time, he noted. Two years before Garfield had mistakenly given the Spanish examination on the wrong day. The proctors had tried to cover up by having the students write the correct day on their test booklets. Someone at the College Board found out and sent a heated reprimand. That was behind him. He mailed the sixty-nine tests with a smile.

The mailing envelope bore a box number for the College Board in Princeton, New Jersey. The Educational Testing Service, which ran the program for the board, had moved from Princeton to the suburb of Lawrence Township in 1958. Officials of the ETS said they kept the old mailing address because Lawrence had no postal facility capable of handling planeloads of test applications and completed examinations.

The ETS headquarters nestled among 400 acres of undulating meadows and scattered woods just outside the university town. The low-slung stone-and-glass buildings could not be seen from Rosedale Road where an ETS entrance sign told motorists to turn. A visitor winding down toward the headquarters buildings first drove past Canadian geese preening themselves in the ETS pond and might have seen a deer or two before sighting any human habitation.

In late May and early June of 1982, 23,825 completed Calculus AB examinations, including the eighteen from Garfield, arrived at the AP grading office in the ETS complex. They were part of a total of 188,933 examinations that would have to be graded by the end of June to give universities time to use the grades in their placement of AP freshmen in advanced courses. Machines could grade the computer sheets the students had used to mark their answers on the multiple-choice section. But the free-response section, the part that made the AP examinations virtually unique among ETS and College Board programs, required human graders—803 of them summoned for one-week shifts of wearying mental labor during the second and third weeks of June.

These "reading" sessions, as the ETS called them, combined elements of a turn-of-the-century sweatshop and a fraternity weekend. They had become enormously popular among the college instructors and high school teachers recruited to participate. Working and living at Princeton area schools, usually Trenton State and Rider colleges, the readers arrived in their most casual holiday clothes to sit on folding chairs for seven hours a day and grade 1,000 to 2,000 free-response questions each in less than a week. The calculus readers rated each answer on a nine-point scale: 9 for a correct solution, 5 for presenting most of the right steps but not the right answer, 0 for a sheet that was blank, completely wrong, or full of irrelevant comments on life in the twentieth century. Answers that fell between those points were scored accordingly.

Accuracy and consistency were crucial. Newcomers were paired with veteran readers and encouraged to seek their advice. "Table leaders" further checked the work of less experienced readers to ensure uniformity throughout the room. By the end of the day, said South Carolina reader Alexia Latimer, everyone felt a deep urge to "talk and drink and tell dirty jokes."

The experience had helped create a national esprit de corps among AP teachers, but no Garfield faculty member had ever participated. The routine was largely a mystery to Bennett, Escalante, Jiménez, Gradillas, and anyone else at Garfield who might care what it involved.

In June 1982, 153 readers arrived at Trenton State to grade the Calculus AB free responses, as well as free responses from the 8,093 Calculus BC examinations. The readers were sent to work in seven classrooms. For efficiency, each would take only one of the seven questions at a time. He or she would read several hundred versions of question 3, for instance, before turning to a stack of question 4s.

Organizers tried to mix the booklets with a "soft shuffle," tossing handfuls of tests into different dispersal boxes, followed by a "hard shuffle," depositing each successive booklet in a different box. The idea was to make sure a reader's senses would not be dulled by grading in succession several students from the same school with, possibly, the same approach to a problem. But that summer a lack of time, or a shortage of the college students usually paid to do such chores, forced them to curtail the hard shuffle. That increased somewhat the chances of one reader seeing more than one examination from the same school.

About midway through the grading session one reader noticed something strange in a botched solution to question 6. The student had begun with an incorrect formula for the cost of the rectangular tank, the question that had bothered so many from Escalante's class.

The test taker had written: $C = 5(10w) + 5(2)(4h) + 5(2hw)$. That was wrong; the first term should have been $10(4w)$ rather than $5(10w)$. The student compounded the mistake later in the answer by substituting $9/w$ for h in the term $10hw$ and simplifying it to $10(9/w)$ instead of 90.

It was not the mistakes themselves that bothered the reader. This appeared to be the most difficult problem of the seven, and he had seen it butchered dozens of ways. What disturbed him was that another examination he had read within the hour showed the *identical* errors. He searched his stack and found the other test. He took both examinations to the table leader, who found them interesting enough to take to Patricia Henry, the chief reader for AP calculus.

Henry, then fifty-two, was an intense, brown-haired mathematics professor from Weber State College in Ogden, Utah. She had taught high school calculus earlier in her career, and had been coming to the June reading sessions for fourteen years. As chief reader she reported to work in shirt, slacks, comfortable shoes, and a sweater to combat the air conditioning when it was operating. She shared a spare classroom with two clerks, who helped her stay ahead of a daily stream of odd twists and small crises.

She had seen plenty of silly mistakes and odd coincidences in the booklets passed to her by suspicious readers. Her in-box received a steady trickle of booklets containing erotic drawings, chatty letters to the reader, poetry, and other unexpected messages. Back in May some of the more imaginative students had finished early, or could not finish at all, and sought ways to pass the time. Since the messages often identified the test taker, the chief reader had to grade them herself to avoid any taint of bias.

These two tests were different, however. She had to explore the possibility that one test taker had copied the other. She broke open the special flap, sealed by the students themselves, that covered their name and that of their school. What she saw upset her. She put the booklets aside.

Within a day, she had two more pairs of booklets found by two other readers with the same similarities on question 6. As she opened each one, she became more disturbed. They were all from the same place. All six students had apparently taken the test in the same room at a school called Garfield, in Los Angeles.

She reached for a suspected violation report blank, something she rarely had to do. It was not just the idea of cheating that bothered her. She had read the names. They were all Hispanic.

Pat Henry had been born in Minnesota but moved to Utah as a girl and later married a man named Fernández. Her five children all bore the name Fernández. She did not like this at all.

Luis Cervantes planned to go to Berkeley and transform himself into another Louis—Pasteur. He would become a great medical researcher, but that would be a lot of work, so first he wanted a vacation. He had planned to go to Hawaii with his girlfriend. He had $800 saved from his hospital job. Unfortunately the tickets and rooms cost more than that, and she had no money at all. Well, he thought, how about Mexico? He visited the girl's mother and described in glowing detail a prim and proper Mazatlán vacation: see the sights, ride horses, eat a few good meals, sleep in separate rooms. He would pay for everything. Fine, the woman said. Luis was a very nice boy, a very *smart* boy. She could trust him.

The six days passed in a warm, golden, sweet blur. In mid-July the two returned refreshed and even more in love.

Cervantes rifled the mail, looking for his AP score. It was not there. He called Olvera, who reported with delight his own 5. Bocanegra, Haro, Márquez, Rodíguez, Tapio, and Zamarripa had all received 5s. East LA bubbled with little celebrations and the chatter of proud parents. So where, Cervantes wondered, was his score?

The letter arrived a week later by certified mail. He opened it eagerly, hoping to see his very own 5. Instead he read:

Dear Mr. Cervantes:

I am writing to you because the ETS Board of Review believes there is reason to question your May 1982 Advanced Placement—Math Calculus AB grades. This is a serious problem, and I would like to talk with you by telephone after you have read this letter and the enclosed pamphlet.

The Board of Review is made up of experienced staff members responsible for determining the validity of grades that are questioned. In reviewing your grades, they found close agreement of your answers with those on another answer sheet from the same test center. Such agreement is unusual and suggests that copying occurred. The Board doubts that the grades are valid for you because of these unusual circumstances. My job, as Secretary to the Board, is to help you clear up this problem.

Most often, candidates clear up these problems by:

- *telling the Board to cancel the grades and to refund the fee; OR*
- *providing additional information that will show the grades are valid; OR*
- *taking the test again privately and without charge, to show that the grades are valid.*

The letter, signed by Antonia M. Rosenbaum, said Cervantes could, if he wished, turn the whole dispute over to the University of California, Berkeley, where he was seeking the AP credit, and ask officials there to make their own decision. Or he could appeal to an arbitrator selected by the American Arbitration Association. She continued:

ETS is concerned about your right to privacy and follows procedures designed to protect that right. For example, your grade report indicates only that your current grades have been delayed or that you were absent from the recent test administration. Also, this problem will not be discussed with anyone outside ETS unless you ask to have others informed. Your current grades will be reported if the doubts about their validity can be removed. If you do not respond to this letter or if doubts remain after further action, your current grades will not be reported. Whatever happens, you may register for and take the Advanced Placement—Math Calculus AB test at any time in the future.

Because you have a difficult decision to make, you may wish to talk about it with your parents, a teacher, your principal, or a guidance counselor. You may even want to have one of them on the line when you call. Please call collect if you have any questions or if you are ready to make a decision. My telephone number is (609) 734-1534.

Cervantes read the letter again, very slowly. There could be no mistaking the meaning. They were saying he had cheated.

He began to get angry. He had worked for everything he had. He had worked for his car. He had bought his new motorcycle with his own money. He had paid for his Mexican vacation. He had purchased the right to his calculus grade with three years of worn pencils, headaches, and 2:00 A.M. bedtimes. How could they just snatch all that away?

Bolado had been living in a UCLA dormitory that summer while taking a seven-week summer school program for incoming freshmen. Her sister called with the news that she had received a 4 on her AP calculus test. Not perfect, she thought, but good enough. A week later her sister called again with inexplicable news of a letter saying her score was invalid. Bolado was confused, then frightened. She did whatever she did when she felt the least bit of fear. She made a dozen telephone calls, checking in with her Garfield entourage.

The glorious report of his 5 on the exam, followed quickly by Rosenbaum's vague accusation of copying, led Raúl Haro to think of one thing—the Granada Hills High School band. They were rich; Garfield was poor. Their uniform colors dazzled the eye. Their instruments sparkled in the sun. How many times had he and his friends drilled and sweated to be just right in a city band competition, then found the prize awarded to Granada Hills, as if it were their divine right? Garfield tried its hardest, yet could not ever get more than third place. This was more of the same. It did not matter what you did, but where you came from.

That summer Leticia Rodríguez had dipped a toe into the dark waters of the Ivy League. She'd enrolled in a premedical program at Columbia for minority students, a prelude to her moving to Princeton in the fall. When she returned home in late July, she called Jiménez, her old friend and protector. "What's new?" she said.

Jiménez took a moment to calm himself before telling her. "Go check your mail, Leticia," he said. Her mother never bothered to read her mail, particularly if it was in English. There they were in the stack, both of them: her score of 5, and the letter from Rosenbaum.

Aili Tapio read the letter, her anger rising with each paragraph. She was the class valedictorian, a 4.0, and now this. Her other unhappy encounters with Anglos bubbled to the surface. There had been an English teacher in junior high, when she was bused to a school out in the northwest suburbs. The woman had no praise for her, no matter what she did.

Just a few months before, she had taken a night school accounting course at Cal State. Most of the other students were adults, but she had received the highest score on the first test. The proctor did not believe a girl who looked no older than fourteen could do so well. In a subsequent test, he accused her of cheating after she absentmindedly stretched and looked around the room. When he graded the test, however, he discovered her score was higher than that of anyone who had sat near her.

Fernando Bocanegra considered the news of his 5 on the calculus examination a personal triumph. All his education had led up to that moment. Nearly everyone else, he thought, had been on the gifted list. They had had a special counselor, while all he had was a lump of a man who never got him into any classes he wanted. He showed the grade to his parents. He was so overwrought that he went outside for some air. He was afraid he would explode.

The Rosenbaum letter hit him so hard that, talking about it five years later, he still had to pause to let the bile drain from his throat. He was upset. He was frustrated.

Josie Richkarday did not know what to think when she saw the notice to pick up a certified letter at the post office. She had received her calculus score the week before. Her mother dropped it by during cheerleading practice. She looked at it, then went off to a corner of the Garfield stadium and cried. It was only a 4. She had worked so hard!

She picked up the certified letter and tore it open in the car. She had to read it twice, going back over some paragraphs several times, trying to dampen her panic and discern what it meant.

María Jiménez had gone to Guadalajara, as she did nearly every summer, to see her grandparents. Her parents called to say there was something wrong with the test and she would have to fly home immediately. Escalante wanted to talk to her.

The Escalantes had purchased the ranch house on Orange Avenue in Monrovia for $70,000 in 1977. It was not large, but it had an extra bedroom for a study. Escalante could sit and grade papers until early morning, surrounded by his books, his files, and perhaps a Laker game flickering on his portable TV. In the backyard he put in a small pool where he could close his eyes and pretend he was a Bolivian mine owner relaxing at his winter estate in the Oriente.

Both he and Fabiola were enjoying the pool on a Saturday afternoon in late July when the telephone rang. Fabiola, acting the dutiful mistress to the plutocrat Don Jaime, answered it. It was Bolado, very upset, asking to speak to Escalante.

"Hi, Ellll-sa Bo-laaa-do," he said, playing with the unusual name, the only Bolado in the East LA telephone directory. "I thought you were at UCLA."

"Yes, Kimo, I'm in this program. But this is about my AP grade. You know I got a four?"

"Yeah."

"Now I got this letter saying I copied. Luis got another letter too. I don't really know what it means. We have three choices, it says. You take it over, or you just get your money back, or . . . or . . . gosh, I forget the third one. But what do we *do*?"

"Oooo, this is new to me. I think we just wait a bit. I'll call the principal, I'll find out. Don't worry about it. We'll work it out."

"Kimo, I am so mad!"

"Yah, I understand."

"How could they?"

"Calm down, Elsa. Okay?"

He hung up and returned to the pool. What could this be? His friend Al Santoyo, the counselor, had called the week before to say he had heard all of the calculus students had passed. The principal's office had received the College Board grade roster, which told each school the scores of each test taker. Escalante had assumed the results would be good. His students had been sky-high after the test. He was thinking ahead to the following year. How could he get a summer session going? How many more kids would he have?

Santoyo had mentioned something odd. Three names on the grade roster had been blacked out. He could not tell who they were.

Probably a clerical error, Escalante had said. Most of his kids had called him to report their scores. All the news had been good. He assumed Bennett would show him the grade roster when he returned to school in September.

The following year, having learned his lesson, Escalante would begin hovering around the principal's office, like a pensioner waiting for his check, whenever the grade rosters were due. But in 1982 he had no reason for apprehension, and did not bother to ask Santoyo for a name-by-name accounting of the scores. If he had, he would have realized that six names were missing—three obliterated by the curious black lines, and three not listed at all.

On Monday morning, Ralph Heiland was setting up his lab for another week of summer school physics when Richkarday walked in. Her sunny cheerleader's disposition was gone. "Something the matter, Josie?" he asked.

"Mr. Heiland, you know the AP calculus test? I got my score, a four, not so hot, but okay, I guess. *Then*, I get this letter that says I cheated. What am I gonna do?"

Heiland looked at her closely and realized she was terrified. The poor kid, he thought, hounded by a bureaucracy with powers of which she had no inkling. On Tuesday, two more students told him of getting letters. One showed him a copy. He called Rosenbaum's number, collect.

"Listen," he said, "I'm calling from Garfield High School. We've got several students here who have received letters from you about the AP calculus exam. It looks to me like . . ."

"Excuse me, sir," said the soft voice on the other end of the line. "Who are you?"

"Well, like I said, my name is Ralph Heiland, and I'm a teacher here and I've suddenly discovered that three people . . ."

"I'm sorry, Mr. Heiland. The students have to contact us here themselves. We can't allow any cross discussion of anything. These are individuals and this is extremely confidential."

"I'm just a concerned teacher and I think there's a serious problem. Jurisprudence says you're innocent until proven guilty, and to me the way this thing says is you're guilty until proven innocent."

"I'm sorry, Mr. Heiland. I just can't discuss it with you. The students should call me and I can explain it to them."

Now he was angry. As the representative for United Teachers—Los Angeles, the teachers' union, Heiland decided he ought to take action.

Gradillas was in Provo, Utah, working on his doctorate at BYU. Heiland called a meeting Wednesday afternoon in his room, inviting Escalante, acting principal Henry Ronquillo, and as many affected students as he could find. Two prominent Latino educators also came—Raúl Arreola of the district's Mexican American Commission and Arnold Rodríguez of the senior high school division office. Heiland found Escalante at Occidental, teaching his summer Upward Bound class and trying to decide what to tell the growing numbers of students calling him for advice.

Escalante felt uncomfortable making decisions with so little information. Not only did he not know the value of x and y in this equation, he did not even have the equation. He appeared at Heiland's room at 2:00 P.M. He hoped they would tell him something he needed to know.

Heiland introduced him to Arreola and Rodríguez. "So, Jaime, what do you think about the situation?"

Escalante shifted in his chair. "What is the situation? I really don't know. I've just got a few phone calls. I know these kids have a problem."

Heiland handed him a copy of the Rosenbaum letter. "This is the letter. First they got the green sheet that said they passed the examination and then the letter that said they copied." He described the choices offered the students and asked Tapio and Cervantes to speak. Heiland told the group he was upset that "ETS is taking these kids on individually, not the group collectively." He repeated his strong feeling that "they are innocent until proven guilty. Where does ETS come off to make these kids guilty?" He said he thought they might have a legal case. "This is a typical case of discrimination," Arreola said, noting two Anglo calculus students from another school had recently been cleared of copying after their families had hired attorneys. ETS officials later said they had not heard from any lawyers, but had cleared the cases because of insufficient evidence.

Someone asked Escalante what he, as a teacher, thought of the ETS accusations. "I really don't know what to say or what to do," he said. "The first thing I have to do is talk to the students. I really have to find out, did they copy? The ones I asked, they say no, they don't even know what the letter means. Okay. So . . . look, you have to give me a chance to do something. I don't know what to say."

One of the district officials broke in. "It's a shame that you, as a teacher, don't know what to do with this case."

Escalante looked down. "I'm sorry. This is the first time it's happened to me."

Heiland broke in. "Perhaps we will need a second meeting. We need more information. But I don't think we should put up with this. Those kids *should not have to take that test over*. If we do that, we're admitting we're guilty."

Escalante walked across the hall and opened up his own room. Some of the students wandered in. Jesse López arrived with his own letter. "You see *this*, Kimo?" Gallows humor ensued.

"Hey, Luis, you *copycat*!"

"Did you copy?"

"No, I thought I told *you* to copy."

Escalante sat, puzzled. "Well, what was it like? Could anybody copy?"

"Naah, Kimo," one boy said. "There was no way to copy. Mrs. Pruitt, the head counselor? She watched the whole time."

They discussed the various problems. Which were troublesome? Which were easy? Bocanegra snorted in disgust. "The first part we did in thirty-five minutes. You know one thing, Kimo, you practiced too much. You went over too much."

"Okay," Escalante said, glad to be off his pedestal. "Maybe I did overprepare."

The discussion meandered, full of worry and tension, until Tapio broke into tears. Of the eighteen students in Escalante's course, she was by far the most committed to the goals of Advanced Placement. She wanted to get through USC in three years and then perhaps get a master's degree in business administration. Her father had died in his thirties. This was *wasting her time and money*.

"Kimo," she said, "I took two APs and this would make three. I put all my time into it, and now they say I copied. They're not going to accept what I say. You *know*, Kimo, how much I put into this."

Escalante hated it when his students cried. "Come on, don't worry about it. You could just take the regular class at SC. It be easy for you."

"I can't wait that long, Kimo. I really can't."

155

By 1982 the Educational Testing Service had become a nonprofit giant. It grossed $123,609,402 that year, providing a number of services, mostly the design and administration of 160 different intellectual obstacle courses. The ETS wrote and graded the Scholastic Aptitude Test (SAT). That test alone was the closest the United States had ever come to a national college entrance examination. The steady decline of average SAT scores since 1963 had become, in the popular press at least, a national barometer of the sorry condition of public education. The testing service also studied the impact of "Sesame Street" on ghetto preschool children and produced an examination that determined if a candidate golf professional knew the difference between a mashie and a spoon.

The ETS had acquired great power since its birth in 1947 because it shared with Americans of all classes a belief that opportunity—a freshman slot at Dartmouth, a job at Standard Oil, a place at Stanford Law—should go to the most qualified person, as demonstrated by a fair, unbiased, objective test. The service had begun to feel the heat of critics who said its tests, particularly the SAT, were neither fair nor unbiased, but that did little to weaken the popular belief that merit is what a test says it is.

Toni Rosenbaum became the ETS employee who bore the brunt of the Garfield controversy, and she seemed well suited for it. She was thirty-eight, a short woman with brown hair and a friendly smile. She had taught high school Spanish and had worked five years on test security matters. She was accustomed to handling long, difficult conversations with worried students, parents, and teachers; she had two teenage children of her own. Shortly before the Garfield booklets arrived on her desk at the ETS headquarters, she had been assigned to serve as special liaison at the test security office for AP cases, usually only a small part of the office's total work load.

When the six Garfield test booklets arrived, her first move was almost automatic. She checked with her immediate supervisor, a senior test security specialist, then ordered the examinations analyzed by ETS computer and mathematics specialists. They used a controversial comparison formula, called the K index, which measures the probability of identical answers on the multiple-choice test occurring by chance. The mathematics expert checked the six free-response questions other than number 6 for signs of unusual agreement.

The test security staff investigated about 6,000 exams a year, about one tenth of one percent of the total, and cleared the 70 percent that revealed nothing more than chance similarities or other apparently innocent oddities. The Garfield examinations showed much more than that, Rosenbaum thought. She wrote a short report and gave it to the Board of Review. Suspected copying, she knew, represented the most common problem—49 percent of all scores formally questioned. Another 44 percent involved handwriting that did not seem to match the signature of the alleged test taker.

Usually three ETS officials temporarily diverted from their regular duties made up the Board of Review. At some board meetings on the Garfield issue Louis R. Lavine, the chairman permanently assigned to Board of Review activities, filled in for a board member with a scheduling conflict.

Their decisions had to be unanimous. Any one of the three could have ended the Garfield case. Instead, they told Rosenbaum to retrieve the other twelve AP calculus examinations given at Garfield and subject them to the same analysis. Unlike the six examinations originally discovered, the other twelve had been left alone. They had been graded, the scores sent to the students, and the test booklets filed.

Mathematicians in the ETS College Board programs division test development department concluded that a total of twelve of the eighteen tests had odd answers and mistakes in question 6 that suggested copying. A test security official analyzed agreement between all possible pairs of the eighteen students on the multiple-choice section. Fourteen, including all twelve with similarities on free-response question 6, had answers that, according to the K index, agreed with at least one other examination to a degree expected in only one out of every 100,000 cases. The agreement between some pairs climbed into the one in 10 million range.

The K index would be bruised but not broken in a major legal challenge, a New Jersey case called *Denburg* v. *ETS*, the following year. The case involved four tennis team members at Millburn High School in Millburn, New Jersey, a community at the opposite end of the income scale from East Los Angeles. The four college-bound juniors had taken the SAT at a special time, with their coach as proctor, because of a conflict with a tennis match. The ETS said it could not validate their scores because their right and wrong answers on the verbal part of the test, subjected to K index analysis, were too much in agreement.

The students sued. Their lawyers noted that all four had passed

157

lie detector tests. They argued that students from similar backgrounds with similar instruction could make similar mistakes. But Superior Court Judge Richard S. Cohen ruled that the K index was based on generally sound principles and that the ETS had a right to protect the validity of its tests.

In the Garfield case, the K index analysis and the similarities in question 6 persuaded all the Board of Review members that they had to take action. They voted to challenge the validity of the fourteen exams showing similarities. The remaining four examinations, for Roy Márquez, Juan Cuadras, Alex Guerrero, and René Cano, were validated and sent to the designated colleges.

The letter Rosenbaum signed and sent to fourteen Los Angeles addresses had been used and reused, trimmed and embroidered, sanded and polished for several years. It was designed to alert the student to the gravity of the situation without creating panic or inviting lawsuits. The testing service wanted the recipient to consider carefully all the options, make a decision in reasonable time, and clear the matter off the books.

In the Garfield case, as well as others, the ETS failed miserably in this mission, for a reason that should have occurred to anyone who watched television or read detective stories.

An accusation of wrongdoing creates an overwhelming compulsion to punish the guilty or clear the innocent, at least in citizens of countries accustomed to trial by jury. After decades of televised courtroom drama and paperback murder mysteries, Americans instinctively look for the truth of any charge. Contrary to the popular expectation, the ETS did not want to solve the mystery, but it could find no adequate way to explain that.

The testing service did not have the time, the money, the personnel, or the legal power to question witnesses, secure documents, convict the guilty, and certify the innocent before college began in the fall. All the ETS wanted was to protect the validity and fairness of the scores, using various options, which included retesting of doubtful candidates.

Recipients looked at Rosenbaum's letter as an indictment. The ETS would have preferred that they thought of it as a tax audit, a check of the records that might take some time and trouble, and perhaps some payment in the end, but imply no burden of shame or criminality. The students and faculty of Garfield High—good Americans all—saw the ETS waving a nightstick and pointing them toward the city jail.

Obeying the ETS rules of confidentiality, Rosenbaum first called Bennett with a brief, cryptic warning of trouble. Escalante, after several errant attempts to reach her, finally spoke to her a few days later. He remembers the conversation as very brief:

"Mrs. Rosenbaum. My name is Escalante. I am the calculus teacher of these kids who have gotten a letter from you. Can I do anything to help you straighten this out?"

"Mr. Escalante, I'm very sorry, but I cannot discuss it with you. It is a confidential matter, a one-to-one thing. You're just not involved in it."

"But I think I could explain the problem. I have a certain way of teaching. I . . ."

"I'm sorry, I don't think we can do that."

She fended off other teachers who called and handled the student inquiries like live grenades. Unusual agreement with other examinations indicated copying may have occurred, she told the students. That was all she could say. She gently encouraged them to decide as soon as possible if they wanted a retest, since their college credits would do no good if they came after the fall semester began. This approach struck Rosenbaum and her superiors at the ETS as reasonable, humane, and professional.

But a retest threatened to unleash old fears and doubts the Garfield students thought were safely behind them, as if their dentist had found four *more* wisdom teeth that had to be yanked out.

Many agreed with Heiland that taking the test again would be an admission of guilt. Even more disturbing, it would require them to curtail summer plans and try to revive memories of formulas and functions they had not dealt with in two months. Their textbooks had been turned in long before. They had only their notebooks, themselves, their teacher, and vivid memories of the emotional price they had paid to prepare for the first test.

No matter how carefully and gently Rosenbaum explained their options, the worried, confused, and sometimes frightened students who listened over the soft static of long-distance lines took her words to be the unsympathetic evasions of an ice-cold Anglo bureaucracy.

One of the options the ETS offered—provide information to show cheating could not have occurred—only added to the tension. Students and faculty sent character references and histories of the Escalante method. Cervantes wrote of his 3.79 grade point average and election to the exclusive Ephebian Society, for Garfield's top scholars. "Because of the way in which the class was divided, which consisted of groups of six," he wrote, "by the end of the year we all seemed to apply the same method in attacking a problem. Taking this reason into consideration, it is quite obvious why our answers are so similar and possibly identical. . . . I am a very honest person and would not think of cheating on a test of this much importance to my future." Bocanegra wrote: "Our instructor did not accept any other method of solving problems than his own. Consequently, our steps in solving calculus problems were obviously similar if not the same."

It was useless. Lavine later said the only possibility that came readily to mind was that he would have validated the score of one student if some of the others had confessed that they had copied from that answer sheet without the student's knowledge.

It did not help that one key participant, Bennett, left the controversy early and another, Gradillas, arrived late. Bennett was a gentle, rational man who assumed people would respond to good sense and logic. He could not believe that the ETS would cancel fourteen AP calculus scores. He looked forward to the arrival of Robert H. Parker, the ETS test security director, who had promised to investigate personally.

Parker, then fifty-five, was a balding former air force colonel with the ramrod posture and precise diction of a man who insisted on work done to the last detail. He had some experience in dealing with minorities. One angry black parent had once called him, on the telephone, "a white racist bastard." Parker was too shocked, and too amused, to tell the man he was black also. He traveled often to check test sites. Garfield was just one of many stops.

Bennett gave Parker and Los Angeles–based ETS official Frank Romero a tour of Garfield in late July. When Parker began asking questions, Bennett realized how little he had thought about security when handling the examinations. He had kept the AP tests in the main office vault, which, he was forced to admit, was left open during the day. Still, the office was staffed by adults throughout the day, and the sealed plastic bags covering the tests had shown no sign of tampering.

He gave Parker a chart, prepared by Pruitt from memory, showing where each calculus student had sat. Pruitt and he were honest people.

Did the ETS want them to take a lie detector test? Pruitt had shouted at Rosenbaum over the phone: "Are you saying that I would sit in a room with eighteen students and allow fourteen of them to copy?"

Bennett explained to Parker, several times, that Escalante used intensive repetition and drill. Similar answers were to be expected from his students.

Bennett had promised his wife two weeks in Hawaii in August. Certainly the ETS would see the light and withdraw the charge. He got on the plane without any worries, convinced that good sense would prevail.

Parker boarded a flight in the other direction, back to New Jersey. The unlocked vault, the sealed exams, the seating chart—none of them added anything important to the story, as far as he was concerned. He did not try to speak to any of the students. Grilling teenagers was not part of his job. The trip, he concluded, left the ETS with what they already had, fourteen examination booklets full of suspicious mistakes.

By early August, the ETS officials responsible for AP—President Gregory R. Anrig, Vice President Arthur M. Kroll, and Advanced Placement Program Director Carl H. Haag—had all been warned of the Garfield problem, and the threat of bad publicity. Anrig had spent eight years as Massachusetts commissioner of education during the tumultuous desegregation of the Boston public schools. He knew how charges of ethnic discrimination could inflame a community. It would be discriminatory, he said, if the ETS took such action because the students were Hispanic. But it would also be discriminatory if they *failed* to act for the same reason.

Rosenbaum's other duties were put aside as she tried to persuade the students to make up their minds about a retest before it was too late. Escalante was becoming angry and frustrated at being left out of the rapid exchange of telephone calls between New Jersey and California. Gradillas, late on the scene, was just beginning to sort it out.

The principal had been in Provo tinkering with his doctoral thesis when his wife, Stephanie, called.

"Henry, all hell's breaking loose at Garfield," she said.

He had never confronted anything quite like this. His instinct, whenever faced with alleged wrongdoing, was to get to the bottom of it, to bring the kid and the parents in and give them the Gradillas treatment. He was now a stocky man with flashing eyes—an intimidating presence. But these were some of his best students, taught by one of his best teachers, proctored by his head counselor.

He asked the question—"Did you cheat?"—but not in his usual way. He did not demand that they look in their mothers' eyes and swear to the Holy Virgin.

It was a fruitless exercise. Cervantes left the room annoyed. Tapio sighed with exasperation. Bolado bit her lip and tried to quell a fiery rage that would rekindle for years whenever she heard Gradillas's name.

Finally he called in Richkarday, the girl he had known since he was an assistant principal at Belvedere Junior High.

"Josie," he said, his voice at the high end of his emotional scale, "you know how long we've known each other and I've known your mother and we worked very hard and I admire you and I think the world of you and you're going places. I want you to tell me, Josie. Did *anything* go on in there? I'm talking to you like a brother. I really want to know, because I'm going to make a lot of stink on this, I'm going to carry this to places, I'm going to be criticized. I know in my heart that everything's okay, but someone could have done a stupid thing, and blown it for all. Tell me."

She sat up straight. "*Nothing* went on, sir, I promise you." Her voice broke. "We didn't do *anything*." She reminded Gradillas of a student who hunched over his examination paper and pulled his left arm around so no one could see what he was writing. "That's the way he was at Belvedere," she said. "That's the way he's always been. And now they're accusing *him* of cheating."

Gradillas went off to call the ETS one more time, knowing that he had few weapons, just a bunch of frightened kids. But he had seen what Escalante could do. He saw a way out of this, if those young men and women really knew their stuff.

Of all the people involved in the Garfield drama that summer, no one was as attuned as Gradillas was to the importance of image, politics, and publicity in American education. It struck him, as he composed an angry, ultimately futile letter to Rosenbaum, that the volatile mix of the community's rage and Escalante's skill could put Garfield on the map.

"I am not sure I understand," he wrote, "some unspoken underlying assumptions which prompt you to single out this school, over 90 percent of whose students have Hispanic surnames. The examination involved had as its subject mathematics; and, after all, the language of mathematics is universal." But, he added, "To the extent that your actions have focused attention on, possibly, the finest teacher of mathematics in the United States, we take the consolation that your actions may bring Mr. Jaime Escalante the national recognition he so richly deserves."

Gradillas remembered Fort Benning in 1957. He was a second lieutenant with a ROTC background from a California cow college, and he wanted to win the base marksmanship prize. His competition included generals' sons and men who had hunted deer and raccoons since they were six.

He practiced hard. He provoked a huge laugh from the man detailed to buy the trophy by suggesting that he go ahead and engrave it "Henry Gradillas." He was not kidding.

Gradillas felt good as he sighted down the shooting range. The grounds were mostly dirt and weeds, with scrub pine as a backdrop.

"Okay, Lieutenant, your turn."

Blam. Blam. Blam. Blam. Blam. Hit. Hit. Hit. Hit. Miss! "Hey, wait a minute!"

"Target didn't fall, Lieutenant."

"I *hit* that sucker, clean. It must have gone through one of the holes."

"Doesn't look like it, Lieutenant."

A major came by to check the delay.

"I *know* I hit that last target, sir. How about another shot? That's in the rules, right?"

"At my discretion, sure. . . . Uh, . . . okay, set 'em up, Sergeant. One more shot."

Blam! *Hit!*

He had won the trophy, and that was the way out of this mess. Escalante's students had to take the retest.

Escalante was losing patience with Gradillas. Those men had come all the way from the ETS to look at the school and the principal had not told him.

After his distasteful conversation with Rosenbaum, he asked Jiménez to call the ETS and vouch for him, but Rosenbaum cut short her talk with the younger teacher. She could not discuss the test with someone not directly involved.

Escalante sent his own short letter to New Jersey. He described his drills. "From the way the students were taught to work out the problems in class, it is natural to have a close resemblance in the steps at arriving at their answers," he said. Wanting to check the "intensive teacher influence" theory that so many at Garfield were advancing, Rosenbaum had asked the school to send Escalante's own solutions to free-response questions 3, 5, and 6. Escalante did that, but nothing came of it.

He was becoming uncharacteristically depressed. He had called off his plans to see his mother in La Paz. She did not have too many years left, but he could not leave now. When George Madrid stopped by to talk about their plans for a summer course at East Los Angeles College, Escalante seemed pale and weary. *"Mos alumnos, das chingano* [My graduates have been disgraced]," he said.

Gradillas telephoned to say he planned to meet with Frank Romero, the ETS regional official in Los Angeles, and would like Escalante with him. Gradillas wanted more information on what had triggered the cheating accusation. He needed a mathematician to help him.

Escalante drove his Volkswagen over to the little ETS office building in Eagle Rock, a deteriorating suburb in the northeast corner of Los Angeles. He waited in the parking lot for Gradillas's green Chevrolet, but a half hour passed with no sign of the principal. The teacher loathed tardiness. He could not flunk Gradillas, or send him to his counselor, he could only grow angrier. In that mood, he took the elevator to the third floor and walked in to face Romero alone.

Frank Romero, like Gradillas, like Jiménez, unlike Escalante, was an East LA product, as least in part. He had lived there until age seven, then begun to move through the Central Valley migrant labor camps with his parents. He went to high school in Azusa, northeast of Los Angeles, and discovered a talent for both academics and basketball. He earned a chemistry degree in college, gravitated to teaching and then to educational research. The ETS had very few staff members with his background and promise. He was quickly promoted to head the principal ETS office in the West.

He had dealt with all sorts of difficult situations, but an angry Escalante was something new. Their tense conversation soon broke down as the teacher let his frustrations overflow.

Romero tried to explain how the tests were scored. The graders, he assured his visitor, had no way of knowing a student's name, school, or ethnic group. He could not show Escalante the actual tests, however, without violating the students' right to privacy.

"I don't believe that," Escalante snapped. "That's bullshit. I don't buy that. I want to see the mistakes they made."

"I'm sorry you feel that way. Let me explain to you the whole process and let's see if we can resolve this."

Escalante stared at the tall, slender, youthful administrator. "You know, when I came over here, I expected to see a *gringo*. And then I see you, but you know, you're not one of us."

Romero fought to control his anger. "You're wrong. I'm only doing my job."

"Doing your job," Escalante said, snorting in disbelief. He was getting nowhere, but he wanted the last word. "You're a blind man. You're chasing a black cat in a dark room. You know, I know a lot about computers. Maybe you had a code or something that identified the kids like ours taking the test. You know, the ones that have a last name like yours.

"I know well how to spell discrimination. You're not going to *give me any of this shit*."

Romero mustered his best smile. He was beginning one more patient explanation when his telephone rang and he picked up the receiver.

Escalante felt a little better. He had told the man what he thought of him. He turned on his heel and left without another word.

Escalante sensed everything, including himself, was about to go completely out of control. A local Mexican American activist proposed scheduling him for a speaking tour and leafleting major universities with denunciations of the ETS. Some of his students had heard they might sue the testing agency. "Kimo, Kimo," one said to him excitedly. "If we fight this we can get a million dollars, and with that our college would be free. I could get fifty thousand, you could get fifty thousand."

Escalante was astounded. "Who told you that?"

"One of the lawyers."

"Ah, that's great," Escalante said, shaking his head. "That would be nice."

Rosenbaum began to paper East Los Angeles with letters and telegrams demanding a decision. The response from the students and their supporters became even more heated. "It is nothing short of outrageous that it is incumbent upon Miss Rodríguez to prove her own innocence," wrote Alice Miller, director of the premed program

Rodríguez attended that summer, to Rosenbaum. "Your letter, which violates all principles of fair process and common decency, presumes her guilt without a shred of evidence; it is nothing short of a thinly disguised attempt at coercion by blackmail. . . . Miss Rodríguez, her lawyer, and I will be satisfied with nothing less than a written retraction and apology for your defamatory letter."

Romero several times offered to pay for tutors to help students prepare for a retest, but no one responded. Rosenbaum was having trouble sleeping; this was one of only two occasions a case had bothered her that much. Time was running out, and she seemed unable to persuade anyone to make up his or her mind.

As everyone around him became more excited, Escalante felt himself calming down. The ETS had given no sign of retreat. If they said copying was possible, he thought, they must have some reason, no matter how ill founded. The only way to prove the case to everyone's satisfaction was to have the students take another test. He exchanged tense words about this with Heiland, who thought a retest was an admission of guilt.

By mid-August, time was up. All of the accused students except Richkarday, the only junior, had to take a retest then, or give up hope of college credit for calculus in their freshman year. Bocanegra had already rejected the retest. The freshman program had begun at Columbia. He was going to be a doctor, not a mathematician, and he could not bear to capitulate to Rosenbaum. Sandra López had enlisted in the army and would get no real benefit from a confirmed calculus score. Rosenbaum arranged with López's sergeant to set up a retest at her post, but she turned it down.

It was time for a summit conference in Room 233. Escalante asked Bolado to assemble all the students she could find. They had been appearing frequently at the school for the last few weeks, talking and playing volleyball. Now they would have to make up their minds.

08/24/82

FROM: (MRS.) ANTONIA M. ROSENBAUM
ETS PRINCETON, NJ

SINCE OUR MAILGRAM OF AUGUST 18, 1982, A SPECIAL RETEST OF
THE MAY 1982 ADVANCED PLACEMENT HAS BEEN SCHEDULED FOR

AUGUST 31, 1982. THIS IS THE ONLY DATE THE RETEST WILL BE GIVEN. THE TIME AND PLACE WILL BE ARRANGED WITHIN THE NEXT FEW DAYS. IF YOU CHOOSE THE RETEST OPTION TO RESOLVE THE QUESTION OF YOUR AP GRADE, PLEASE CALL ME, COLLECT, 609-734-1656 BY FRIDAY, AUGUST 27, 1982. IF WE DO NOT HEAR FROM YOU BY AUGUST 27 IT WILL BE NECESSARY TO CANCEL YOUR GRADE.

"You have to make up your minds now," he told them. "I think you ought to take the retest."

Bolado was still angry. "Kimo, you're not going to take the test. We have to take the test. Why don't you go someplace and give us a chance to talk?"

He strolled out, glad to have someone else take over. Bolado shut the door and turned to the small group. Cervantes thought Rosenbaum was a monster. To him, a retest was an admission of guilt, and how could they possibly prepare themselves in less than a week after three months away from calculus? Olvera said he didn't need the credit anyway.

Bolado sucked in a quick breath and heard her words pour out: "I want to take the retest. I want to take it to show Escalante that what he taught me I didn't forget, and that I really appreciate all the time he put in, that it didn't go to waste, and to prove to the school that we didn't cheat and to ourselves that we can do it again."

Tapio quickly added her assent, and the rest fell in line. "Yeah, well, I don't need their dumb test," Olvera said. "But we ought to do it for him. He deserves it."

Zamarripa had just had a raging argument with her father. He had refused to pay her tuition at USC, forcing her to go to Cal State and making her calculus score even less important. But she would do it for Escalante. He put so much into us, she thought. She could not let him down.

Bolado strode downstairs to find Escalante. There he was in the main office, talking to that two-faced Gradillas. For one white-hot moment she forgot her mission and turned on the principal. "You know what you are, Mr. Gradillas? You're a real hypocrite. You're wasting our time in the classroom all year coming in and telling us how great we are, and how proud you are of us, and when the time comes for really helping us out you're not around. I'm really *disappointed* in you."

"Well, I had to do things . . ."

"I don't care. *Everybody* just let us down."

She pulled Escalante off to 233 to decide their next move. They would have to call Princeton. The telephone in the math department room, just across the hall, seemed the best to use. Earlier in the year, alone in the building and curious about the telephone system, Escalante had rearranged the switches so the long-distance line connected directly to the department office. It would be a month before someone in the main office noticed an unusual volume of calls in late August and put a stern note in the school bulletin.

The students, excited now, lined up in the hall to speak to Rosenbaum one more time. "Bulldogs, bulldogs, *bulldogs!*" That was the school mascot. A pep rally had begun. It was Friday. They had a little more than a weekend to prepare for the Tuesday test. "Tuesday. Tuesday! *Tuesday. Tuesday!*"

The old magic was back—Calculus Team '82 against the world. Escalante soaked up the laughter and issued orders for all to appear the next morning with notebooks in hand. Their textbooks were locked away somewhere, irretrievable. Many old notebooks had been sent to ETS in a futile attempt to prove they knew the material. But if they worked all weekend, maybe . . .

Olvera was last to the telephone. Rosenbaum was not there, but he told the frazzled test security specialist on duty that he, too, would be taking the retest. He slammed the receiver back into its cradle with the finality of the great Wilt Chamberlain, Escalante's idol, stuffing the ball through the hoop.

Olvera winked at his teacher. "Don't worry, Kimo," he said. "We're gonna *kill* Rosenbaum."

After eight years at Garfield, Escalante had quietly acquired copies of keys to nearly every lock of nearly every door and Cyclone fence gate in the school. He arrived at 7:00 A.M. the Saturday before the retest and prepared his ground. Front door open. 200 Building open. Room 233 open. Fresh chalk on the blackboard shelf and a pile of old tests ready for reference.

Richkarday heard herself saying, over and over: There isn't enough time, there isn't enough time. Cervantes thought about his summer in Mazatlán, the long horseback rides at night, the hang gliding. How could he remember anything he knew before that? Was this any way to finish a beautiful summer? Bolado found herself feeling curiously lighthearted, the last-minute euphoria of the trapped and the condemned.

Escalante took them through several hours of review of main points, functions, and tricks certain to be tested. A squad was dispatched to bring back provisions from McDonald's. They sat and ate and chatted for more than an hour. Escalante tried to revive interest in another stretch of afternoon drill, but they had had enough. He wished them well and sent them home.

When Rodríguez arrived early Tuesday morning for the 8:00 A.M. test, she found she was shivering. Gradillas had designated a science room down the hall from 233 for the examination. It had individual desks and an air-conditioning system someone had turned to high cool.

Two older women in business suits, people Rodríguez had never seen before, waited with expressions as cold as the temperature. They were ETS employees from the Eagle Rock office, dispatched when Gradillas refused to allow any of his staff to proctor the retest. Pruitt, still angry at the ETS, had come, but only to observe. Rodríguez felt as though she had stepped into the freezer at her parents' restaurant. She was glad she had worn a sweat suit.

Tapio had spent the weekend at an intensive preseason practice of the USC band. Now she had one more distraction, an entrance examination in English that would begin at the university campus promptly at 11:00 A.M. The proctors had agreed to let her begin the calculus test a half hour earlier than everyone else and waive the midway break; she left after only two hours.

The proctors carefully placed the students at widely spaced desks. They read the instructions in tones appropriate to the Ten Commandments and told the students to begin.

Twelve examination booklets opened with a nervous rustle. The room became very still as several students went into mild states of shock.

Zamarripa thought she had been told the retest would be no more difficult than the first test. This was *much* harder. María Jiménez felt numb. She began to work problems almost blindly, frantically looking for any element she found familiar. Oh God, Bolado said to herself, I'm not familiar with any of this. Cervantes wrestled with it. He knew the principles, if only he could dig them out of a brain encrusted with summer memories. He sensed little tricks in some of the free-response questions, little razor blades cutting him down as he moved along. He pressed down so hard on his pencil that he left marks on the table underneath.

Escalante had promised himself that he would stay at home to avoid the slightest suggestion of undue influence. He did not realize until that moment how much he had depended on the distraction of teaching his other classes when his students had taken previous AP examinations. He walked around the house, watching minutes tick by. Fabiola wondered at this and suggested he mow the lawn.

"I cannot, Mommy," he said. "We are out of gasoline for the engine."

"Well, then, why don't you relax? Watch television."

"I tried that."

"What *is* the matter with you?"

"Oooh, I'm sorry, I didn't tell you. The kids are taking the retest. I am waiting for the phone call from Elsa Bolado."

Finally, at 12:30, it came. "Oh, Kimo, it was *hard*," she said.

"Don't worry about it. You play defense?"

"Yeah, sure, but this question six, it had a lot of problems with trigonometric identities and related interval change. Who remembers all that stuff?"

"Don't worry about it. The game's over."

"But I want to know how I *did*."

"I'd like to know too, but you gonna have to wait."

Gradillas sat back in his desk chair, contemplating the year's opening faculty meeting. Escalante rumbled in. It was September 13, two weeks after the retest exams had been sent back to the ETS. Escalante ached to know what had happened. "Henry, you got to call them up," he said.

Gradillas, lost in other thoughts, looked up, not quite comprehending. "Huh?"

"Princeton, you got to call them up, Henry. I want to know what the calculus results are. It nearly two weeks."

Gradillas nodded and reached for the telephone. Someone else answered Rosenbaum's line. Did they have the Garfield results? They said they were not sure.

"I'm getting a lot of pressure from the community," Gradillas said, looking at Escalante. "I can't wait any longer." Call back in thirty minutes, someone said. He waited twenty minutes. His faculty meeting was about to begin.

"Okay," the voice on the other end said. "You have a piece of paper?"

Suddenly Gradillas realized his desk was empty. He motioned frantically to Escalante, who handed him a light blue computer sheet. "Okay. Yes, Four. Yeah. Three. Five. Five." His eyes began to widen. He started to bounce in his chair. "Three. Three. Four. *Eeeee-iiiiiyyyaaaa*. This is *great!*" He waved the sheet at Escalante, who returned a small smile and immediately left the office.

They had done it, he said to himself. Good. He slid into his Volkswagen and drove home. He was supposed to go to the faculty meeting, but he had never liked meetings.

Hanging up the telephone in a glow of delight and relief, Gradillas looked for Escalante, hoping to take him to the faculty meeting for a celebration. When Escalante could not be found, Gradillas went himself and waved the scores in triumph before his assembled teachers:

Elsa Bolado, 4; Luis Cervantes, 3; Raúl Haro, 5; Gustavo Hernández, 5; María Jiménez, 3; Jesse López, 3; Martín Olvera, 5; Josie Richkarday, 4; Leticia Rodríguez, 5; Hortensia Sánchez, 3; Aili Tapio, 4; Margaret Zamarripa, 5. Five 5s, three 4s, and four 3s. Everybody had gotten at least the requisite 3 for credit. They had all passed.

The Educational Testing Service would reveal later that only one of the twelve had done as well or better on the second test as the first, according to the raw scores, which are usually kept confidential. In some cases the drop was significant. Five students—Cervantes, Jiménez, Jesse López, Sánchez, and Tapio—scored one grade lower than on their original test. Only two of the twelve retest scores, both 5s, were high enough to be automatically reconfirmed under ETS rules. Five more had dropped to a lower level but were reconfirmed by the Board of Review on the grounds that they were close enough to the original score. One person who was given a 3 actually fell into the 2 level, but was left at 3 by the board.

Such subtle distinctions were ignored by most Garfield community leaders. The second test, after all, had been much more difficult than the first. (Officials at the ETS insisted the two tests were "comparable," but *they* had not had to take them.) There had been little time to prepare. Mathematics teachers at other schools were astounded that students would even attempt such a difficult examination after that long a vacation.

What was important was that all twelve had passed and vindicated themselves, Garfield, Escalante, East Los Angeles, the Los Angeles Unified School District, and—many community members declared—Mexican Americans everywhere. The students were heroes. All that was left was to choose suitable villains.

When the news finally reached the press, in a September 29 front-page story by the weekly *East Los Angeles Tribune*, the ETS was immediately confirmed as the evil antagonist and remained in that position during the story's brief, erratic run. The *Tribune* story began, "Administrators and teachers at Garfield High School have reacted angrily to a national testing service's decision to make 18 [sic] students retake a calculus test." It named three faculty members, including Heiland and Bennett, who "hinted that racism might have been the reason for the retest."

The major media of southern California do not read the *East Los Angeles Tribune* very often. It was not until November 16, in an editorial broadcast on CBS-owned KNXT-TV (later KCBS), Channel 2, that the story won wide circulation:

"The people who give college entrance exams have wronged some Mexican American students here in Los Angeles. The incident suggests that the test givers harbor stereotypes about Hispanic performance levels: when the kids do well, people don't believe it."

By the time the story hit the major California newspapers in December, and a few national publications shortly after, the Mexican American Legal Defense and Educational Fund (MALDEF) had been contacted by several students and had begun planning legal action. When the ETS refused to validate the scores of Bocanegra and Sandra López without a retest, MALDEF attorneys suggested a lawsuit, but the students and their families began to lose interest. The *Denburg* decision in New Jersey said the ETS had the right to question scores. A suit would take time and money. Also, MALDEF proposed suing Garfield and the school system for failing to defend the students' rights, which did not appeal to many of the potential litigants.

Eventually MALDEF lobbied for a bill requiring a higher standard of proof for ETS cheating cases. The governor vetoed the bill and, after another year, signed a weaker one that raised the standard of proof from a "reasonable basis" to "substantial evidence" of cheating before a score could be canceled. An ETS attorney said the practical effect of the change was negligible.

Escalante had ignored the legal maneuvering. When the controversy moved to the legislature, state senator Art Torres, one of the most astute and articulate politicians in California, asked Escalante for support against the ETS. These people discriminated against Mexican Americans, he told the teacher. They didn't want to talk to you. How can you not support us in this?

"I'm sorry, sir, but this is a different situation," Escalante said. "This kind of test motivates the kids to do something. If you take it, it's a good gauge. It's the only way to do it." He had seen enough mediocre teachers in eight years to last him a lifetime. "There are a lot of teachers just killing time, sir. This is the only way to prove the teacher is teaching. Say I'm preparing for the Olympics. *You* say I'm ready for the Olympics, but the only way I can prove it is if I compete against the Russians. We don't have anything in the district like that."

Stung by its beating in the press, the ETS sent Frank Romero and ETS spokeswoman Joy McIntyre to show some school officials and reporters actual copies of the disputed Garfield answers to question 6. They did not show all the tests on which they suspected cheating and allowed only brief looks at the students' answers. The ETS said its analysis of the retest scores showed none of the close agreement found in the first test.

But the new data had little impact. The story of twelve East Los Angeles teenagers who bested an upper-crust Princeton think tank was too good to die. And it reached some very distant corners.

Olimpia Escalante de Ortuño had arisen early, as usual, on that cloudy December morning in 1982. It had been a pleasant summer. She pulled out some pans and started to cook breakfast while flipping on the radio to *La Voz de América*. It reported the news. United States banks save Banco do Brazil from default. Poland plans suspension of martial law. Nicaraguan diplomat warns against isolation from neighbors. Then came the special features. Her mind wandered.

What was that? She moved closer to the radio. ". . . the American testing service said the students had cheated, but Señor Escalante had them take the test over again and they all passed. A wonderful moment

173

for a very good teacher. . . ." She began to cry, her dark face wrinkling in smiles and sobs.

She would have to check before she called her mother. But it had to be Jaime. Who else? All that heartbreak, all the times she missed him, and now she was paid back.

She *had* to call Mama. So many Bolivians went to America and disappeared. Not Jaime.

All great successes produce jealousy and suspicion. Escalante's temper and distaste for compromise hurt feelings. His influence over Gradillas and the media stardom he achieved after 1982 brought resentment. A few students harbored grudges over his cavalier approach to grades and his sharp reaction to sloth and sloppiness.

Even before the 1982 triumph, rumors and dissent had haunted his program. When filmmakers Ramon Menendez and Tom Musca in 1987 began shooting their riveting feature film, *Stand and Deliver*, starring Edward James Olmos as Escalante and based on the ETS controversy, more than the usual amount of hate mail landed in Escalante's mailbox. One telephone call was threatening enough to convince Escalante, at his wife's insistence, to stop teaching a night school class at Garfield, where there was very little security after dark.

Some of the anonymous letters suggested he was getting too much credit, or that the true story had never been told. Some people suggested that the movie—and this unrelated book—would exploit Garfield, and would interfere with the educational process. Some letters repeated second- and thirdhand charges that some calculus students in 1982 had actually copied. Many students and East Los Angeles community leaders, taking the opposite view, argued that more ought to be done to expose what they felt was ETS ethnic bias in challenging the 1982 scores.

The argument came and went, never drawing much attention because—as almost everyone knew—the 1982 retest had proven that Escalante's students knew calculus and deserved their AP credits. The controversy shrank to a historical footnote, although an interesting one.

Asked by me to put the issue to rest, and perhaps reveal once and for all how ETS had erred in its investigation, ten graduates of the 1982 calculus class signed releases allowing ETS to give me copies of their original examinations and any other materials the testing service thought relevant. Although the students authorized me to look at the entire test, I asked ETS only for copies of their work on question 6. I felt the other free-response questions were not relevant because they had not been challenged and the alleged agreement on the multiple-choice questions was a statistical issue that could not be resolved by inspecting the actual answer sheets. Along with the ten answers to question 6, ETS provided a three-page memo by ETS Board of Review Chairman Louis R. Lavine. It gave the most detailed justification ever of the board's 1982 actions, although it dealt only with question 6 and ignored the other questions that were not challenged.

According to the copies, nine of the ten students began their work with near identical—and incorrect—formulas for the cost of the rectangular tank. All nine produced the same wrong answer to the problem, $360—to be expected, perhaps, since they began the same way. (The tenth test-taker, Leticia Rodríguez, approached the problem differently and produced the right answer, $330.)

Lavine noted other odd similarities, but focused on the error in substitution that all of the nine with incorrect answers had made in the middle of their work. Using their approach, they had to simplify the term $10hw$. Each noted, correctly, that $9 = wh$. That meant h $= 9/w$, and $9/w$ could be substituted for h in the term $10hw$, simplifying it to 90. But in each of the nine tests, the simplified expression read not 90, but $10(9/w)$ or $90/w$. Each had failed to cancel out the w.

Lavine concluded: "The overall picture is one of a variety of errors, some common to more than one candidate, but all followed by group agreement that does not follow logically from the preceding errors."

Rodríguez and another, unknown student who did not sign a release were not challenged for their work on question 6. Instead, Lavine said, their tests were ruled invalid because they, like the twelve students who showed similarities on question 6 (nine of whom signed releases), gave an unusual number of similar wrong answers in the first half of the test, the multiple-choice section.

ETS may have placed too much confidence in its K index as an abstract indication of copying on multiple-choice answers. But the nine incorrect solutions to question 6 in the second part of the examination remained unexplained. As promised, each of the ten former students who signed releases were sent copies of their work on question 6 and Lavine's report, and were given an opportunity to respond to the new material.

After being promised anonymity, the first two former students approached for a response contradicted their earlier statements and said the unusual agreement on question 6 was not accidental. They said they and some others—they did not know how many—had copied the work of another student. They said the other student, whom they would not name, had wanted to be helpful and had passed around a piece of paper with a suggested solution to question 6 near the end of the examination, when there was no time to check for errors. They said that no copying had occurred on the first, multiple-choice section of the examination or on any other free-response question.

Andreda Pruitt had proctored the examination alone that day. In an earlier interview she had mentioned that at some point during those three hours she had worked in the examination room on her master schedule. But when asked later if a note could have been passed without her noticing, she strongly denied any such possibility. Any glances at her schedule were very brief, she said, and she could clearly see both the tops of the tables and the space underneath them. She toured the room every fifteen minutes. "I knew at all times what was going on in that room," she said.

One of the two graduates said he had always felt ETS was wrong to challenge the scores. The copying had done him little good, he said, because the formula, solution, and answer were largely incorrect. And the retest had proven beyond doubt that they all could have passed the first examination without help.

The other graduate said she did not know how to handle question 6 and felt under enormous pressure to pass the test. The entire class had been looking toward that day for more than two years, and as she faced that question she cringed at the thought of having wasted all that time.

I heard a very different story from the next four former students I approached. All denied copying at any point in the test, and expressed extreme disappointment and distress that this subject was being raised again. "We've answered all those questions before," one said. Another said their answers on question 6 could not be judged fairly unless their answers on all the other free-response questions were also examined. The remaining three students with similar answers on question 6 could not be reached for comment.

When I told Escalante about these interviews, he said he was certain there had been no copying. Most of the former students sent him personal letters saying they had not copied. He expressed his confidence in the 1982 students to the parents and siblings who approached him with worried questions about my interviews. Eventually, the former students produced a joint letter denying that any of them had copied. It was signed by nearly everyone who took the 1982 test, including one of the two students who had originally said there was copying.

When I reinterviewed that student, he said he signed the letter because he felt I had dishonestly coerced a statement from him by promising I would tell no one what he had said. I apologized and told him I had had a different understanding of our agreement—that I would keep only his name confidential.

He then told a somewhat different story: he said no note was passed but he had copied the original incorrect formula from the paper of another student and had surreptitiously shown that formula to a few students sitting near him. He said it was possible that some students accused of copying had instead innocently used a mistakenly learned formula, as the person he copied from may have done, and that the identical errors in substitution occurred by chance.

Three days after this conversation, further muddying already opaque waters, I received a letter signed by the same person saying everything he told me was a "joke" to test a theory that I was an agent for the ETS. "I told you lies, nothing but lies," the letter said. "What I told you was I felt all that you expected and wanted to hear. The truth was probably too boring for your book, we passed and re-passed without any cheating whatsoever. We only wanted to see what you would do with these 'private' facts, and prove to us if you were an ETS investigator or an honest friendly author as you claimed to be. Only time will tell."

When I reinterviewed the second former student who originally described copying, she said she thought the issue was dated and irrelevant and did not wish to discuss it anymore.

My questions created much emotional turmoil and controversy in East Los Angeles. There were intense discussions over what might have motivated some students to copy—youthful bravado, obsessive perfectionism, nagging doubt about their own abilities—and similar speculation over what might have led two former students to tell me there was copying when there was not. The ETS agent theory was mentioned often. Some people familiar with the students and the community suggested even before I received that last letter that I had been the victim of a prank, motivated by weariness over the constant rehashing of the events of 1982.

Having explored in the limited time before publication what I thought were the most likely explanations, I decided simply to report what I had seen and heard, and hope it would be taken in context. I was convinced that, whatever occurred during that first 1982 examination in Room 411, it had ceased to have much meaning for what was happening at Garfield.

What was important was that twelve students, obviously frightened and upset and handicapped by lack of preparation time and textbooks, had taken the retest and had passed. Under the close supervision of two ETS staff members they earned valid AP college credit and proved that they had had sufficient grasp of the material all along.

After 1982, John Bennett moved to eliminate the chance of the issue ever being raised again by thoroughly overhauling what he acknowledged had been an amateurish security system. The test booklets were locked up. At Escalante's suggestion, he put two proctors in every testing room—many of them no friends of Escalante. I closely watched both the 1986 and 1987 AP calculus tests and concluded that little, if anything, could get by this system. In fact, no one at ETS has detected any irregularities since 1982.

As this book was nearing publication, Escalante reaffirmed his strong belief that there was never any copying in 1982. "I stand behind my kids," he said. "I believe in my students. They are the true dreamers."

There will continue to be rumors and suspicions about 1982, above and beyond what has been reported here. That may seem unfair to many, but the odd truth is that Garfield and Escalante eventually benefited greatly from those bad times. The initial distress and rage created a mood that made the story of the successful retest irresistible and persuaded more students to take calculus and more administrators, parents, and donors to support Escalante.

There is something in Escalante's frequent explanations of absolute value that casts light on what happened at Garfield. X inside two vertical lines, $|x|$, means absolute value of x, a quantity that may be either negative or positive. Escalante explains the concept a dozen different ways. One way to remember it is this: The value within is more important than its positive or negative sign, just as a large failure can turn out to be an enormous success.

Sometimes in mathematics, as in life, negative and positive are just different directions toward the same goal.

PART TWO

—

CONTINUITY

‖ 12 ‖

The sun poked up above the power lines on Atlantic Boulevard and lit the dull yellow stucco of the Garfield High facade on Sixth Street. One gardener edged the threadbare September grass with an electric trimmer. Another slowly and carefully ran a large rider mower over the lawn as if he were a barber tending the balding skull of his richest customer.

A tall boy wearing a striped polo shirt and black slacks carried a folded American flag to the pole directly in front of the main entrance. Looking bored, he attached the flag to the hanging rope and hoisted it up as a small detachment of ROTC students saluted.

It was 8:00 A.M., the first day of school, 1986. All the bells were set to ring late and ease 3,575 nervous, excited, resentful teenagers into another year's routine.

A tide of students surged slowly through the front doors. Those heading for academic classrooms mostly turned left, down the freshly polished linoleum of the 400 Building hall to the 300, 200, 100, and 700 buildings beyond. Those seeking the automobile shop or music rooms or gymnasium turned right. If they looked to their left as they exited the eastern end of the 400 Building, they saw a beige stucco cube with two doors, no windows, and a broken drinking fountain. That was MH-1, domain of Jaime A. Escalante. He was inside, bundled in a blue windbreaker and motorman's cap, sniffling and feeling out of sorts.

July had not gone well. The ELAC classes were larger than ever, but there were no more teachers or money. George Madrid administered Escalante's weekend and summer ELAC program, but even

183

Madrid had received a chilly letter from community college head-quarters saying there was no money to pay him. The oil price slump had devastated the ARCO Foundation, meaning perhaps no money at all for next summer's program.

Escalante had spent the latter part of August in La Paz. He learned once again how easily he could catch cold on the altiplano. He returned to face 184 students in five periods of mathematics—29 in first-period Calculus AB, 47 in second-period Algebra 2, 36 in third-period Trigonometry, 21 in fourth-period Calculus BC, and, in what was always the most difficult period, the postlunch fifth, a record 51 in his second class of Calculus AB.

Escalante would have to instruct aspiring rock musicians in RUN-D.M.C. T-shirts and tight blue jeans, friendly altar boys in love with computers, surly football players in blue-and-red game jerseys, and tiny pep-squad members with cotton-candy hairstyles and enough chores at home to keep any full-time suburban mother busy. On his class rosters he found boat people, beauty queens, straight-A students, unwed mothers, petty thieves, and children sent up from Mexico without papers or parents.

Escalante blew his nose into a Kleenex and worried. Fifty-one students were twice as many as any sane AP calculus teacher would tolerate in one class. How were all those kids, their brains sodden with cafeteria nachos and Pepsi-Cola, going to absorb this material?

He had made calculus popular at Garfield. But that did not mean these dozens of students would be able to pass the AP examination. The whole system threatened to collapse of its own weight. He was no longer dealing with a thin crust of intense achievers, like the class of 1982. He and Jiménez alone had more than 350 students in some stage of what he called the "developing process." He felt the school lacked enough good teachers to handle them all, and with such large numbers came students with problems he had never encountered before.

On their first day of school in the autumn of 1986 Escalante, Jiménez, and every other teacher at Garfield found copies of the district's *Senior High Schools Division News* in their wooden cubbyhole mailboxes. Across the top of the front page the paper announced the selection of an English and speech instructor at Gardena High School as Senior High Schools Division teacher of the year. She would vie for the honor

184

of California state teacher of the year, who would in turn go to Washington, D.C., for a national competition.

The teacher had changed many lives for the better, but her record did not approach the scale of Escalante's achievement. Dealing with students who had somewhat fewer disadvantages, Gardena High had thirty students take an AP English test in 1986 (Garfield had twelve). Gardena had thirteen students take an AP calculus test. Garfield had ninety-three. The newspaper announced sixteen other finalists, including Escalante, who were not selected.

It was the fourth time Escalante had been passed over for a major teaching award. Despite the accolades from students, parents, filmmakers, politicians, businessmen, and columnists, the leaders of his own profession could offer only an awkward silence.

Joe Hoffman, a California Department of Education mathematics consultant, chaired a 1984 committee that had failed to nominate Escalante for a presidential award for excellence in teaching mathematics. Asked about it then, he said Escalante "had a lot of high recommendations, but some people thought there was a lack of professional sharing." Hoffman thought Escalante was a wonderful teacher but wondered if he could be a model for others.

Years before Hoffman had done an academic study of what he called "sweatshop teachers." "When they're teaching their classes everybody is on the move, things start happening. Work harder, work harder. It generates a kind of frothing at the mouth. The kids are very excited," he said. "But what happens to those kids when they go to the next class? They can't keep that up all day."

Gradillas flushed in anger when the remark was first repeated to him, and he still had not forgotten it. The students would not burn out, he thought, but Escalante might. Teachers and principals and politicians called the calculus teacher out to weekend workshops and invaded his classroom to watch and ask questions. The man was sick. He was working too hard. Fabiola persuaded him to drop two of his four night school classes, but only because some unknown critics had telephoned to say they would "get him" one of those nights.

Some way or another, Gradillas thought, all this stuff was going to suck Escalante dry. Gradillas tried to tell him to slow down, but Escalante did not listen to anybody.

Knowing the risks he was taking, Gradillas had persuaded Escalante three months before to join him at a National Education Association conference on concerns of minorities and women. The NEA

185

emphasized collegiality, consensus, and political organizing to win more federal government support for education. Escalante preferred to go his own way, make his own decisions, and find what extra money he needed in the private sector, where he did not have to deal with so many bureaucrats.

On the way to Louisville, trapped by his seat belt and strict rules against leaving the aircraft, Gradillas listened to Escalante's complaints—some counselors were still letting students drop his classes, his department was full of amateurs, a search of the junior highs had found not a single good teacher willing to join his program.

At the NEA conference, Escalante nearly walked out when one luncheon speaker prayed for deliverance from the murderous foreign policy of the Reagan administration. The White House had done him a favor, and weren't they supposed to talk about education? At a workshop, Escalante tore into another speaker for presenting detailed statistics on the dropout problem without suggesting any solutions.

Gradillas did not want to lose the best teacher he had ever seen, but his farmer's instincts sensed something bad coming, not a storm, but gusts of foul wind, which, over time, could wear down a person who insisted on standing as straight as Escalante.

UTLA   9/25/86

Brian,

I would like to call for an election of a new dept. chair for math. Can you fill me in on the procedures? I mentioned this to Mr. Escalante last year but haven't this year yet. He is not fulfilling any of his responsibilities as d.c.

Dorothy Fromel

UNITED TEACHERS–LOS ANGELES
2511 West Third Street
Los Angeles, California 90057
(213) 487-5560

For two years Dorothy Fromel had silently suffered the Escalante management style. As the mathematics resource teacher for the Chapter 1 program, she was responsible for maintaining the level of mathematics instruction to the 2,500 Garfield students eligible for federally funded remedial education. Yet each year she found herself doing more of the department chair's work, since he would not do it himself. She read the reports and announcements and guidelines coming to him in the mail and tried to pass the information on to teachers who might need it. When a school or district meeting for department heads was held, she went in his place because he refused to go to meetings.

Everybody complained about meetings, of course, and not everything that came in the mail was useful, but she thought someone ought to take on these responsibilities. To her, the only solution was a new department chair. She dropped her note in the box of Brian Wallace, Garfield's teachers' union representative, and circulated a petition requesting an election.

Escalante was the first to sign the petition, but when Wallace gave him a copy of Fromel's note, he changed his mind. What had first appeared to be a helping hand now seemed to be shaking a finger at him.

Yes, he missed meetings. Nobody ever talked about anything but how many minutes to advance the bells, or somebody might ask him, for the ninety-eighth time, how he motivated his kids. How could he ever motivate his kids if he was off at a meeting someplace talking about motivating his kids? Fromel, he was convinced, simply did not like him or his ideas, and perhaps suspected he and Gradillas planned to cut the number of basic mathematics classes to a bare minimum. It was time for another letter to his principal.

"Some faculty members of the Math Department do not understand my dedication to develop a Math Department of the highest order," he wrote, his pen biting into the paper. "My time is often spent late after school with students and faculty that need extra assistance and guidance with Math. This has not allowed me to attend Dept. Chair meetings. However, this should not give anyone the excuse to say that I am not fulfilling my responsibilities as Department Chair. . . . Please accept my resignation, effective today, September 29, 1986. This kind of ungratefulness hurts me and diminishes my desire to continue as Department Chair."

Word spread quickly. His friends thought he was under an unusual strain. He had been ill and he still refused to see a doctor. The hate mail he had been getting felt like a slap across the face. Fernando would be in college in a year, and he had to worry about money.

Al Santoyo walked into MH-1. If Escalante was not there to cut back the easy courses in the department and weed out the bad teachers,

Santoyo said, the whole program would go to hell. Gradillas came to plead that he reconsider. Wouldn't he miss the $500 a semester extra department chair's pay?

If that was all they had to say, Escalante thought, then they did not understand. Did he really feel the aching need anymore to prove he was right? Look what was happening to Gradillas. He would grow old in that job. Downtown was so annoyed at the way he had been pushing they would never promote him.

Maybe Garfield was on the verge of a year that would finally make everyone pay attention. Poor, beat-up Garfield could pass Hunter and Exeter, New Trier and Evanston, do things no inner city minority school had ever done in mathematics. Escalante's classes already accounted for one out of every four Mexican Americans taking AP calculus in the *whole country*.

But, he thought, after all this time, all this sweat and youthful anxiety, if he still had to defend himself against little people sitting at desks and tending their in-baskets, maybe he was wrong. Maybe it really could not work.

||13||

It was the spring of 1983, shortly after the wave of publicity about the 1982 test results, when the three young men descended on Escalante. If he had seen them coming, he might have had time to hide. He knew every corner of the 200 Building. He had all the keys. They caught him off guard.

The leader stood about 5 feet 6, 170 pounds. He wore a bandanna, jeans, and white T-shirt. He had a familiar face. A former student, Escalante supposed, probably not one of his most dedicated basic mathematics graduates. He could read, unfortunately. He had seen Escalante's name in the papers.

"Hey, man, how ya doing?" the youth said, his entourage hanging back. "Don't you remember me? Come on, Kimo! You remember me. I was in your high school math class."

"Oh, yes, sure, how you doing?"

"You know, we have a job now. We're working over in the body shop. We hear you still driving the same bug, right?"

"Yeah," Escalante replied uncertainly. "What about it?" Did they want to buy his car?

"We came to congratulate you."

"Well, thank you."

"And you know what? We're gonna take your car!"

Escalante stiffened.

"Come *on*, Kimo. We're gonna fix it. We're gonna paint it."

"No, no, no. Really. I don't need it."

"Come on, give us the key. We're gonna do it right. Don't worry about it."

189

"Really, no," he said, as nonchalantly as possible. These *llockallas* looked *very* strong.

"Look, you only have to put up fifty dollars for paint. We gonna do it for you."

He groped for a polite way to put them off. "Listen, it's one o'clock. Maybe you guys can come back at three and we'll talk about it."

"Sure, man. We'll do it." At 3:00 P.M. they were there in the parking lot. He sighed and surrendered his keys. They said they planned to take the ancient Volkswagen to a small shop in the shadow of the Pomona Freeway, a place of rusting barrels and vicious dogs and late night rendezvous. "Just take a week, Kimo. What color you want?"

"The same color, I guess."

His admirer looked disappointed. Light green was not appropriate for an East LA celebrity. "You look worried, Kimo."

"I think I have to say bye-bye to my car."

"Oh, come *on*, Kimo. You know me. You remember *me*."

Escalante could remember almost nothing about him. He meekly requested and received a ride home, where Fabiola shook her head sadly. She had seen her husband's benefactors.

Jaimito took him to work the rest of the week. On Friday, the young volunteers returned with their handiwork. Escalante thanked God that his wonderful souvenir of America had survived. The paint looked fine, about the same color. What was that on the sides?

"You like it, Kimo? *Pinstripes!*"

He was too stunned to speak. He groped for some intelligent comment. "Uh, why those colors? Blue? Red?"

"Kimo, come *on*. The *school* colors. We're *bull*dogs."

I hope, Escalante thought, they didn't leave any graffiti inside.

Appearances were very important. Escalante's brief notoriety lured a few more curious youths into his web, but he had to find a way to make them stay.

Room 233 had become a showcase, a pedagogical Disneyland that delighted visiting principals. His huge color photographs of Wilt Chamberlain and Jerry West shared wall space with posters of the space shuttle and the white-wigged inventors of what was originally called the calculus.

Next to the clock, a principal focus of attention in any classroom, he placed the formula DETERMINATION + DISCIPLINE + HARD WORK = THE WAY TO SUCCESS. Another poster over the blackboard extolled his watchword: *ganas*. The Spanish word loosely translates as "the urge"—the urge to succeed, to achieve, to grow.

The forty-two students who made up his 1983 calculus class had been with him long enough to chant the relevant slogan in perfect unison—"Determination plus hard work plus concentration equals success, which equals *ganas*." Occasionally, from the back of the room, someone would softly add, "We've got the *ganas* but we don't have the money."

During much of the publicity barrage after the 1982 retest, Escalante had sulked in his third-floor redoubt. The principal, the superintendent, Downtown—they were all taking the credit for what had happened. He heard the rumors that some students actually had cheated. He had to prove something with his next calculus class.

Like every successful preacher, coach, sales director, and chairman of the board—like any good motivator—Escalante never settled on one method. He improvised, using different devices with different students, but Jiménez and other careful observers discerned a basic philosophical approach.

Social commentators and columnists sometimes speak of personal contact and warmth as characteristic of Latinos, as if no other ethnic community possesses such traits. In fact, Garfield students shared with all American teenagers the compulsive need to belong—thus the power of the gangs and the church and the extraordinary popularity of activities like the band and drill teams. That intense feeling of community may have explained in part the wave of hysteria that swept the stands during a Garfield football game in 1982 when the loudspeaker announced that some people had gotten sick from snack bar soft drinks. Eventually 126 people, who had been hearing of poisoned Tylenol in Chicago, went to hospitals complaining of stomach cramps, nausea, and chills. An analysis of the drinks revealed nothing.

Escalante gradually came to appreciate the force of togetherness and the power of suggestion among his students. He moved slow learners to desks near his own. Gloria Bujanda, a quiet, thoughtful Escalante star who eventually turned down Harvard for Berkeley, watched him ingratiate himself with as many newcomers as possible.

Most received some kind of illustrative alias, since he still could not remember real names. There were usually one or two Elizabeth Taylors and, later, a few Madonnas. Bujanda herself had to put up

191

with Gordita, "Little Fatty" in Spanish. His students accepted their new names, no matter how embarrassing, as a sign that he recognized and cared about them, a crucial first step. His jokes and occasional digressions into Lakers lore lightened the load of complicated mathematical reasoning and added to their sense of obligation.

Next came the inevitable guilt trip.

Escalante was their friend. So why were they not doing their homework? He could lay this on in several ways—a friendly word, a sudden coldness of intonation, an injured expression, or in some cases a request for the student's textbook, the equivalent of stripping a corrupt patrolman of his badge and gun. Some of his critics saw this as bald, insensitive coercion, but his students almost always felt his warmth and concern, and understood the message.

He joked constantly about the threat of an "F-U-U," the report card triple whammy of a failing academic grade plus unsatisfactory marks in work habits and cooperation. His students laughed, but the humor also served as a reminder that their lovable bulldog had teeth.

Early in the term he called the parents of each of his newcomers—usually Algebra 2 students—and exchanged pleasantries. The students always heard about these calls. They were a tacit threat that he would call again if they caused trouble. In many cases, just the hint of plans to call someone's mother brought sudden reform.

He experimented with classroom routine. Sometimes he became so unpredictable that the most orderly of his students would request a transfer to Jiménez, who had given Escalante's style of discipline and instruction a very steady and, to some, reassuring hand. Escalante required students who botched homework assignments to do them again. He ordered ten copies of some solutions. He put a concept on a quiz, went on to something else for a few days, then put the old concept on a quiz again to see if it had been retained.

Time was his tool, his melody. He welcomed—and sometimes ordered—students in for hours of after-school study to steal time from television and parental chores and talking on the telephone and band practice. He sang of time, scratchy and off key, "Yesterday, all my troubles seeeeeem so *far* away, . . . but tomorrow, TUUUUU-morrow, I test you, tomorrow, it's only a day AAAAA-WAAAAY."

If, as Jimmy Breslin often said, political power is mostly mirrors and blue smoke, then Escalante was a politician. He strutted in front of the blackboard. He called himself "The Champ," a nickname he preferred to the milder "Kimo." Once he understood how the residue of the 1982 publicity helped him, he ceased to shrink from it.

He sent errant students to a counselor friend who kept a phony list of names in his typewriter. Escalante said the man needed "just one more to fill up the next bus to Jordan High," seven miles, and a very long bus trip, from Garfield. Escalante left some doubt as to who actually ran the school, Gradillas or himself, and the principal went along.

"Sir! We have some students we have to send out of here."

"Of course, Mr. Escalante. Anything you say. We don't want people taking up space."

What worked best, in the minds of students who thought about it years later, was simply hard work. Escalante, Jiménez, and the core of other Garfield teachers who began to push the Advanced Placement program spent so much time with students—early morning, nutrition break, lunch, after school until dark—that they could not be ignored.

Inside most American teenagers, including those at Garfield, lurks a visceral respect for honest labor. The feeling transcends class and ethnic background. They might give in to sloth and diversion themselves, but it was more difficult to do so when dealing with a teacher who worked as hard as Escalante did, no matter what they thought about his accent or wardrobe. "I'm not going to class because I want to," a struggling calculus student, Delia Mora, announced to a group of friends in 1983. "But when you see all the effort he puts into the class, you begin to want to put out just as much."

It was the second week of calculus. He gazed wistfully at the huge poster on the back wall showing a close play at home in Dodger Stadium. He sighed. "Every time I see this poster, it reminds me of my last game. A couple years ago I play against . . . It was at Montreal at night."

Muffled laughter rose from several corners of the room. "What? You don't believe it? The photographer screwed me up, he took it from the wrong side. You don't believe? I don't care."

He pulled something out from behind the lectern. "Here's my glove, and here's the ball they gave me." He stuck a baseball, with the prominent signature of Fernando Valenzuela, in the faces of several front-row occupants. "Until you understand the pitcher and the catcher, you don't understand anything."

He had prepared a small white board with an x- and a y-axis drawn on it, as well as a tiny plastic ball suspended in front from a string. "Imagine you watching a Dodger baseball game, and the Dodgers are in the field. This distance between the catcher and the pitcher is fixed, the pitcher throw the ball, the ball is going a certain velocity and the distance, the distance . . . *Orale! Orale!* [Hurry up!] I forgot the pitcher. What else I forgot? . . . uh . . ."

"The catcher!" said several young voices.

"Oh, yeah, where's the catcher?" He pulled out a small toy hand with flexible fingers, its palm magnetized and its forefinger sticking straight up. He hastily adjusted the fingers and brought the toy hand to the board while several boys hooted and laughed.

"Okay, the ball is now traveling a certain velocity, it's getting closer, closer, closer to the glove of the catcher, the ball is traveling a certain ve . . . ve . . . ve . . ." He looked confused.

"Velocity!"

"Oh, yes, right." The ball, with its own small magnet, plopped into the disembodied plastic hand of the "catcher." "You know, I would say the distance between the ball and the glove of the catcher is decreasing, but I hate to use that word. In calculus we do not use that word. I would say the distance between the ball and the . . . uh . . ."

"Catcher."

"Oh, yup. Is approaching zero, that's what I mean. So this is what I'm going to write." On the blackboard, he chalked: "$x \rightarrow 0$." "You know if I write this way"—$x \nearrow 0$—"I cannot say approaching zero. It has to be, it has to be, horizontal.

"You know, the way the pitcher throws the ball determines the path the ball will take, am I saying right?"

"Yeah. Yes."

"Here what we have, the screwball. What else we have? Uh . . ."

"Curveball."

"Oh, yeah, and then something else, it's . . . it's . . ." He snapped his fingers in frustration.

"Fastball."

"You know, the trajectory of the ball, ah, yes, the *trajectory* of the ball, is what I'm gonna call f of x." He wrote "$f(x)$." "Now," he said, pointing at the plastic hand, "what is it they call this? I forgot."

"*Catcher.*"

"Oh, yeah, catcher. It's really important, the catcher is the most important in the case. You know, the pitch could be a ball, or it could be a . . . a . . . what's the other name?"

"Strike," said several voices, all trying to help this apparently absentminded bumbler.

On the white board with the x- and y-axes forming a cross, he had drawn a vertical line intersecting the horizontal x-axis at point a. "$x = a$," the board said. He indicated the point on the vertical line where he held the plastic hand. "It could be a strike, or"—he pointed to a point above the hand—"it could be a ball. That's what the *limit* is. The catcher has to go up and down, to the left or the right. That's it. That's what the limit is. So we write:

$$\lim_{x \to a} f(x)$$

"The catcher is at x equal to a, so that is the position of the catcher. Now, notice this. I said the pitcher took the ball, and is coming from the right, so I would say coming from the right, I put $x \to a^+$. Or from the left it is $x \to a^-$. And so I write:

$$\lim_{x \to a^+} f(x)$$

since we come from the right." He repeated it two more times, writing the function for both the left and right approaches.

He looked hard at his audience, gauging the level of comprehension and trying to spot a whisperer, or a wandering eye. There was one, a boy, fourth row back. Escalante grabbed a small red pillow and flew up the aisle to pummel the unfortunate victim. "What wrong with you? Are you mentally in *shape*? *Huh?*"

He returned to the board and summarized again before moving into no limit (pitches from right and left that do not meet) and oscillation function (an impossibly erratic knuckleball). He presented the material again, using drawings of pitcher and catcher superimposed on a graph and shown on an overhead projector. He passed out mimeographed sheets with the same drawings, then told some students to open their textbooks and read him the first few problems. He solved them on the board and asked once more for questions before leaving them to work on their own. "Remember, every time I have to deal with this kind of problem, I have to identify the catcher.

"You know, sometimes I don't understand this. It's difficult to me. It took me three years to understand this, but you're gonna learn in one day."

From his Garfield beginnings in basic math, Escalante had struggled to translate the jargon of functions and binomials and values into the American idiom, just as he was trying to do the same with his own Spanish.

Eventually he developed an Escalantese, a multilingual collage of sports, television news, high school patois, and soap opera vocabulary. To an outsider, it was just as incomprehensible as a Caltech text on relativity, but it made sense to Escalante's students. Its odd twists of meaning helped them remember, and its obscurity gave them the special feeling of being part of a secret society—a gang without graffiti or violence.

A visitor observing an Escalante class required an interpreter. Escalante leaned over the shoulder of a boy puzzled by a wrong answer. "Face mask! Face mask!" the teacher shouted, and gave him a soft slap on the back of the head. He snorted at another student's question. "Marching band," he said. The student seemed satisfied.

"You missed the secret agent."

"Give and go!"

"No, no, red light. *Red light.*"

The students understood every word. *Face mask* meant the student had made an error at the very beginning of the problem, and had to go back and find it—similar to a 15-yard penalty in football for pulling a linebacker's face mask at the beginning of a long gain. *Marching band* meant the solution was easy, just follow the usual steps—Escalante still insisted band was an activity for dunces. The *secret agent* was a minus sign in front of a parenthesis, which could reverse all the signs inside. *Give and go* meant breaking down an absolute value function into its alternatives, minus or plus or zero. *Red light* meant factoring would be difficult, and perhaps impossible.

He developed hand signs. Three fingers meant a student would have to come after school, at 3:00 P.M. Thumb down meant an F on a test. Thumb up was an A or B. Thumb sideways meant a C.

A group of young Escalante watchers, Olga García, Gabriela Pantoja, and Raúl Orozco, eventually produced an observer's guide to Escalantese. A class requirement, they said, was "nodding your head in a positive way even when the teacher is wrong." If Escalante said, "Go to the beach," he meant, "See your counselor. I don't want you back." They quoted his favorite proverb for misbehavior by a senior nearing graduation: *En la puerta del horno se quema el pan.* (At the door of the oven the bread burns.) (See Appendix 1.)

Escalante made it clear that no one was going to spoil his plans to spend August 1983 peacefully sampling *salteñas* in the cafés of La Paz. By the time of the AP calculus examination he had thirty-three students ready to avenge the troubles of 1982.

For much of the spring term he displayed a foul temper. The 1983 group, he insisted, was just not as good as previous teams. They were not working hard. No matter what the newspapers said, he repeatedly announced, no one should think that he could wave a magic wand and they would pass the test. He watched with concealed satisfaction as his words had their desired effect.

The 1983 class took their examinations in the library on the second floor of the 200 Building. Two proctors scattered them to distant tables and watched their every move. Escalante grunted agreeably at the results: thirty of the thirty-three passed with 3s or better. Josie Richkarday, the only veteran of the 1982 test still at Garfield, had tried to prepare for Calculus BC. But she was head cheerleader, her ulcers were causing terrible pain, and there was no other BC student to study with. She tried her best, but received a 1.

Escalante consoled her, and scanned the AB results. There were six 5s, eleven 4s, thirteen 3s, and three 2s. He waited with only mild apprehension for more nasty letters from the ETS. None came. The testing service made no special effort to check Garfield tests. Its rules forbade that. The Garfield experiment could proceed without fear.

Now Escalante and several others began to look for ways to expand the program. They continued to share a vague feeling they were on to something important that had never really been tried before.

In their own small empire across the campus mall in the 700 Building, John Bennett and Tom Woessner noted, with a mixture of envy and excitement, the acclaim Escalante was receiving. None of the reporters who had briefly flooded the campus had noticed that their own little experiment in AP American history had also had an upsurge, and in a subject that many considered more difficult than mathematics for these particular youngsters.

In 1979 Bennett had persuaded Jessie Franco to let him expand his small AP history course by taking Woessner in as co-teacher. They hoped to lure more juniors who might have previously had little interest in the subject. After two years of modest success—four 3s and a 4 in 1980 and four 3s and two 4s in 1981—they heard grumbling from other teachers about their good fortune in being allowed to work together.

So they suggested something more. They would combine AP American history, taught just by Woessner, with an honors American literature course taught by Dennis Campagna, one of the school's most gifted English teachers. If they could find at least twenty-five willing students, they could augment the political history with a healthy dose of literature from the same period. The students who took the AP history test would thus be forced to practice writing English essays, a weakness for youths who usually spoke Spanish at home.

Bennett and Woessner had noticed that no matter how successful they had been drilling facts into young brains for the multiple-choice section, their students stumbled over the free-response questions in the second half of the examination. An English class tied to history would attack that problem and, at the same time, help provide the critical thinking skills that several new commission reports said were missing in American public schools.

Woessner was a modest man whose father had been a mechanic. At Notre Dame High School in Glendale, he had been a mediocre student with a stutter and an inferiority complex. The first counselor he saw in junior college suggested he quit and go work in a gas station. A flamboyant political science professor eventually saw something salvageable in him, and his grades and self-esteem soared. He wanted to pay the favor back to a collection of similarly unappreciated teenagers.

Gradillas agreed to let Woessner and Campagna schedule their courses one right after the other. Each took a preparation period while the other taught. If Woessner needed two hours for an examination or a special project, he kept the students during Campagna's period, and Campagna would do the same when he needed extra time. All that remained was to find the students.

Woessner worked up a speech that he delivered in the spring to sophomore English classes. "You'd be absolutely crazy to take these two courses," he began, and paused to collect some quizzical looks, "except for the following reasons. You have to be serious about going

198

to college, but not only will this help you get into college, it will help you stay in college."

At that point, he saw several listening attentively. Garfield students often had older sisters, cousins, uncles, and aunts struggling with the demands of time and money in higher education, even at Cal State, LA. "No matter what your major is, medicine, PE, engineering, aerospace, whatever, ninety percent of your work is going to be reading, writing, vocabulary, and thinking, and that's what these two courses are about."

In 1983, their maiden year, their students produced one 5, four 4s, six 3s, six 2s, and two 1s. No Garfield class had ever had nineteen students take the American history examination before. Bennett looked for other places to inject AP, just as the College Board and the ETS were beginning to see a use for the program none of its creators had ever imagined.

Harpo Hanson cheerfully admitted years later that he had been hopelessly wrong when he guessed, at the very beginning of the Advanced Placement program, that it would peak at 220 schools. As an assistant dean at Harvard, and later the College Board AP director, he watched with pleased surprise as the program began to raise expectations and competitive urges in one unlikely corner of the country after another. Mormons in Utah were fond of high standards in discipline and education; the state's schools quickly embraced the idea. Coming into the 1980s, as national commissions and school boards began to assess the damage of the lowered standards and free-form curricula of the 1960s and 1970s, several states considered special appropriations to support AP. In 1983, the year the Garfield program began to accelerate, the regents of the University of California announced that an extra grade point would be awarded for every AP or other honors course on a student's record—a significant boost in the heated competition to win places at Berkeley, UCLA, and other fair-weather campuses rich in Nobel laureates.

By 1983 AP had found its way into not 220, but 5,827 of the nation's 23,000 secondary schools. That spring 157,973 students took 211,160 AP examinations, a 12 percent increase over the previous year and far above the growth rate of the ETS–College Board prime ticket, the Scholastic Aptitude Test.

The SAT had other problems. In 1983 author David Owen was

in the midst of preparing a razor-edged book, *None of the Above: Behind the Myth of Scholastic Aptitude*, that gave heart to a small but growing band of educators who wanted the SAT scrapped. It was much better, they argued, to test high school students on *what they had actually studied in their courses* than to administer a test of amorphous, allegedly value-free "aptitude" that was really little more than a vocabulary and arithmetic quiz.

Owen found little good to say about the ETS. He recommended it be abolished along with the SAT. But the AP program received what was, for him, a backhanded endorsement. He noted reports from some readers of erratic grading of the essay sections. As then set up, he said, the AP program "is a joke, but the form is appealing. The nice thing about the concept is that it emphasizes serious learning and promotes the notion that taking challenging courses is a good thing."

The ETS and the College Board were not about to quote Owen in their AP promotional material, but his comment did not displease them. The College Board was spending $500,000 a year to encourage the spread of the Advanced Placement program into more schools and its acceptance by more colleges. After surviving the stinging Garfield publicity and the threat of a lawsuit, several people at the College Board and the ETS began to realize that the East LA school's story might help this effort.

They invited Gradillas to speak at a few conferences. When he arrived late to a College Board workshop in San Francisco because he had had to intercede for a woman struggling with a man outside his hotel, the staff from New York began to spread the word they were dealing with a wonderful, unrestrained original. Do not mess with Gradillas, they said, just use him whenever possible. The College Board also spread the word of AP successes at a few other inner city schools, in Texas and Florida.

Advanced Placement, or something like it, had the potential to replace the SAT as the principal standardized test for college-bound high school students. Schools like Harvard had begun to discuss dropping their SAT requirement and using AP or achievement test scores instead. A few educators were becoming increasingly enthused about what AP could do to the whole thrust of American high school education. Fred Nelson, a former College Board official working for the ARCO Foundation, called it "the only thing I know in American education at any level where assessment of how well the student has learned is independent of the teacher giving the instruction. It makes the teacher the ally of the student against this outside force."

Rather than slowly building up a program until it was ready for AP, some principals found it better to create the AP course first and let that produce pressure below. A calculus course for seniors forced teachers to arrange suitable doses of trigonometry and analytic geometry in the eleventh grade and advanced algebra in the tenth. That in turn forced ninth and eighth grades to provide full courses in geometry and beginning algebra.

College Board studies reported that students learn subjects like calculus more readily in a small high school classroom with a teacher hovering over them than in a huge college lecture hall with a distant professor at the podium. If AP high school students took the same calculus test given to college freshmen, they appeared to score at least as well, and often better.

High school principals discovered the program helped them keep their best teachers. Other teachers vied for the privilege of teaching AP. Woessner found himself digging much deeper into the analysis of the Compromise of 1850 and the election of 1876 to prepare his students for the test's daunting essay questions. He assigned regular "cold shots," a favorite East LA expression for an unexpected, underhanded blow. Each student would have to sit down at the beginning of a designated period, examine a list of five essay questions never seen before, and write for forty minutes on one of them, just like in the AP examination.

One day Bennett realized he no longer hesitated to say "Garfield" when asked where he taught. Fewer people praised him as a martyr to his social conscience for teaching in a school "like that." The people who ran the gifted program Downtown responded warmly to his every request. In return, when the district entertained educators from places like Israel, the Philippines, Fresno, Phoenix, or San Diego, they sent them to Garfield and let Bennett give his short lecture on the perils of underestimating the disadvantaged.

Gradillas approved an experiment in AP European history, almost unheard of in an inner city school. He told Bennett the class could begin with just five students, if that was all that could be found. The teacher would have time to build confidence. "It's like a TV program," Ed Martin explained to visitors. "The first year of 'Hill Street Blues' may not be too successful, but if you keep trying, it picks up."

The AP program had its difficult moments, and not all were Escalante's fault. Woessner was at one point so discouraged by a hint he might lose his preparation period that he told Gradillas he was dropping out of AP. The principal felt blindsided on an already bad day and angrily accepted the teacher's resignation on the spot. It took Bennett two hours of negotiation to bring everything back to order.

Slowly, gingerly, Bennett and a few other ambitious teachers added AP biology, physics, French, government, and computer science to the list. Bennett had always been content with small gains, but up in the 200 Building, Escalante still wanted much more.

Escalante telephoned a father whose son, an algebra student, had missed two homework assignments and penned a decorative bit of graffiti in his notebook. "You have to help me solve this problem, sir," Escalante said in Spanish, assuming the grave persona his students called "The Priest."

"Look," the father said, "this is the way I solve the problem. I work nights and my wife works days."

"And who controls the kids?" Escalante asked.

"My kids have food and everything they need. I don't want anything from the welfare. I take care of everything, and the boy knows that. Maybe he's just not right for your class, Mr. Escalante. He'll probably work in the body shop when he graduates. That's a good job. Or he can get work as a janitor."

Escalante felt the back of his neck get warm, but he kept his temper. "But, sir, I want him to be the *boss* of the janitors. He could do it."

The man laughed. "That's very nice of you, Mr. Escalante. But like I say, we're doing fine. I'll tell him to behave."

There was not much else Escalante could do. If they actually kept the boy out of school with chores and family employment, he could call upon his collection of bogeymen—the child welfare people, the police, *La Migra*. The most ignorant, those recently arrived from Mexico, sometimes believed he had the power and inclination to summon these demons. In fact, he could not even count on the support of the school system.

One afternoon he saw one of his target students, a bright boy teetering on the edge of failure, enter 233 without depositing the required homework in the basket. He would later recount this particular conversation many times, rendering the student's part in a surly, low-octave growl.

"Where your homework?"

"I didn't do it."

"Why you didn't do it?"

"I had a bad dream."

This was a new one. Escalante recoiled, uncertain how to proceed against the forces of darkness. The excuse only demonstrated, to his mind, how intelligent the youth was. He reached for a dismissal slip.

"Okay, all right. This ticket is one way, one way. You got to talk to your counselor, or you bring in the homework. You want to drop the class, you bring in your mom, your dad. They sign the paper and you fly. Then you have to take three buses to get to the other school. Have to wake up about six o'clock. Less time for bad dreams. So you want the ticket? Or are you gonna bring the homework?"

The student studied the floor for a moment. "I'm gonna bring the homework."

Within hours the school psychologist was climbing the stairs to 233. "Mr. Escalante," he said. "This boy has a real problem, and he is not always going to be able to do the assignment right away. I want you to keep that in mind. You just don't understand this kid."

Escalante had heard enough. He had seen too many teenagers equipped with excuses borrowed from adults. He assumed his most formal manner. "I am sorry, sir. I don't believe in what you're saying or what you're doing. Please. If you want to take the kid, welcome. But I don't accept a kid who behaves like that in my class. Even if I believe a hundred and ten percent in what you're saying, I believe a hundred and twenty percent in what I'm doing."

The psychologist was a specialist in self-control and bristled only slightly. "I'm not going to accept this," he said. "I'm going to talk to the principal."

In this matter, Escalante thought he knew his "Big Brother," his nickname for Gradillas. They had discussed such excuses before. "If you send this kind of crap over here," Escalante had said, "excuse me for saying, but I'm going to have to look for a transfer."

Gradillas listened to the psychologist's story and sighed. "Do what you can," he said, "but stay away from Escalante. He has his own school of psychology."

As far as Gradillas was concerned, Escalante would never be under control, but the teacher had passed all the important tests. He was loyal to the school. He stayed in touch with the principal. He loved the kids. He taught with a passion that filled Gradillas with wonder. By 1983 the principal was asking Escalante for a list of his needs. "Whatever you need, I'll get. You have *carta blanca*."

Escalante said he wanted more books, a teaching assistant, and a new room.

"What room, Jaime?"

"Sir, I have done my homework. You have this big room over here, MH [for music hall] one. It is really in bad shape. It has no chalkboards. All the walls are full of graffiti. There are some old instruments there, violins in completely bad shape. They've been using it as a music room some but also a storage room."

Gradillas shook his head. "Well, then, somebody is using it already."

"*No sir!* I told you, I do my homework. Period one, guitar"—he strummed his fingers across his abdomen and trilled his imitation of an Aymara balladeer—"fourteen students. Period two, twenty-one students. Choral. They don't even sing. They cannot sing. Why don't you put them in the PE building and put me in there? In two periods already, that room is vacant. They don't use that room."

Gradillas investigated. He saw the fourteen students strumming idly in first period. He listened to twenty-one young voices—they sounded fine to him—attempting a Spanish folk song in period two. The room was empty for two periods, and it was, indeed, a mess.

He told Escalante to go ahead. *Carta blanca*. He would consolidate some music classes and move the guitarists and singers elsewhere.

Escalante rubbed his hands with glee and called Paul Possemato, the man who had helped sweep away the ill-fated Avilez regime. After the 1982 triumph, Possemato had called to congratulate Escalante and offer his help. Escalante now gave him a list: paint, new desks, new chalkboards. "You may have problems finding people to do the work, Jaime," Possemato said. "The maintenance crews are all backed up."

"Don't worry about it, sir," Escalante said. The less professional interference, he thought, the better.

Like a balding Tom Sawyer, Escalante lured in students one weekend to paint the MH-1 walls a subdued off-white and give the narrow adjoining storage room a set of baby blue cabinets and enough space to put his desk and files. The classroom was very large and designed like a college lecture hall. It had broad steps climbing up toward the back, with enough space to put a line of desks on each level. Escalante surveyed his home collection of discarded stereo equipment and brought in enough components to pipe his favorite Bolivian dances—and some occasional heavy metal—into the classroom for motivational purposes.

He had been scanning the school's daily bulletin for reports of teacher transfers. Pregnant English teachers, disgruntled shop instructors, ambitious administrators—anyone announcing his or her departure from Garfield found Escalante at the door, inquiring politely if they had any equipment they did not plan to take with them. He acquired file cabinets, office supplies, and a few additional chairs. School board member Larry González, a man who sensed Escalante's potential, agreed to appropriate $25,000 to air-condition the large room. That would attract marginal students wondering where to spend a hot afternoon.

The transformation of MH-1 so impressed Gradillas that he quickly acceded to Escalante's next demand—hand over its nearby companion room, MH-2, to Jiménez.

Carta blanca developed a hitch. Not yet understanding Escalante's method of operation, Gradillas warned him it might be a few months before he could arrange to have the broken instruments, old uniforms, and other debris removed from MH-2 so it could be used.

"Don't worry about it," Escalante said.

Within a week he had assembled Jiménez and several students, plus George Madrid and Paul Powers from East Los Angeles College. They worked until midnight clearing MH-2. They left a huge pile of debris in the asphalt courtyard between MH-1 and MH-2.

Gradillas saw the heap and exploded. "Jaime, you know what you did?" His face was flushed. "This is against the law. If a kid steps on this he's going to break his neck."

"Okay, sir," Escalante said. "Don't worry about it."

He recalled his team and told Jiménez to bring his new pickup truck. Beginning after dinnertime to avoid unwelcome supervision, they loaded the truck several times until they had eliminated the pile. Gone were all the old uniforms, sheet music, and other debris bearing the unacceptable taint of the marching band.

Jiménez asked if they needed permission to remove them. "Nah, let's go," said Escalante. With that fondness for playing by the rules,

205

he thought, Jiménez could never have led the takeover of the Hugo Davila School, as Cordero and he and the boys of El Piquete did in 1951.

Jiménez showed no further hesitation as he trucked the forsaken garments and equipment over to the janitors' building and tossed them into the dumpsters.

It took the band director three days to discover his old uniforms were missing. "I don't know anything about it," Escalante said. "I didn't see anything. Maybe you better talk to Jiménez."

Jiménez had his own answer: "You better talk to Escalante. Escalante knows everything."

Gradillas soon appeared. "Okay, Jaime," he said. "Where did you hide those uniforms?"

"Oh, they're gone with the wind. We threw everything away. You told me I could do it. *Carta blanca.*"

Gradillas took a breath. "But how could you do that? Throw them out like that?"

"I don't know. They stink. They look terrible, big rat holes in them. Now look. It's nice. All we have to do is paint."

Soon after the two men appeared at a community luncheon, one of several called to celebrate the victory over the ETS. "They'll probably ask us to say a few words, Jaime," Gradillas said.

"I know, and I want to assure you I'm going to give you plenty of credit. I'm going to tell them you were the one who gave me the *carta blanca.*"

"Uh, Jaime, why don't we keep that our little secret?"

George Madrid was frustrated, and a bit frightened. He had been operating on the fringes of a real job at East Los Angeles College for some time. He wanted to help Latino kids become doctors and engineers and lawyers. They deserved the financial security and social clout he did not have.

But sometimes he pushed too hard. He had sued the county in a job dispute once and gotten enough money to finance his education. But a reputation as a troublemaker lingered. Few people at ELAC wanted to give him a permanent slot. The director of the Upward Bound program, his current assignment, did not like him. He needed something different, something better.

He thought he saw what he wanted, but it would require some administrative sleight of hand. Since 1980 the college had been receiving more than $100,000 a year from the U.S. Department of Health and Human Services under its Health Careers Opportunity Program (HCOP, pronounced "H-cop"). The government wanted to encourage minority youths to become doctors and dentists. It gave most of the money to medical schools for scholarships. ELAC had captured some of it by arguing that attracting Latinos to medical careers required getting their attention in college. What better place to start but the most accessible college in the largest concentration of North American Hispanics anywhere outside Mexico City?

Madrid had one goal—to lure Jaime Escalante to ELAC. The 1982 affair had made the Garfield teacher's name a household word in East Los Angeles. He knew how to motivate Latino students better than anyone Madrid had ever seen. Whatever program could be arranged for him would certainly turn to gold. All Madrid had to do was create the program and persuade Escalante to take it over.

If only Escalante was not such a hard ass. If the smallest thing went wrong, he threatened to quit. That was how he motivated me, Madrid thought. Madrid was husky and intense, a Roosevelt High graduate who had served with the marines in Vietnam. He thought of Escalante as a big rock cod who had just bitten into his hook. The fish was struggling wildly, he was close to breaking the line, but if Madrid could keep him hooked, what a prize!

Madrid and his closest comrades in the ELAC bureaucratic wars, Dean of Instruction Kenneth L. Hunt and campus HCOP Director Paul Powers, had agreed to funnel some of the federal money into a summertime and Saturday morning program for Escalante's Garfield students.

Escalante and Jiménez could radically accelerate the pace and substantially increase the size of their program by teaching the two semester-long calculus prerequisites, trigonometry and mathematical analysis (analytic geometry), in an intensive two-month summer course. Saturday morning classes during the regular year would help them prepare their weaker students and inject mathematics into hours the teenagers usually reserved for sleep, basketball, or television cartoons.

Madrid, Hunt, and Powers had given themselves only a few weeks to put together the first summer program in June 1983. Time and Escalante bore down on them. Powers, already slim, was losing weight. Hunt's bosses were making testy remarks about the amount of time he devoted to this little project. Madrid was not sleeping much. He had spotted blood in his urine. Each day he awoke early, showered, and drove quickly to school, mentally noting the things he had to do.

Escalante complained that the books had not arrived. "School starts next week," he said. "If the books aren't here, I'm not going to be in the program. I'm going back to Oxy [Occidental College]." He called Madrid's office. "George is not there? It's eight o'clock."

Escalante had no telephone in MH-1. When Madrid received such a message he got in his van and drove, very fast, the six blocks to Garfield. If he had to kiss Escalante's ass to find out what was bugging him, so be it. He did not want to miss this shot.

It is an ill financial crisis that does no one any good. Proposition 13 had killed the ELAC regular summer school, so Upward Bound, and now Escalante's program, had the campus to themselves. The supervisor of the nursing department building they wanted to use at first resisted. "High school kids here? Are you crazy? We'll have graffiti all over the place," she said. But the department chair had read about Escalante and welcomed them.

Madrid had learned many bitter lessons of campus politics. Now came more. Short of money for student lunches, Hunt had arranged to pick up surplus food from a federal storage facility and give it to the ELAC cafeteria in exchange for sandwiches and soft drinks. One ELAC administrator, discovering this, was about to charge them with misappropriation of federal dollars when Hunt found someone high enough to collar him.

In 1980 the ARCO Foundation, stuffed with petrodollars in an era of thirty-five-dollars-a-barrel oil, held a retreat on Balboa Island near Newport Beach, California. Ernest Boyer, former U.S. commissioner of education, and A. Bartlett Giamatti, president of Yale University, told the group of executives they felt the American high school had become the critical weak link in American education. Almost overnight, the foundation switched its emphasis from higher to secondary education, eventually adding to the Carnegie Foundation support for Boyer's influential 1983 report, "High School: A Report on Secondary Education in America."

The turnabout allowed Fred Nelson to offer ARCO Foundation aid to Escalante. East Los Angeles College asked for $7,000; ARCO gave $10,000. Madrid's elation cooled briefly when he learned the

ELAC mathematics department chair, seeing the announcement in the press, was demanding the money for her staff and insisting a high school program had no business on campus. Hunt cut her off, and Madrid went back to his chosen assignment as Escalante's Sancho Panza.

In mid-June of 1983 Escalante and Jiménez began their first classes at ELAC. Hunt, Powers, and Madrid, exhausted, thought they were ready for the expected fifty students. More than one hundred appeared. Escalante dismissed this sudden expansion as youthful enthusiasm he could do nothing about. Madrid chose to assume the same attitude; the alternative was madness. Powers could barely speak. "One hundred? One hundred students they've got? Why, . . . uh, . . . well, that's . . . *wonderful*."

Working through county and private agencies, Madrid found afternoon jobs for eighty students with below-poverty-level family incomes; Escalante had insisted on some kind of financial incentive to draw kids with little money to intense summer mornings of mathematics. To fold the cloak of HCOP respectability over the program, Madrid arranged Friday field trips to medical facilities and local universities. He served as counselor, taking each student into his World War II barracks office near the classrooms. He advised them on the proper choice of high school courses and on financial aid plans that would get them into the colleges they wanted.

From the beginning there was never enough money. Madrid's job and salary always teetered on the edge of extinction. By the end of the summer Washington had told Hunt it did not like what he was doing with its dollars and would soon cut him off. The program was "inappropriate" for HCOP, one Health and Human Services letter said. It had "limited upward linkages to . . . a health professions curriculum."

In the initial burst of publicity over his 1982 triumph, Escalante had received feelers from the White House. Here was a teacher who exemplified the Reagan administration's call for new, rigorous educational standards, and he was Latino to boot. Escalante declined invitations to come to Washington, and when the Department of Education and the White House arranged a California unveiling of the new federal report on education, "A Nation at Risk," Escalante turned them down again.

"Change his mind," said Hunt.

"How?" asked Madrid.

"The kids," said Hunt cryptically.

"Gotcha," said Madrid.

He briefed a few of the more persuasive members of the class of '84 on the opportunity their teacher was wasting. They descended on MH-1: "Kimo, he's the *president*. Your Big Brother. You gotta go, Kimo. Tell him what he's doing wrong."

In the gymnasium of Pioneer High School in Whittier, Ronald Reagan and Jaime Escalante exchanged pleasantries. Escalante thanked the president for signing his teaching credential in the last year of his California governorship, 1974. Reagan grinned. Hunt, sitting in the bleachers with the Los Angeles Community College's chancellor, pondered the next step in using this fortunate encounter to get his HCOP money back.

In America as in Bolivia, Escalante and Hunt knew, it was always good to have friends in the government. As time ran short for summer 1984 funding, Hunt reminded White House Special Assistant and former California Congressman John Rousselot of the president's warm regard for Escalante. Escalante himself contributed a letter reaffirming his and the president's mutual goals—"personal and national self-sufficiency and excellence through education and work." The HHS official who had cut them off wrote back to say they had been reconsidered, and renewed for a year. When the department threatened to cut them off the following summer, Hunt called the White House again and eventually won a two-year renewal.

But all the warm headlines, all the glowing presidential adjectives, all the talk about Escalante's Pied Piper reputation only kept the program just above the cutoff mark. HCOP officials complained that the ELAC proposals were not properly "focused" and the college was not working to strengthen them. Eventually the federal funding ended altogether, just as Escalante and Jiménez had soared to an unprecedented level of success. Washington's money went not necessarily to programs that worked but to programs that fit into the legislative and regulatory definitions.

Madrid and Escalante went looking elsewhere. A great teacher, Madrid knew, was a whirling vortex who could suck in money from all sorts of odd places, if word of his miracles was brought to the right quarters.

John Saxon, a maverick mathematics textbook author from Oklahoma, had begun a friendly correspondence with Escalante. Saxon knew Jack Dirmann, an executive with the small, Los Angeles–based Foundation for Advancements in Science and Education. The foundation had been more involved in science than in education. It promoted a program of drug and poison detoxification developed by L. Ron Hubbard, founder of the controversial Scientology movement, of which Dirmann was a member. Despite its roots, the foundation had managed to generate interest and support from mainstream institutions.

Dirmann liked Escalante's energy and his insistence on a quantifiable measure of his work, the AP examination. He arranged small grants to pay for tutors' wages, extra textbooks, and stationery supplies, then bought Escalante a copier and a computer and helped when minor emergencies, like an unpaid ELAC food bill, intervened. Such assistance came to about $13,000 a year, not counting Dirmann's own time, which was donated. The foundation became Escalante's key link to the world outside Garfield, and Dirmann one of his closest friends and supporters.

Dirmann set up a small board of advisers to look for more donors and suggest ways to publicize Escalante's work. Madrid discovered the Community Service Organization on Olvera Street could find $3,000 or $4,000 every year for the project. Lorraine May, a local businesswoman who had read about Escalante, began to chip in $1,000 a year. The ARCO Foundation contribution jumped briefly to a high of $40,000, before the oil market collapsed and forced a more modest $25,000 annual commitment.

Hunt and Madrid realized that finding money required as much creativity and ingenuity as solving a free-response question in conic sections. Escalante told his students, "When you have a problem, first look for the key word."

Hunt found it. The community college district itself had money for the program if Hunt could somehow define it as a part of the college curriculum. Why not include it as adult education? He could call it a noncredit course, enroll all 200 Escalante students, then all he would need was a category, a place to file it, because district rules required all adult courses to meet certain criteria.

He scanned the list of possibilities. He did not see one that fit.

He had to be imaginative. Could he call it remedial? The rules allowed remedial courses for students from disadvantaged backgrounds. What could be more disadvantaged than East Los Angeles? Garfield's standardized test scores still looked bad next to those of

Palos Verdes or Beverly Hills High, and more than 80 percent of the students qualified for the federal lunch program.

He made up a name for his new remedial course: Transition Mathematics. With a small intake of breath, he sent it in.

No problem, the district official said. Just send us a short outline.

A course that prepared its students for one of the most difficult examinations in American secondary education became a "remedial" course, and everyone was happy.

14

Ralph Heiland had gray hair, a potbelly, and more than thirty years' experience teaching physics and other subjects at Garfield High. He loved Jaime Escalante, and because he was an honest man, he knew he also resented him.

Heiland had worked across the hall from Room 233 long enough to learn how Escalante performed his magic. Escalante worked his kids hard. He threatened them. He could, when he wished, speak to them in the language in which their parents spoke to them and catch every veiled reference and insulting pun in either Spanish or English.

He ate with them. He agonized with them over divorce and neglect and violence or rejoiced with them at marriages and births in their families. He would not leave them until it was dark, and Fabiola or his night school class absolutely demanded his time. He discouraged sports, cheerleading, field trips, and anything that took time from his class.

And that meant, inadvertently but inevitably, that he discouraged spending time with Ralph Heiland and his beloved physics. There was no help for it. Heiland realized he did not have Escalante's gifts. Perhaps no one did. Other teachers realized the same thing, but few were willing, as Heiland was, to confront their feelings. That meant trouble.

There was, for instance, the Medfly Lady, whom Escalante felt threatened the future of his mathematics department as much as that insect pest menaced the California fruit crop. She was an Italian major with a minor in mathematics, so she had been given three Algebra 1 classes. Escalante distrusted teachers who did not have a major in mathematics. When he visited her class, he realized the lesson was arithmetic—remedial high school math, not algebra.

"That's not fair. You can't *do* that," he told her after class. "These kids should be taking algebra. They already *took* high school math."

The Medfly Lady was one of the few teachers who did not melt immediately in the heat of the Escalante temper. She was proud of her Latino heritage; as an extra activity, she taught *folklórico* dance at the school. She had chosen Garfield because she wanted to help the young people who shared her heritage. She felt she knew as well as anyone what was best for them.

"You're not going to tell me what I'm going to teach," she said. Either follow the program, he told her, or go see Gradillas. "I'm teaching high school math to these kids because they are not prepared for algebra," she said. "They are not capable of doing algebra."

Nonsense, Escalante said. They have all had high school mathematics already.

Gradillas eventually questioned one of her students. "Have you taken high school math before?"

"Yessir, five times."

"*Five* times?"

"Right, sir, this is my fifth year."

Escalante beamed. "You see that? That's why these kids not doing. I assume in five years they at least know the times tables."

He became even more indignant when barred from dealing with what he thought were shirkers in his own classes. When he had refused, as usual, to sign a slip permitting one student to transfer out of Algebra 2, the student's surprised counselor, Martha Gurrola, sent back a message: If he would not sign, she would.

Escalante, his face a dark cloud, appeared within minutes at Gurrola's little cubical office on the main building's second floor.

"Excuse me, you said *you* were going to sign this?"

Gurrola stood and walked to the door. Both the student and her mother, a teacher's aide at Garfield, had insisted on another teacher. Gurrola resolved to stand her ground. "Mr. Escalante, you don't have the right to keep the students in your class. You know that. It's against the law. The student has the right not to take your class."

The few students sitting in the outer office struggled to retain proper expressions of boredom while they tuned their ears to this conversation. Escalante's response was not difficult to hear.

"It's my policy not to sign any of these things. Number one, we have to teach these kids some kind of responsibility, and *plus* we have to teach the counselors some kind of counseling. I am afraid you are not doing your homework."

Gurrola's eyes flashed. "*You're* not going to tell me that."

"I can tell you this, I'm not going to sign this, and you gonna have to talk to the principal."

Gradillas, though fond of Escalante's tactics, did what the rules required. He let the student transfer.

The Medfly Lady eventually became an administrator downtown, and Gurrola moved on to another school, neither apparently suffering any damage from their brush with the buzz saw in MH-1. Other teachers lost some skin. Escalante's complaints about one mathematics teacher's ponytail were thought to have accelerated his transfer to another school. Escalante persuaded Gradillas to dismiss a shop teacher who had been ignoring his students while making a fireplace set for his home. Another teacher was cautioned about skipping class for long weekend vacations after Escalante complained.

Once other faculty learned of the mathematics department chair's unforgiving attitude, a backlash began. A Garfield athletic coach sent him a taunting note: "There are other things that are important to kids besides calculus." Someone entered his name without his permission in the district's master teacher competition and told him, "This will give you a chance to move to another school." He overheard teachers discussing him in the faculty cafeteria; he appeared there so rarely, his face was not known. "Yeah, well, I hear one reason he spends so much time in class is he's got a problem at home," said one. "Can't get along with his wife, so he stays over here."

His notoriety after the 1982 triumph had brought many accolades, but also the kind of hate mail and threatening telephone calls that trouble many celebrities. Some writers asked why he was wasting his time on Mexicans. Some suggested his methods would get him into trouble. "We'll be looking for you," one caller said.

Someone even left huge scratches and dents on his beloved Volkswagen. Escalante's personal body shop crew appeared almost before the police report was filed.

"*Kimo!* We saw what happened. We are very sorry," said the husky young man, examining the scratches and giving his pinstripes a fond look. "We're gonna fix it for you. Good as new."

215

"No, no, no, don't fix it. That's all right. I'm going to sell that car. Don't worry about it. I not going to keep that car. No, no."

"Please, sir, we saw you have a long dent over here. We gonna fix it *right here*. No waiting."

Within moments, mallets, hammers, and paint appeared. The dents vanished. Escalante felt relieved that this time he had a car to drive home in. He gave the group's leader a ten-dollar bill.

The young man seemed shocked. "No, no, no, it's free for you. But you must have a beer. Come on, we got some over in the car."

He accepted the offer. Fabiola did not have to know.

Possemato once asked Escalante if he was interested in an administrative job. Escalante thought most administrators were stupid, like the assistant principal who demanded that all his students get a special pass to spend lunchtime in MH-1. But he respected Possemato, so he considered it. He would be dealing not with students but with scores of veteran teachers and administrators who did not do things his way. The old-timers, he called them—they did not want to change the system. One of his geometry teachers had nearly fainted at a hint of changing the textbook to a series that acknowledged the existence of computers.

Escalante saw only one way to make a difference. He had to stay in the classroom and look for young teachers who might accept his ideas and personalize them as Jiménez had done. He scoured the junior high faculty rooms. He pulled more students into Algebra 2, the first step to calculus. They in turn spread the message.

He rejected the mentor teacher program. It was the California version of what educators and politicians called the master teacher concept, an old idea revived during the surge of interest in school reform in the early 1980s. As Escalante saw it, the chosen instructor, in return for a salary bonus of $4,000 a year, spent a great deal of time developing curricular materials that would only gather dust in Downtown's filing cabinets. He had worked with enough weak teachers to know they would reject his advice. The old-timers would not listen to him either, Escalante thought. What a waste of time to deal with them instead of students.

He also dismissed the gifted student program, even when it became

216

the responsibility of men he respected, such as John Bennett and Ed Martin. For each student judged gifted on the basis of intelligence tests given in the second or third grade, the district received $65 from the state. The extra money was to be spent providing enriched instruction to those students proven able to appreciate it.

For Latino children just growing accustomed to English, an intelligence test at age seven had many drawbacks. The system made it difficult to test new students later on, and forbade retesting children already on the gifted list. "If we retest them and find that they are not achieving at that level anymore," said Bennett with a slight smile, "we don't get money for them. Besides, it costs seventy dollars just to test somebody."

Intelligence tests were written and administered by psychologists, anathema to Escalante. He hated the idea of putting students on tracks—this one to college, that one to McDonald's. He wanted to leave his door open to anyone with *ganas*. He proudly displayed his calculus roster, where gifted students were always a minority.

This did not surprise Bennett or Martin. They estimated that by the high school level, half of the students rated gifted in elementary school were no longer performing at that level. By the time AP calculus classes grew large enough to provide a roughly accurate sample, gifted students proved themselves the least successful of any identifiable group. They made up only about 20 percent of the calculus team, and only about half of them passed the AP examination with a 3 or better.

Escalante practiced psychology, of course, but like many gifted amateurs, he scorned those who had learned it from books. Bennett watched Escalante's students perform and thought he saw little flashes of cult worship. Escalante made calculus into a religion. Students followed his idiosyncratic ways because he amused them and made them feel part of a brave corps on a secret, impossible mission.

Tom Woessner used a variation of that approach. He compared AP American history to the annual October football classic, Garfield versus Roosevelt, the championship of East LA. "That's peanuts," Woessner told his class. "The Garfield-Roosevelt game is just in East LA. You're going to be competing against the best in the country."

Escalante outfitted his calculus team with special jackets or sweatshirts and conducted a preclass, pretest, preanything warm-up. It was a chant, often accompanied by rock music from the stereo, which made up in volume what it lacked in precision. Students who did not like cults or Escalante's erratic, captivating passions eventually opted for Jiménez's class and his logical and orderly, if somewhat drier, approach to mathematics.

Martin thought special teachers succeeded because they extended themselves. Escalante received students at all hours. He gave them his home telephone number and saw them inside or outside the classroom, at 7:00 A.M. or 7:00 P.M. Although Woessner had little Spanish or previous contact with Latin culture, he also developed a rapport with the Garfield community during the years he conducted an annual spring vacation student tour of the California gold country.

Garfield teachers had to inspire trust because their students had so little faith in themselves. There had been a point to the "East LA Blowouts"—the walkouts and demonstrations at five high schools in 1968 to protest a legacy of neglect. Teachers like Sal Castro, a leader in that protest, understood that decades of underestimating Latino abilities had left a mark.

In the spring of 1983 Woessner had his usual doubts about some of his AP students. Some could not write. Some could not organize. Some choked at the sight of a long list of dates. But there was one bright spot, Chris Martínez. He was brilliant, the only student Woessner had ever had who looked at his first sample document-based question (a standard part of the AP examination) and took it apart as if he had already done fifteen of them.

Three weeks before the AP examination, Martínez spoke privately to the teacher. "I've been thinking, Mr. Woessner. I shouldn't take the test. I'm not doing well enough."

Woessner counted a few beats, trying to control his shock and exasperation. "Chris, you're a better student now than I ever was in my life. Okay? If you don't take the test . . . Well, it's ridiculous. Forget about the score. You have *earned* the right to take the test. Take it as a learning experience. Take it as a challenge. Take it as what you will. It's a reward in itself, whether you win or lose. It's an honor, okay?"

He ran out of words. He felt blown away. Jesus, he thought, what had he done to these kids?

For one thing, he had reassured Martínez. The youth scored a 5 in AP history, the first for any Woessner student. He also had a 5 in Calculus AB and a 4 in Spanish. As a senior, he had a 5 in European history, a 4 in Calculus BC, and a 3 in English composition. It was a school record—six AP grades, all suitable for college credit. He went to Stanford a bit more certain than before that he might be doing well enough.

Success breeds jealousy. Familiarity brings contempt. Prophets are without honor in their own lands. By 1984, many members of the Garfield faculty had grown sick of hearing about Jaime Escalante and his calculus teams.

The AP results were so good that year that Gradillas began to wonder about national ranking. A friend at the College Board gave him some data which he copied and passed around the school. The number of Garfield students taking AP examinations had increased from 71 in 1983 to 122. The number of calculus examinations had doubled, from 34 to 68 as Jiménez taught a calculus class for the first time. All but five of the calculus scores were 3 or above, for a pass rate of 93 percent compared with the 76 percent national average. In 1983 Garfield ranked 544th in the country in the number of students attempting an AP test. In 1984 it climbed to 150th place. Chris Martínez's six examinations placed him in the top 0.3 percent of the country.

Here and there at Garfield influential teachers and counselors began to wonder if all this was missing the point.

Brian Wallace, a rotund, bearded, Spanish-speaking English and social studies teacher, had chosen to teach because he cared about kids and thought he could have some impact on the system. His father, a barber, and his mother, a seamstress, were English and had emigrated when he was ten. Those early years in the English school system had left him with a lingering affection for drill and memorization, and a stubborn disdain for the American lack of scholastic rigor.

From the beginning of his career he showed a profound interest in what was going on outside the classroom, making him a prickly thorn in the side of nearly every principal he ever worked for. His family had believed a class system ruled the world, and they had to do what they could to weaken it. The black and Latino children Wallace encountered at school seemed to be living proof that class and poverty, influenced by racial discrimination, had stamped a black mark at birth that no one was bothering to erase.

He lost his first job at Manual Arts High because he supported a demonstration in the black community against poor facilities there.

He was dismissed from the Gompers Junior High faculty for supporting a boycott of the cafeteria. The principal at Marshall High, his alma mater, suspended him for wearing a beard. He angered the Hamilton High principal by refusing to tell him which students had met to plan a sit-in.

He married, traveled around the world for a year, then returned to teach Spanish in southcentral Los Angeles at Locke High, one of the most depressing places he had ever been. He saw one teacher beaten up. Another was Maced. When he transferred to Garfield in 1973, it seemed, despite its gangs and indiscipline, a country Sunday school by comparison. The students seemed passive and docile. So did the faculty, who immediately elected him the Garfield representative of United Teachers–Los Angeles. Except for a short break in the early 1980s, Wallace would remain the union man at Garfield, sparring with every principal he encountered.

Escalante intrigued Wallace. He liked the mathematics teacher's emphasis on drill and his commitment to high standards. He applauded the outcome of the 1982 ETS controversy. But when Escalante became a celebrity, courted by film producers, conference program chairmen, and politicians, Wallace became concerned. He had promised to "fight for the rank and file teacher and the rank and file student." He wanted to get something for the teachers no one ever invited to lead a workshop, the people who taught tenth-grade algebra or the nonhonors history classes. Escalante no longer needed any help, and perhaps, Wallace thought, the calculus program's success had obscured an important reality of inner city education.

What Escalante and Jiménez and the other AP teachers had done was fine, but how many kids were they helping—400, 500? They never touched the majority of the school's 3,500 students. The 15 percent or so pulled into upper-level courses was three or four times the percentage found in other inner city schools, but the majority could not enjoy higher standards, Wallace argued, until the city established full-scale ethnic integration of every classroom.

He began to tell people, in a gentle reminder of his own bulk, "It's like weight loss. Almost anything works for a while because you get involved in it. But it is the longevity of it that really counts."

Jo Ann Shiroishi came to the problem of Escalante from a different direction. While Wallace was cheerfully casual in dress, she was trim and immaculately groomed. While he charged up the stairs to the principal's office, she loathed confrontation and resorted to it only at moments, like the case of the racist bulletin item in 1974, when she felt she had no choice.

Shiroishi, unlike Wallace, had grown up in East Los Angeles, part of a small community of Asian Americans who had always been in the area's immigrant mix. Her father sold furniture and appliances. Her mother owned a lunch stand. She had gone to Roosevelt and remembered the days when most East Los Angeles children were steered into vocational courses without much consideration of their actual talents.

She could not remember when she had not wanted to be a teacher. Her parents had given her a small blackboard when she was eight. "Ding Dong School," with Miss Frances, was one of the only television shows she had been permitted to watch. She took her degree at Cal State, LA, and started work almost immediately at Garfield. As the calculus program expanded, she found herself the counselor responsible for all 180 computer science students at the school. That brought her into bruising contact with Escalante.

Since 1967 Garfield had had a computer program, for years one of its very few special academic attractions. The program had begun under a husky navy veteran and former Burroughs programmer named Jack Knight, who arrived to teach mathematics in 1965.

Knight first drove student keypunch cards over to a Control Data facility near the airport, where friends would let him run and print the programs. In the early 1970s he organized a business-oriented computer program that drew students from several other schools. That died off in the budget crises of the late 1970s, but in 1982, as part of a court-ordered desegregation plan, Garfield was designated a magnet school for computer education. Students from all over the city were invited to apply for 180 places in Knight's program.

Eventually the magnet program gave Escalante's efforts a helpful boost—27 percent of the students who took the 1987 AP calculus examination would be magnets. But from the start he reacted sharply when the computer program interfered with his plans.

Escalante had hoped to coax Michael Litvak, the man who had introduced him to mathematics games his first day at Garfield, into the calculus program in 1982. When Litvak decided to join the magnet program instead, Escalante threw a magnitude 8 tantrum. He told Litvak he was a "back stabber," and worse. Escalante later said this was a calculated burst of temper, a ploy to try to shake Litvak into reconsidering, but it did not make relations between the calculus and computer camps any easier.

Shiroishi became the designated magnet counselor, and eight faculty members joined the school-within-a-school. The magnet students were selected for racial balance, not academic achievement. About two-thirds were Latino, while Garfield overall was more than 95 percent Hispanic. The program brought in more Asians, and even a trickle of blacks and Anglos. Each sought Shiroishi's advice on what courses to take.

Some of the magnet students, Shiroishi discovered, had applied for the program under intense parental pressure. The parents often did not precisely understand what computers could do, but they were convinced they meant success and financial security for their children. Some of the magnet students wanted to concentrate on something else, but their father or mother said no. The long bus trip to and from school added stress. Shiroishi listened to a succession of teenagers weeping and cursing life in a computer cage. She calculated that at least half of her magnet students were getting some emotional counseling, or needed it.

There were only so many hours in the day. Magnet students were required to take a full academic load; carefree electives like photography or cabinetmaking were forbidden them. Why, Shiroishi thought, could these people not have a little time to enjoy high school? They needed to go to a few football games, join a club, have some memories to cherish in something other than PASCAL computer language.

She began to talk of the perils of student burnout and to discourage students loaded with heavy courses from adding any more. Occasionally, if she found a particularly thin-skinned or ill-prepared student signing up for calculus, she would recommend Jiménez over Escalante, or suggest that calculus be put off for a while. The Escalante-Shiroishi relationship deteriorated markedly when one of those students turned out to be Greg Rusu.

Grigore Augustus Rusu was a quiet boy with square features and short brown hair. He had left his native Romania with his parents and two older sisters when he was eight. Years before, his veterinarian father had become an admirer of American liberties from listening to Voice of America reports of the Watergate investigation. When his attempts to protest fraud at his own workplace were ignored, he applied for an exit permit and—with no connections to anyone in

222

the United States—a U.S. visa. Romanian government officials harassed him. He declared a hunger strike and smuggled letters to the West that produced a report of his plight on Voice of America. The government relented, American sponsors were found, and in April 1978 the Rusus arrived in California.

Greg did not get on well at school. Other children made fun of his formal, Romanian schoolboy clothing. He cursed and fought and let his grades slip. Then, when he was transferred to a different school in the eighth grade, his bad reputation evaporated and he blossomed. He skipped the ninth grade, gained quick entry into the Garfield magnet program, and immersed himself in computers and mathematics.

The first time he came to see Escalante, the teacher did not bother to look up. Rusu had only geometry and no Algebra 2, but he wanted to take the summer course in trigonometry and math analysis so he could have calculus in his junior year. Escalante was hunched over his desk, scribbling figures on a piece of paper.

"Mr. Escalante, I'd like to take your class in the summer."

"Yup," the teacher said absently.

"I've only had geometry, but I have a pretty strong background in algebra and I think I'll be able to do well."

"Yup," Escalante said. He continued to scribble with his right hand while he handed Rusu an application with his left.

The summer went as Rusu expected. He received an A. He signed up for calculus. Knight, in his role as magnet program head, called the boy in. Shiroishi was there also. Both looked concerned.

Knight asked: Was Greg sure he knew what he was doing, taking calculus from Escalante? Escalante's kids failed other classes because they spent too much time on calculus, Knight said. They sacrificed their other studies. They stayed after school. They stayed during lunch. Shiroishi broke in: Escalante's students did not join clubs, they did not participate in school activities. She was concerned that Rusu, already younger than most of his classmates, would become a social outcast. If she were him, Shiroishi said, she would not do it.

"But I want to be a physics major," Rusu said. "I'll need calculus later on."

Knight smiled reassuringly. "Look," he said, "I'm a math major. I have a master's in math, but you don't need that much math now. All the math you'll need you'll learn in college. Don't try to grow up too fast. If you invest all that time, you're going to flunk all your other classes. Your grade-point average will go down. Nobody's gonna give you scholarships. Your parents are going to get mad."

Rusu began to worry. His parents' wrath was not lightly dismissed. Knight pointed out that he did not have Algebra 2. That would come back and haunt him, no matter how well he had done in the summer. Rusu remembered summer homework assignments so long that he stayed up until 1:00 A.M. and still could not finish. He was frightened, but also stubborn, like his father. He enrolled in calculus anyway.

Escalante heard the story, and added it to his list of alleged Shiroishi outrages. Rusu would score a 5 on AP calculus, and a 3 on AP American history, followed by a 5 on calculus BC and a 3 on English composition, while beginning a romance with Veronica Vásquez, class of '87, 3 on the AB, 3 on the BC.

Advanced Placement calculus and the computer magnet program proceeded down their dual tracks, eyeing each other suspiciously. When Escalante allowed Jiménez to take over a calculus class in 1983, large numbers of magnet students signed up for it. By 1987 Jiménez had twenty-two magnet students in his one class, compared with thirteen scattered over three Escalante classes. Escalante thought Shiroishi steered people to Jiménez out of contempt for him. Shiroishi said, "I can talk to Mr. Jiménez. I am responsible for the whole child, his academic program and his emotional well-being. Sometimes it's easier to approach Mr. Jiménez to talk about a student's problems at home."

Escalante noticed the magnet program's dismal AP record. There were fifty magnet program seniors every year, but few took the AP examination, and their success was erratic at best. Nine took the test in 1984, and two passed. In 1985, six took it and all passed. In 1986 seven took it and none passed.

Litvak, then a magnet program mathematics teacher, acknowledged the results were embarrassing. In the beginning, the program had too many classes in BASIC, one brand of computer language, when the AP tested PASCAL. And, he added, in preparing students for that test, "our computer teachers aren't that good."

When Roy Márquez, a 1982 calculus graduate approved by all factions, took over preparation for the 1987 computer science AP, the numbers improved dramatically. Thirteen students took the test, and nine passed—two 5s, one 4, six 3s, one 2, and three 1s.

There was a smattering of applause for Márquez. But many faculty at Garfield had come to distrust numbers, and Escalante. They did not like to be judged, and that was what the AP numbers and Escalante were doing. Some doubted the Saturday classes at ELAC had any purpose other than to provide Escalante additional salary. Some disapproved of his using first-marking-period F's to shock the slow or the lazy into more effort. Some said they thought the school should emphasize learning, rather than AP scores.

"I feel that exposure to academic courses is important," Shiroishi said, "but it's not necessary to have students get all fives on the AP test. . . . My students are already under stress. They're already carrying heavy loads. I'm trying to help them cope with all this, and then to have the students say to me that they're being asked to put in more time for a particular AP course really upsets me, because my goal is to try to help them to do whatever I feel is in the student's best interest."

These words filtered back to Escalante's new base in the southeast corner of the school—his narrow, long, high-ceilinged office off MH-1. He listened, leaned back in his chair, pulled off his glasses, and rubbed his eyes.

"They don't understand that these kids need the competition," he said. "They need something to motivate. They're lazy, most of them. You give them more time, they go home and watch television, or ride their motorcycles, or go to McDonald's. Empty set. But if they got through calculus, they have something."

‖ 15 ‖

Gradillas had been friendly to the girl, so she approached him boldly. "Mr. Gradillas, do you know what the kids are saying about you?"

"No, Sonia."

"They're saying that you demand too much of us, that you expect too much, you push too hard."

He gave her his most malevolent smile. "Yes, you're right!"

That was putting it on a bit thick, he thought, but he was not very troubled by what she said. There were so many people telling these kids to relax. Take it easy, they said, or you'll get sick. They told Escalante, you should take more time to relax, cut back a class or two.

Why, Gradillas asked himself, did he never hear anybody worrying about burnout at Beverly Hills High?

Many people were on his back. The euphoria of 1982 had dissipated. A few parents and teachers said he was pushing too hard. These kids had problems, they said.

So what? Everybody had problems. Blacks had problems. Hispanics had problems. Poor white trash had problems. Did that mean the school should not challenge them to do their best? How could he make parents, students, and particularly faculty see that they did not have to mirror the community?

Why should poverty excuse students from proper discipline? If the kid did not have discipline at home or in school, it was just going to be tougher later.

In a first rough draft of his long-delayed doctoral thesis, Gradillas quoted the findings of educational researcher William White: "The effective teacher of deprived children is not the romanticist with missionary zeal. He is not filled with pious platitudes about searching for 'beauty' and 'goodness' among the faces of the students. In order for the teacher to be truly successful with disadvantaged children, he or she must view the limited world of the deprived as a place to learn and study."

Gradillas's plan was to bring student discipline and decorum to a proper level, then go to work on the faculty. Persuade those who were not doing well to leave. Bring in younger teachers who could do better.

For several days someone had been setting off fire alarms in the school. Finally, one went off in the 300 Building, close enough for Gradillas to react. He dashed down the hall, yelling at teachers and supervisors to follow him.

A dozen students stood around looking curiously at the broken glass. "Everybody freeze!" he said. Alarm busters always stayed in the vicinity to enjoy the commotion. He lined everyone up and saw one boy's Adam's apple bobbing. Gradillas grabbed his wrist.

"No, no, I didn't do it. It was a girl. She went in there, that room."

There was a way to separate a needlelike miscreant from a classroom haystack. It worked 100 percent of the time in elementary school. Perhaps 75 percent fell for it in junior high, 25 percent in high school, and no one in college. Still, it was worth a try.

"Ladies and gentlemen," he told the class, "we have reason to believe the person who broke the alarm is in this room. Whoever did it, please, please come outside and meet us in the hallway. If you admit to what you did, the punishment will be lessened because I value your honesty and courage. It's a great thing to admit a wrong. You will be suspended, and your mother and father will come in, but it will not become a legal matter with the police. You will not be kicked out of school, but you will have to pay for the damage. It's not a bad deal."

No one moved. He thought of trying the black light trick—"You know, I sprayed the alarm beforehand with fluorescent spray that will show when we shine this black light on your hands"—but no one older than twelve was ever fooled by that one.

He noticed one girl give him an odd glance. Okay, he thought, that is all I need. "I'll ask all the boys to leave the class now . . . starting

227

here." The boys filed out, most looking relieved. He told the girls to follow them, also in single file. When his target was almost to the door, he pointed at her. "Now, you. Yes, you! Will you admit to me, or do you want the sheriff?"

She trembled, but said nothing.

"Okay. I want a sheriff's police car here and a lady matron. I don't want anything to go wrong with this one. This is a clean one. This is a *good bust*."

"Wait," the girl said.

"*What?*"

"I did it."

He gave her the no arrest deal, with one final word. "If you ever even go *near* one of those suckers, you'll never graduate from this school."

A student came to school wearing a bandanna around his forehead—a favorite sign of gang membership and an irritant to Gradillas. The youth insisted he had the right to wear it. Gradillas had an idea. The youth was looking for work. He sent him to a local bank two blocks away on Atlantic. Pick up an application, Gradillas suggested. See what happens.

The guard flinched the minute the boy entered. We have no jobs, thank you, he was told. The guard carefully escorted him to the door.

A week later a student appeared in Gradillas's office with a tattoo that had gang overtones. He too insisted on his rights. Gradillas sent him to apply for work at a local Jack-in-the Box. The manager, also Latino, called Gradillas. "What the hell are you doing sending this joker over here?"

"Hey, he's just part of the community, looking for a job. I thought you might want to help the downtrodden Latino."

"I consider those kids liabilities, handicaps," the manager said. "I can't hire a guy who's all messed up like that and deal with food, deal with the public."

Gradillas recounted the incidents to his faculty and his parents' group to make a point. He would not tolerate vandalism or inappropriate dress at school. Why should he, if the people in the barrio did not? "Why should we allow such behavior in a school that is supposed to teach standards that will serve its students in the outside world?"

Stephanie Gradillas watched her husband push and push, and she harbored a certain dread. She had taught long enough herself to know there was also an unwritten code of conduct for principals, and he

228

was getting close to the line. She could not believe some of the things he got away with. He told students they would not graduate unless they took a class he thought they should have. The way he put it, it was not quite lying, but awfully close.

She had to admit, grudgingly, that his instincts seemed right, most of the time. She had brought her child into the marriage, a tall, blond boy named Erik, who sped through Alhambra High School and went on to the University of California, Santa Cruz, to study English. When a brief tour as Prince Charming at Disneyland convinced him he could be an actor, he dropped out of college and announced plans to live at home, in a guesthouse in back, while he went to auditions. He wanted, he said, to experience the real world.

This is not, his stepfather replied, the real world, not when you are living rent free in a nice little house beside our pool. If you leave school, you'll have to live somewhere else. His wife was angry and afraid. But, sure enough, Erik discovered he could not pay his car insurance on his meager amusement park salary, so he went back to school. Score one for Henry, Stephanie said to herself.

It was time, Gradillas thought, to do something about his dozens of introductory and basic courses. He wanted more algebra and chemistry. No matter how often he asked teachers and counselors to challenge students, to push them into tougher classes, the enrollment in high school mathematics remained constant.

He took a deep breath and began to strike courses off the schedule. He cut Basic Math from thirty-eight sections to twenty. Counselors complained that they had students who simply could not adjust to the rigors of algebra. At the end of the first year, teachers reported a 40 percent failure rate. That, Gradillas noted, was only 10 percent above the usual 30 percent failure rate in basic mathematics. With better teachers, he would get better results.

Escalante wanted to take eager young junior high faculty and add them to the mathematics department, but he had difficulty finding teachers willing to put in long, unpaid hours after school. Just keep looking, Gradillas told him.

Gradillas rocked any safely anchored boat, if it had money in it. Downtown had provided special funds for the new books and extra teachers he needed to build the AP program, but he was never satisfied. He told them they were giving more money to schools that were much worse than Garfield. Those schools made no attempt to do *anything*. They just threw money at their problems. He ran a school that had proved it could get results for the money, but Downtown said, No, you have enough. We have to spread it around.

It was, Gradillas thought, an incentive for bad management.

Some things he could do on his own. He sharply cut the number of shop and home economics courses, already suffering a decline as students sensed these skills did them very little good in the marketplace. No longer were counselors shuffling Latino kids into such classes automatically, as they had when Gradillas was a sophomore at Roosevelt.

He had been reading something about the great eastern immigrant high schools of the early century—Boston Latin, Stuyvesant. They had an immigrant community with a lot of problems, and yet they had really tough high schools. Great men had graduated from those places. They made a significant difference to a lot of lives. Why couldn't Garfield do that?

Every revolution has its factional strife. Jiménez and Escalante would not be spared. As growing numbers of Garfield students filtered up into calculus, some seeing Escalante, others getting a dose of Jiménez, two camps evolved.

In the Escalante group were the quick-witted underachievers, students who knew boredom and academic failure and lived for the energies and juices and antics of a day in MH-1. If Escalante threatened them with F's, or called their parents, or gave a quiz two days later than he said he would, it was all part of the game. So much in high school was predictable. Escalante's class was fun, even if time consuming and sometimes stomach churning.

Into the smaller Jiménez camp came a few methodical, shy youngsters who had not enjoyed the circus in MH-1. Stella and Margie Zavala, sisters a year apart, had compiled admirable academic records through hard work and obedience to the rules. They found the cheering and digressions and guilt trips in Escalante's class distracting rather than stimulating. They studied conscientiously the night before an announced Escalante quiz, then sat in rage as he spent the day going over some point someone in the fifth row did not understand.

Jiménez had taken the Escalante method and remodeled it to suit his very different personality. He rarely bullied. He accepted the prevailing view of his formative years in 1960s America and refused to force students to come after school or on Saturdays. They had rights.

He encouraged all who needed help to see him at nutrition break, at lunch, after school. He had no intensive care, no quarantine, no three-fingered salute or any of the designations Escalante had for those required to appear at 3:00 P.M.

But he was there. When an F quietly appeared on a report card at midterm, the student would often seek him out. A failing grade became an even more powerful weapon in 1983, when the school board joined a national movement to close after-school sports and other activities to any student with an F, or less than a C average.

Most Escalante students thought their final grades were fair, but often it was unclear how he arrived at them. He combined quiz scores and tests and homework and overall effort in a formula known only to him. He could always be persuaded to boost the grade of a student who did unexpectedly well on the AP examination.

Jiménez did not like mysteries. He told his students precisely what they had to score on each test and quiz and assignment to keep an A or B. His grade book was easy to follow.

In 1976 Jiménez had married Sara Salcedo, an energetic bank clerk he met in a karate class. He jogged or lifted weights on a regular schedule, sometimes arising at 4:00 A.M. to find the time. When mentioning Jiménez to his students, Escalante would occasionally hunch his shoulders and tighten his fists in a parody of Mr. America.

But the younger man immersed himself in his classes as much as Escalante did in his. At home, Jiménez would rub his hands in anticipation of a surprise quiz he was about to fire into the lethargic ranks of an inattentive class. Sara Jiménez complained that her husband contracted colds and other illnesses only during vacations, when his body knew it did not need to be at its best. He grumbled to himself about students who seemed to emerge from other algebra teachers' classrooms innocent of fundamentals. He silently endured Gradillas's and Escalante's public relations ventures, which seemed to ignore any role he might be playing in the school's success.

In the last few weeks before an AP test, he became obsessed with his students' level of preparation. He rarely slept more than four hours a night during those periods, and had difficulty eating properly. He did not have as many calculus students as Escalante did, but his results were impressive all the same. Each June he totaled the number of his students who passed the AP examination and reviewed the results with satisfaction. He did not recite the numbers unless someone asked. In 1984, fourteen of his sixteen students passed with a grade of 3 or better. In 1985 it was thirty out of thirty-four. In 1986, twenty-three of twenty-six.

Despite his shyness, Jiménez was an emotional man, and he felt strongly by 1986 that Escalante should have split the BC students with him. So when Margie Zavala suggested they form a small, secret conspiracy to grant her the privilege of a BC course without Escalante, he wavered, and then gave in. Zavala persuaded Martin to let her take an independent study in Jiménez's room. With Mai Phung, another quiet, cerebral sort who preferred the light Jiménez touch, Zavala sat in a far corner of MH-2 doing quizzes and assignments, wondering what would happen when Escalante found out.

She was disappointed. Jiménez was forced to broach the subject in order to qualify her for tutoring work on Saturdays. Escalante acted as if it had all been arranged at his insistence, and the tiny class continued in the less interesting light of day.

In August 1983 Escalante returned to La Paz. He wanted to relax after the first hard summer at ELAC and allow his Bolivian entourage to celebrate properly the victory of '82. Roberto Cordero, now a customs officer, escorted him through the airport formalities. More than two dozen of his old San Calixto *llockallas* threw a banquet. Government officials presented proclamations. Journalists requested interviews. Educators sought advice.

His siblings had done well. Olimpia and Bertha were teachers who had risen to administrative posts. José was a university administrator, Raúl a banker, and Felix a financial consultant. But they all doted on Jaime. His mother and sisters displayed the scrapbook of clippings they had collected, from not only the United States but throughout Latin America. One Puerto Rican headline proclaimed in Spanish: INTELLIGENCE OF LATIN PEOPLE SURPRISES U.S.

A teacher at San Calixto could expect to encounter a few future cabinet members in his classes. Escalante had had his share. Fabio Machicado, minister of the economy, called his old teacher in for a long chat while bank presidents waited impatiently outside. He offered wine. Escalante, no longer a man of the Prado, asked for a Coke instead. Machicado said he planned to be president someday. Escalante, he said, should return home so he could vote.

The teacher made no promises. It did not seem like the country he remembered. The students who used to take over new buildings so they could have more classes now boycotted classes altogether. Marxist ferment pervaded the place, leaving a bad smell in his nostrils. Nobody was doing homework.

He went back to California, glad that his mother's voice and spirit were still strong, sad that her heart was weakening. Six months later she died, in characteristically orderly fashion.

The day before she had insisted on telephoning her son in America. "This is the last time you're going to hear my voice, Jaime," she said. "I want you to always treat Fabiola very well and take care of your sons." It was a gentle reference to her constant admonition against ignoring his own children in favor of those strangers at school.

At 3:00 P.M. the next day, lying in Bertha's arms, she whispered that she was going to find her sister Margarita, dead months before. Then she was gone. Bertha called Escalante, but he could not make it to the funeral. The air connections were difficult. Fabiola did not like the idea of such a long trip so soon after his gallbladder operation. And the AP examination was only seven weeks away.

A year later he received another telephone call from Bolivia, this time unexpected. Roberto Cordero had died, killed when the car in which he was riding was struck by a truck on one of La Paz's steep highways. He was a good man, a funny man, a wonderful person with whom to share a beer and *salteña*.

That was, Escalante thought, a long time ago.

Escalante made two trips to Washington in 1984, one to appear at a conference for Hispanic educators, one to attend a White House dinner for the president of Mexico. On the conference trip, he traveled alone. Jaimito drove him to the airport, checked him in, guided him to the proper gate. His father did not look up more than twice during the journey. He had a new book on the integration of pi, and he wanted to finish it. At the gate, Jaimito seemed doubtful. "You sure, Dad, you're going this way?"

"Yeah, just go ahead."

So Escalante walked down the ramp and found his seat. He next became aware of his surroundings when the plane landed and the passengers disembarked. The book had made the trip seem unusually short. No one from the conference was in the terminal to meet him. He sat, puzzled, then began to study his surroundings.

"Jaimito?" he said on the telephone.

"Hi, Dad, you make it okay?"

"Jaimito, I'm not at Dulles Airport. I'm in Dallas."

No one could ever persuade the faculty of Garfield that Escalante's accent had not betrayed him, but that a travel agent had typed the wrong flight number and Escalante in his absentmindedness failed to detect the error.

His immediate family had long since written him off as a dreamy child who could not be trusted with the simplest errand. It did not help that neither Jaimito nor Fernando had inherited any of his fondness for deceit in the interest of humor. They were serious young men, like their Tapia uncles who began the family migration to America.

The week before their father had to take his driver's license renewal test, they fretted loudly about his reluctance to prepare. "Piece of cake," he said. "Don't worry about it."

He returned from the test late in the afternoon. Fernando thought he looked uncharacteristically sheepish.

"Dad? What happened?"

"You know what? I blew it. I missed seven questions. They're gonna pull my license."

"Why did you *do* that?" the boy shouted. "You didn't even look at the book. The only thing you do is math. You don't pay attention to anything else. Mama, listen to this. Dad flunked his test."

Fabiola appeared, fearing the worst. "Jaime?"

Escalante grinned. "Nah, I'm just kidding. I just miss one."

Fernando glowered. "That is *not* funny, Dad. We do *not* like those kinds of jokes. You understand?"

Escalante's reputation for unworldiness was not far off the mark no matter how he exploited it. All he wanted was to coax and coddle and orchestrate and manipulate and mystify and educate his students. Each year brought more of them, in startlingly wider varieties.

When Escalante, Jiménez, and Gradillas later looked back on the years after 1982, they wondered how the social misfits, athletes, curiosity seekers, social climbers, unsung geniuses, and gang members drifting into the program became the critical mass that made calculus at Garfield a self-perpetuating success. Sal Quezada, an East Los Angeles native who taught at middle-income, suburban South Pasadena High School, provided a clue. He helped teach the Saturday sessions at ELAC and noticed a striking difference between his weekday students from South Pasadena and his weekend students from Garfield.

"My kids don't *need* calculus like East LA kids do," he said. "They have other priorities in their lives."

Steve Robles was a lean, darkly handsome boy who spoke in rapid, infrequent bursts, like a machine gun probing an enemy's defenses. He lived near Salazar Park in a geographically and economically depressed area called "The Hole." His mother rented a green, tattered wood-frame house jammed together with other small homes at a bend in the road. To scan the surrounding area from their low-lying neighborhood, the residents had to look up. It put a premium on self-respect, which Robles sought in a little gang called the Hole Stoners and in the back row of MH-1.

He had been born in Tijuana and came to America before he could walk. His parents divorced. His mother took odd jobs to support her four children, but money was always short. The tiny two-bedroom house was often a mess, walls full of aimless bric-a-brac, toys on the floor, half-eaten meals scattered about.

Yet teachers who encountered the Robles children marveled at what could grow out of such meager soil. Steve's elder sister Blanca was admitted to California State Polytechnic University, Pomona; his younger sister Roxane would eventually become an Escalante star and attend the same college. Besides being brilliant, they were attractive, quiet girls who would have sailed through anywhere. Steve was different.

He was on the gifted list, but Ed Martin, his counselor, despaired of him. He often had to call Robles in for some transgression, such as truancy or failure to do homework. The boy sometimes just turned on his heel and walked out, leaving Martin shouting at his back. He rarely exchanged more than a word or two with any teacher. That interested Escalante.

Robles met Escalante in tenth-grade Algebra 2. He sat in the back and watched with detached interest as the teacher with the funny accent threw two latecomers out of the class. This was fun, he told himself. He liked mathematics and thought a teacher like that might reduce the usual boredom ratio. He would lean back, listen, and stay out of trouble.

It took more than his usual amount of patience. Escalante lusted for some response from students, particularly those as taciturn as

Robles. And the boy wore a badge of resistance that the teacher could not resist—shoulder-length hair. Escalante would tug at it, threaten forced haircuts, and accuse Robles of devil worship. He called Robles *Greñas*, "Longhair," which did not bother him, and "Stevie," which did.

Mathematics rarely interfered with Robles's social calendar. After finishing homework he strolled through the streets with other Stoners, drinking, occasionally fighting, sometimes neglecting to sleep. He accumulated small scars from street brawls and an occasional haggard look from sleeping on his porch. He played the drums in a succession of bands, like Wreckage and Kaos, that catered to the jarring metal rhythms and satanic cult symbols then in vogue.

His friends in the Hole taunted him in disbelief when he mentioned he was in calculus. After that simply said he had a math class. He enjoyed the frightened looks he got from older women in elevators, and he liked his reputation in Escalante's class as a sociopath who unaccountably knew the answers.

Escalante tried to get under his skin, but Robles took that as a compliment. The man was not boring, and the toys and games and slogans he used in class did help him remember certain functions. He took the summer course in trigonometry and mathematical analysis. For calculus, he was assigned to Jiménez, who was less electrifying in class but won Robles over with his patience and care.

Robles pursued his usual social activities the week before the AP examination and received a 5. He returned to Escalante's room for Calculus BC his senior year and received a 5 on that test also. He tutored at ELAC on Saturdays, but found it difficult to tolerate students who could not see the solution to each problem as clearly or as quickly as he could.

When he came to school in a particularly tattered shirt, Escalante bought a new shirt for him. He refused to accept it. Weeks later, he came by with a calculus problem he could not solve. "I'll help you, but first you have to wear my shirt," Escalante said. Robles reluctantly agreed, on the condition that Escalante drink Robles's gift of lemon juice. Escalante did not like lemon juice, but he drank it anyway.

Gradually Robles's conversations with Escalante expanded beyond monosyllables. When Escalante had not seen Robles for a few weeks, he told Madrid to hold up the boy's tutoring check. That forced him to stop by for another chat.

Escalante encouraged him to enter a $500 essay contest for prospective young engineers. "Of course, Stevie, if you win the five hundred dollars, you will have to give me a hundred, that is the deal," he said. Robles solemnly agreed. Don Mroscak, the college counselor, expressed amazement at Escalante's success in opening a dialogue with the boy. When Robles won the essay contest, Escalante negotiated another deal. He would advance the boy money for suitable clothes for the banquet. In return, Robles would get a haircut.

He arrived at Escalante's office the next week, almost unrecognizable in new clothes, his ears clearly visible. He was businesslike. "I got the cash. Here's the hundred dollars."

"It's a joke, Stevie," Escalante said. "The money is yours."

The boy looked startled, then smiled, then laughed, then frowned. "I'm sorry," he said. "I didn't know. Nobody ever did nothing for me. I have a father, but I don't see him much. Now I know you, and you know me."

"I'm sorry it took me three years to get to know you, Stevie. You were one of my best kids."

Sprinkled among Escalante's sea of Latino youths, like stray bits of multicolored foam, were the few Anglos, blacks, and a somewhat larger number of Asians deposited at Garfield by the magnet program and some shifts in the East Los Angeles immigrant tide.

Escalante called all students of Asian descent his "Kung fus." In 1985 one of his Vietnamese students was escorted into MH-1 by a noon aide, a neighborhood woman who signed visitors and late arrivals in to the school after the bell rang.

"This student in your class, Mr. Escalante?"

"*Sí, señora.*"

"Well, he just used some very foul language with me."

The student looked puzzled.

"If you'll excuse me, Mr. Escalante," the woman said. "I asked for a hall pass and I heard him call me a . . . a . . . a fuckin' lady."

Escalante gave the boy his hardest look. "Did you say that?"

No reply.

"Come here and have a seat, Johnny. I'm gonna teach you when you use that word."

He directed the youth to a very small blue chair in front of the room. It was the Escalante equivalent of a dunce cap, a lonely spot where wrongdoers would have to face the rest of the class and endure boos in several different pitches and keys.

"Listen," he said, looking down at the boy. "I don't think you're going to go far. Assume you're working in a company. If you use that word, believe me, next day, clock out." The boy seemed to be listening. "Okay, I don't have time to talk about this now. You be here at three o'clock."

Within an hour, the same student, looking even more perplexed, stuck his head in the door. "I'm sorry, Mr. Escalante. I'm not going to be able to come at three o'clock."

Escalante was annoyed. The kid was not getting the message. "It's up to you, but we're going to have to talk about this."

"Let me explain. You know, they told me I'm out of school. They kick me out of school. The lady went to the dean's office, and he asked me, 'Did you say that?' And I said, 'Yes,' and he told me, 'You're out.'"

"That fast?" said Escalante, snapping his fingers.

"Yes."

Escalante marched over to the 400 Building and climbed the stairs to the vice principal's office. The man refused to budge. "That's the rule, Jaime," he said.

Shiroishi, the boy's counselor, caught Escalante in the hall. "What can we do?" she asked.

"I'll talk to Gradillas."

The boy had been going with him from office to office. Now he spoke up. He was seven when his family left Vietnam. His father worked in a gas station. "Mr. Escalante, this is nothing. My dad uses that word every day. It doesn't mean that much to us. I even hear teachers use it. 'Go get the fuckin' absence slip.' It's normal, right?"

Escalante shook his head and sighed. Some days the world was too much for him.

He found Gradillas, who rescinded the suspension. Escalante pulled the youth back downstairs for a long talk. It was a rerun of the speech he gave once or twice a term whenever the circumstances warranted:

"There are three reasons why you *bandidos* are not going to succeed over here.

"*One*, phone calls. You got your girlfriend and boyfriend, you kill the time.

"Number *two*, involved in the gang activities.

"Number *three*, lazy. You're lazy guys and you don't have the control at home, so I get paid for controlling you. The principal gives me extra money. If I find one of those cases I get fifty dollars for each case, so I want you to tell me your troubles. I gonna share with you. You give me a case, you get ten dollars.

"Now go home. Nobody gets nothing for this one. This happens again, I charge *you* ten dollars."

‖16‖

The bell had just rung for the first day of school, September 9, 1986. This was the year that could prove, as much as anything in American education can ever be proved, that Escalante's system would work on a school-transforming scale. Jiménez and he had 151 calculus students, plus at least 400 other youngsters in the developing process. If they could arrange a successful conclusion to such a year for most of their students, people outside East Los Angeles might finally take them seriously.

Olga García, dark hair framing her face, strolled along Woods Avenue, unconcerned that she was slightly late. She was enjoying the walk and the time to herself. She lived in a brown stucco duplex about ten yards from the six-lane Long Beach Freeway, with no wall between to muffle the noise. She shared a bedroom with her mother and two sisters. She did her homework stretched out on one of the bottom bunks with a pillow propping up her chin. Her sisters chattered. The television blasted studio applause from the living room. The telephone rang. A truck on the freeway changed gears.

After school, between long stretches in Escalante's class, she ran cross-country, her legs pounding the hard cinders of the worn-out school track or, occasionally, the concrete of the neighborhood sidewalks. Small one-story wood-frame and stucco houses slid by as she ran. Most had low roofs, numerous dogs, low Cyclone fences, an occasional car on blocks, and every imaginable kind of garden, with roses in great profusion.

Many of those people had come to America the same way her parents had, without papers, uninvited. She laughed at her father's story of the federal agents boarding their bus, scanning the faces. "American citizens," her father had told them, using the only English words he knew. It was a busy night; the agents passed him by.

She liked the stillness of a good run. The noise of babies and carburetors and Mexican soap operas and German shepherds could not keep up with her. She could collect herself, relax, soothe her mind with thoughts of slopes rising into third quadrants and parabolas vanishing into infinity.

She was an Escalante favorite, wedded to his system and more certain of her future than she had ever been. She had already crossed the point of exhaustion and doubt which most Garfield calculus students encountered. But many remained on the other side, uncertain of the subject and of themselves.

It was 8:15 that Tuesday morning, the first day of school. No one rushed into MH-1. Young people lingered outside to greet old friends and keep an eye out for enemies. Many were not certain where Escalante fit on that scale. Raúl Orozco, a junior with braces on his teeth and a restless look, remembered how the teacher had abused him that summer. Now he had Escalante for first period, by far the worst part of his day.

Orozco lived with his mother and three sisters in a little house across the street from a public swimming pool in the hills above the Pomona Freeway. Since there were not enough bedrooms, he worked, played, and slept in the living room, a cramped collection of plastic-covered red couches and television sets. The pace of life in a crowded household often kept him up. He was never at his best in the morning.

Orozco's father, who had never married his mother, was eighty-three and lived in a rest home. Orozco studied when inspired, loafed otherwise. He had spent much of the eighth grade pretending to be sick. At Garfield he sometimes disappeared for days to sleep, watch television, and work on his impressions of Ronald Reagan and Richard Nixon. Teachers loved his unpredictable humor and fretted at his aimlessness and what they called his immaturity.

The summer had been hard for Orozco. He had taken Escalante's trigonometry and mathematical analysis course at ELAC. Pupil and teacher clashed. Friends hid Orozco's backpack one day, forcing him to search for it frantically during class.

Escalante tore into him. "I don't like this shit you're giving me. I don't *like* this b.s. You gonna fly. Which school you wanta go to? I'll

241

tell Gradillas to throw you out." This isn't fair, Orozco thought. I wasn't doing anything wrong, they stole my backpack.

Escalante, as usual, withdrew the threat, but the episode left Orozco uneasy. He had let them talk him into taking Woessner's AP history course too. His Reagan imitation had become quite polished, but it was not going to help much.

The summer he was twelve he ran into Aili Tapio, that brilliant girl, a few years older than he, who lived around the corner. She was so polite, he thought, she would be the envy of the queen of England. To his shock, that day she was swearing like a Royal Marine. It was something about the stupid, goddamned AP test, and a lot of dirty SOBs at something called the ETS. It did not sound like she was having fun, and she went to school *every day*.

Désirée Esparza stepped off the RTD bus after a fifteen-minute ride from her home in the northwestern hills. She was a short, slim junior with brown hair and perfect skin who spoke quietly, and listened more than she spoke. She looked for her friends, Norma Huizar and Juana Valdez, as she walked through the main Garfield entrance and turned right toward MH-1. The sky was blue. The trees were green. Life was sweet. She was in love.

For most of her life she had been a serious student. Her parents had divorced when she was seven. Her father, a Guadalajara physician, decided not to join her mother in Los Angeles. Two daughters and a baby boy had to live off the woman's salary as a bank clerk. Family lent extra support, and they settled into a one-bedroom house with an upstairs attic converted into a second bedroom for the two girls. When her elder sister married, Esparza took sole possession of the upstairs. There she plowed through algebra and trigonometry and nursed a growing desire to go to USC and become an accountant.

Ramiro Casillas, the man in her life, did not seem to mind her ambitions. He had dropped out of parochial school after the eighth grade, but was working with his father in the family upholstery business. He was a year older than Esparza. He radiated calm and self-confidence. Small and wiry, with broad shoulders, he joked about his brainy girlfriend and her nerdy friends. Norma and Juana liked him anyway. He encouraged Désirée to plan for college.

Her mother was far less enchanted with the relationship. Esparza had joined the cheerleading squad that summer and had been practicing every day from 3:00 to 5:00 P.M., after trigonometry with

242

Escalante at ELAC. At the end of a tense argument over the time she spent with Casillas, her mother told her she would not permit her to be a cheerleader. Esparza decided it was best to have the extra time anyway. Besides AP calculus, she had signed up for Woessner's AP history, and she had just seen his reading list.

José Pulgarin came to the United States when he was twelve, lying beneath a carpet in the back of a station wagon driven across the border at the Tijuana–San Ysidro checkpoint by coyotes, professional smugglers hired by his mother. He had suffered recurrent fears and disappointments in America. His mother had arrived illegally before him and expected *La Migra* to find them any moment. He had anticipated casual riches, trash cans full of used but perfectly serviceable television sets. Such had not materialized. His only chance, he thought, was to do well in mathematics at school, but there were distractions.

Pulgarin was not Mexican, but Colombian. His father had driven a taxicab in the city of Pereira, 100 miles west of Bogotá, until he was murdered for his cash box. Pulgarin was three when it happened. His mother worked in a toilet paper factory for a while, then began to dream of a better life in Los Estados Unidos, and a good education for her son. She struck up a friendship with a man at work who helped her secure Mexican identity papers, fly to Mexico, and sneak across the U.S. border in 1980. A year later Pulgarin followed, apprehensive and frightened. When his flight landed in Mexico City, the flight attendant forgot for several minutes that she was supposed to take him off the plane, leaving him alone and terrified. His mother's friends eventually got him on a bus to Tijuana and guided him across the border.

He had always been slim, with delicate features and very curly hair. Some days he looked malnourished. His slow, halting speech left the impression of a boy with limited intelligence. But some teachers noticed a spark. Escalante had let him into the summer program at ELAC and it had not gone well.

Pulgarin and his mother lived in a tiny shack in the back of a house on Townsend Street, a fifteen-minute bus ride from Garfield. A boarder took the one small bedroom to help them pay the $240 rent. Pulgarin and his mother slept in the living room, usually on the floor, since the fourth-hand furniture could not comfortably bear their weight. There was little money. Pulgarin found few pleasant distractions other than watching American football games on their battered black-and-white television set.

When a young neighbor suggested one day some beers and a dip in the public pool, he accepted. He was in his fourth week of Escalante's trigonometry course. It was mid-July and very hot. By late afternoon he was drunk. When his new friends suggested they buy some cocaine, he did not object. Two small lines of white powder, snorted in his friend's house, cost twenty-five dollars, money he did not have. He promised to get it by morning, but as the effects of the beer and the drug wore off, he became terrified. He would have to tell his mother something to get the money.

She was not home, he discovered. He was certain she had been kidnapped and held for ransom. Or perhaps they would just kill him when he failed to get the money. She finally appeared and, relieved, he told her everything, punctuated with deep sobs.

She cried with him, soothed him, and suggested they pray. She prayed for strength, for help, for God's grace in letting her son see the light. At that moment, she resolved to leave the Catholic church and become a Baptist, an idea she had been considering for many weeks. She suggested her son think about committing his life to Jesus. He promised he would. He felt refreshed, saved, reborn. She gave him twenty-five dollars, and he walked off to Fifth Street in search of the dealer. It took two visits to the man's house to find him, but the debt was paid.

He sat at home for a few more days, thinking and praying, then returned to ELAC, hopelessly behind. He was certain Escalante would eject him from the class, perhaps even from high school altogether. His mother came with him to speak to the teacher. "Mr. Escalante, please let him stay. He was sick."

"Why didn't you say anything before?" Escalante asked the boy.

Pulgarin said in his soft voice, "I didn't want to lie."

The mother interrupted. "Okay, Mr. Escalante, there is more to it, but you must keep him. Ever since my husband was killed, José has been my treasure, and I don't want him to lose this opportunity."

Escalante studied the two frightened people in front of him. "Look, I make you a deal," he said to Pulgarin. "I take you back in class, but you take trig and math analysis again in the regular year, same time you take calculus."

The boy looked even more worried than usual. "I don't think I can take two things at the same time. It's very hard."

"No, no, no! Who says it's hard?"

Feeling trapped, yet relieved that he was back in school, Pulgarin agreed. He was still not sure this was a burden even God could bear.

The little brick house where Juanita Gutiérrez lived rarely revealed an unswept floor or an unmade bed. Her mother kept the tiny lawn mowed and the three bedrooms immaculate. Inside her own room of puffy cushions and stuffed animals and precise schedules on the bulletin board, Gutiérrez pursued good grades and college. She arrived at Garfield looking forward to her junior year, but there were problems.

She was the eldest of six children. Her father and uncle ran a small garment-cutting business, but work was irregular and her father's health problems had set him back. A sharp blow to the head in a 1984 traffic accident caused occasional seizures. Then his appendix burst. He gave in to rages, and the marriage had run into rocky ground. Gutiérrez had been balancing the family checkbook and mailing off the bills since she was fourteen. She supervised the homework of her five little brothers and served her father's dinner, as well as helping her weary mother whenever she could.

She had been born in Mexico and brought to Los Angeles when she was three. Her father thought she inherited her talent for mathematics from her Guadalajara grandmother, a wily old woman who ran a general store for many years. Grandma Chuy could neither read nor write, but she was able to compute complicated accounts in her head.

Gutiérrez slipped into Escalante's fifth-period calculus class in her usual costume—gray, skintight jeans, multicolored floppy sweater, running shoes, brown hair ratted into a glorious crown atop her head. This was going to be hard, she thought. She was taking Woessner's AP history and was determined to join her friend Sandra Aguirre on the school pep squad, no matter what Escalante said.

Jesús Armando Beltrán, Armando to his friends, had gone to enormous lengths to get himself into calculus. His academic record would have raised doubts in the minds of most teachers, but Jiménez and Escalante were optimists. Beltrán was heading for a C average. He took Algebra 2 the summer after his sophomore year but lasted only a week.

Friends of his—he had many friends—admired his warm smile, his athletic talent, and his good looks. He wore a suggestion of a mustache and jet black hair cut short on top, trailing down his neck in back. His genuine warmth would lead to his selection as "best personality" of the class of '87, but he knew that would not impress Jiménez, his fifth-period calculus teacher.

He played center on the Garfield C basketball team, the small player division. He ran cross-country and pitched or played center field for the baseball team. When he arrived at Garfield in 1984, he noticed the Escalante students in their AP calculus sweatshirts and wondered if this might not be another team to go out for.

His B in sophomore geometry proved he could handle the material. He dropped out of Algebra 2 that summer because he could not stand the idea of wasting a three-month vacation doing homework. Also, there was brief trouble at home over a sister's drug problem. At the beginning of his junior year, he persuaded Escalante and Jiménez to let him take Algebra 2 and trigonometry/math analysis simultaneously.

He never had any burning career goal—he thought he might try being a physical therapist, since it looked like easy work. He simply wanted to be with the crowd, to be part of whatever was happening. At Garfield, that was calculus.

Jiménez sat in his little office attached to MH-2 and glanced at the room's single air conditioner, groaning in agony over one of the doors. He envied Escalante his $25,000 worth of cool air. Perhaps he ought to snap off the machine and leave the doors open.

His fifth-period calculus class totaled 50 students, nearly as many as Escalante's in the difficult post–lunch period. They had to find more good teachers. That was just too many students at one time. And those 50 were his only AP students. Escalante had a total of 101 in three classes.

Jiménez's wife, Sara, at least, was not likely to complain much about his time away from home. She and her brother, Saul, were about to open a hamburger stand in a new minimall not far from their yellow wood-frame and stucco home in La Puente. Saul lived with them in the three-bedroom house, which they rented from Sara's father for $150 a month. Their son, Daniel, age two, could spend the day with Sara's sister. If the hamburger stand made money, perhaps they would have enough to buy a better place.

As Escalante's first-period class drifted in on the first day of the new school year, Richard Strauss's Opus 314 played on the stereo, the soft music almost inaudible above the chatter of teenagers in the large room.

The desks in MH-1 were arranged neatly on risers that marched up to a back row that was three feet higher than the front. The layout gave the room a collegiate atmosphere, although at times the arrangement made Escalante seem a wounded lion screaming in the pit of the Colosseum as callous Roman nobles in jeans and T-shirts looked on.

He began the day, as usual, with his Aymara ritual:

"*Kamisaki?* [How are you?]"

Class: "*Walliki!* [We're fine!]"

Then an interchange in Quechua, in honor of his in-laws:

"*Imaynalla?*"

"*Walejlla!*"

This was Calculus AB, mostly Escalante veterans who knew his routine. He skipped up and down a few aisles, pulling hair, commenting on summer sloth and sluggish brain cells.

A tree maintenance crew outside turned on an electric saw, forcing him to raise his voice. "I say, I want to talk to your mom. You say, My mom works till ten o'clock. Okay, I'll be there at eleven o'clock. One thing you have to keep in mind, the subject is really easy. Easy. Like a game, it has three rules. The power rule, the product rule, the quotient rule.

"Over here the dy/dx is the derivative, or slope, and another is geography, plane geometry, or prime of x. So, let's say for instance if $f(x)$ is equal to $3x$ plus 4 prime x, f prime of x is . . . help me out, please, one shot." He filled the board with numbers.

There was a brief discussion of ordering jackets with the calculus team logo, a fierce bulldog wearing Escalante's motorman's cap and dark glasses. "The jackets cost twenty dollars," he said. "I'll charge you twenty-five, five dollars for the teacher."

After forty minutes, he ended the period with his maxim on homework: "Remember, you have the ticket, you watch the show. You don't have the ticket, you sit on the floor, or you're out the exit."

He had been thinking all morning about second period, Algebra 2. Tenth graders. His new recruits, the AP calculus team of '88, or for those who skipped summer school, '89. The bouncy, avuncular Kimo of period 1, a pleasant facsimile of Dr. Jekyll, became Mr. Hyde, or in Escalantese, Dr. Black, a sour, malevolent figure full of warnings and bad news.

Each algebra student received a single white sheet of paper decorated with the head of a spike-collared, scowling bulldog:

SUBJECT GRADE

Tests		Quizzes
A	90–100%	7
B	80–89%	6
C	70–79%	5
D	60–69%	4

TEST (100 points each): All tests will be on *Fridays* and you must take them in class. *No make-up* tests will be given.

QUIZZES (10 points each): Almost every day and must be taken in class; *no make-up* quizzes will be given.

HOMEWORK (10 points each): All homework assignments will be collected. When turned in the paper should have your name, period, and homeroom number. They must be written in the upper-right corner.

WORK HABITS: No late homework or make-up work will be accepted.

COOPERATION: Five tardies = U.

NOTEBOOK (possible 50 points): Each student will keep a notebook, not a pee-chee folder or any other type of loose file, in which he/she shall keep his/her work composed of two sections:
  i. Class notes (you should take notes carefully in class)
  ii. Quizzes and tests
On Fridays each student shall submit his/her notebook to the teacher for credit.

ATTENDANCE: You are expected to attend the class daily. If you are absent five (5) times during the semester, you will be referred to the Dean. If you miss three (3) tests during the semester, you may be referred to your counselor.

PLACE THIS PAPER IN YOUR NOTEBOOK
FOR A BETTER EDUCATION

_____	_____
Student's Signature	J. A. Escalante
	Mathematics Teacher

"You have to sign this," he said. "Friday the kids call payday. That means you going to have to take the test every Friday. We do not issue the books the first week, because at the end of the first week"—he snapped his fingers loudly—"we switch a lot of students to another school. So I hope you going to understand and follow the instructions."

He spoke softly, in low, menacing tones. "You have to be on time. Put the homework in the box marked period 2. Every time you don't have your homework, you may have to talk to Mr. Santoyo." He wrote the name on the board. "If it's the first time, maybe you just have to sign the contract. I don't know what his procedure is. But if it's the second time"—*snap*—"you're gone with the wind."

His voice went lower. "They going to put you in another school, so the only problem is going to be this: To get to that school, you going to have to take three buses.

"The only thing you got to do over here, you got to work with *ganas*. You don't have to have a high IQ, not like the ones that have one twenty, one forty IQ. Myself, I have a negative IQ. So the only thing I require of you is the *ganas*."

He walked up an aisle and stopped at one boy's desk. "You don't have your equipment, sir? You need your paper and pencil. You don't have your equipment? *The Bus!* You want to watch the show free? No!" There was a rustling noise as several students pulled out paper. "Where you from, Belvedere? That's a bubble gum school.

"My two doors are open all day long, till six or seven o'clock. . . . You gonna make it if you follow my instructions. Remember, this is Garfield High School. See my bulldog over there? This is no bubble gum high school. We prepare kids for college. . . . If you going to be in chemistry, physics, biology, or electronics, the language is mathematics, so if you have the domain of the language, you gonna make it.

"If you don't, forget it. You gonna be working at Jack-in-the-Box, shoveling McDonald's or something. And that's no problem. You could make the minimum wage. However, you have to work maybe twelve or fourteen hours to succeed. If you have your degree, you only have to work eight hours to get the same money."

He ran through some Algebra 1 problems.

"Am I doing right? Yes? No?"

"If you don't have your notes or anything, the *bus*!"

He tried out his repertoire of tricks: instant multiplication by 11, the three-digit rule, instant squares, guess the number. The bell rang. "If you going to be in calculus, I'm going to show you the secrets to read the problem, get the key word, and solve it in one shot. . . . Your counselor probably told you, when you came into this room, you cannot drop this class. You have to go all the way with me, and next week you sign the contract and I talk to your mom, your dad. There's no way to drop the class."

Wondering how many believed this, he wrapped up. "Tomorrow we have a little quiz in order to warm up. In the summer you work with me, you take math analysis and trigonometry and you make a thousand dollars in eight weeks. But you have to be a top kid. I can't bet the money on someone who doesn't work."

They left, chattering, laughing.

His trigonometry class filed in to take their place.

"Most of you already know me. Do the assignment. Don't smoke. Don't drink. Don't have bad dreams."

The body contact began outside the stadium, glowing brightly under its lights in the soft air of a southern California autumn. At the ELAC gates, campus police frisked everyone who entered, more than 25,000 people. Some knives were confiscated, but most of the items accumulating on a side table seemed innocent—beer cans, sharp combs, skateboards, hairspray.

One young man wearing a leather jacket and impossibly tight jeans smiled broadly as a policeman tried to find contraband in pockets with no room even for lint. His grin caught the attention of the crowd surging outside the Cyclone fence. "Hey, look! He *likes* it," one boy shouted. Others laughed and rattled the lengths of fence wire against their steel posts.

This was the Garfield-Roosevelt game, the East LA Classic, bigger than Texas-Oklahoma or USC-UCLA to anyone living east of downtown and south of the San Bernardino Freeway. Both schools were almost 100 percent Latino. Both produced small, wiry players who rarely won football scholarships. That only seemed to add to the ferocity of their play and the enthusiasm of the crowd. This was the social event of the fall, with rituals found in many other American cities, large or small.

Gradillas had graduated from Roosevelt in 1953 but there was no mistaking his loyalties now. He wore a bright blue blazer and red carnation over white shirt and dark slacks.

The stadium at ELAC, reserved every year for the event, provided plenty of room for supporters from both sides, Roosevelt on the north, Garfield on the south. Gradillas fretted at the sight of so many exuberant young people on a Friday night. He scanned the crowd intently for some sign of trouble, some provocateur he would have to dash up and collar. He had legions of his best teachers, including Jiménez, staked out in the tunnels to direct latecomers to the empty sections and to spot trouble early.

Escalante was at home, correcting papers. He refused to dignify such frivolity with his presence. Sandra Muñoz, a Calculus BC student who would be voted most spirited senior, badgered him for days before he would let her wear his lucky bulldog motorman's cap to the game. José Pulgarin, Désirée Esparza, Raúl Orozco, Olga García, and their families and friends were all in the stands talking and waiting for the game to start. Juanita Gutiérrez sat within the solid mass of the pep squad in their white blouses. Armando Beltrán was on the field, stroking his bright blue tuxedo and carrying out the sacred responsibilities of the senior class's elected prince to the Homecoming Court.

No matter where their parents or grandparents had come from, these were just a few thousand more American teenagers celebrating Friday night football. The stands pulsed with bright colors—blue, red, and white for Garfield, red and yellow for Roosevelt. True to the habits of U.S. youth, few sang the words to the national anthem, but most knew at least one fight song: "On Wisconsin, on Wisconsin, the cheese more people chew!"

The head Garfield cheerleader, armed with a microphone, unlimbered a voice that sounded like Phyllis Diller on a bad night: *"Hey, Dee, aaaaa . . . tack! Aaaa . . . taaaack!"*

Both schools were built in the 1920s to serve the growing immigrant neighborhoods and factories spreading east of the old Los Angeles pueblo. Both had been named after Republican presidents, but with a difference. James A. Garfield had been killed by a frustrated job seeker after only months in office and nobody knew anything about him. Theodore Roosevelt had an indelible reputation and image and was even on Mt. Rushmore. To express their contempt for TR's popularity, Garfield fans took teddy bears to the game, waved them in the direction of the Roosevelt stands, ripped them apart, and tossed the pieces in the air. By kickoff time, the stands were full of fuzz and scattered toy limbs.

Gradillas watched the crowd so intently he missed the first play. Garfield fumbled and Roosevelt recovered. A Roosevelt field goal, then a touchdown, followed quickly, 10–0. The Garfield head cheerleader had expended her foghorn voice fruitlessly on the *"Big Dee"* defense, so now she encouraged the offense. "Yes, we *do*. We believe in *you!*" The band broke into a wild flurry of Latinized percussion.

On orders from Gradillas, the loudspeaker announced: "Those who are taking the SAT exams tomorrow, get a good night's sleep." Somehow, that helped. Garfield scored once, scored again. The half ended with Garfield leading 23–10. The hugging began.

The Garfield band members embraced in triumph when their spirited, complex half-time show ended without a mishap. The dancers in white blouses and tight blue pants and the pompom girls in tight blue tunics and pillbox caps laughed and hugged as if seeing each other after a long absence. Returning graduates hugged their teachers. The Garfield cheerleaders hugged the Roosevelt cheerleaders.

On nights like this, the *abrazo*, the Latin embrace, had a special place. It was the only thing that made the evening at all different from a hundred thousand other Friday night games from Fargo, North Dakota, to Sarasota, Florida.

Margie Zavala, her hair piled high, had been leading cheers at the far east end of the stands but now moved toward the middle for one of her specialties. *"Party!* Don't let your mother know. *Paaaarrteeeee!* 'Cause she won't let you go."

"Bulldogs, we are A-live. *Bulldogs*, don't take no . . . uh . . . *jive!"* The score climbed to 33–10 and the Roosevelt stands, to Gradillas's

relief, rapidly emptied. He went to tell coach Steve Robinson to put in all the remaining players.

Gradillas had suffered for this night. When he asked Coach Vic Loya, a fourteen-year veteran with health problems, to give up the job two years before, his telephone rang for days. The district school superintendent returned from a Washington lobbying trip to complain he could not get the leaders of the Congressional Hispanic Caucus to stop talking about the coaching change and discuss his need for funds.

Gradillas felt himself relax, a celebratory mood sneaking up on him. Josie Richkarday, calculus '82, spotted him wandering around the field, looking for something to do. She had spent the second half down in front of the stands. In jeans, tennis shoes, and old varsity sweater, she had jumped and kicked and clapped and yelled and felt rather ancient as part of the traditional alumni cheerleading squad. Now she ran toward Gradillas.

"Josie! Hi!" he shouted, and gave her a big *abrazo*.

Outside MH-1 on a chilly October morning, twelve trigonometry students stood shivering next to the stained drinking fountain. Some stared into space; others leafed intently through their textbooks.

Escalante opened the door. "You ready?" He had a question for each, their ticket to class. The half of the class inside, safe and warm, had answered correctly on their first try. The rest had to stand outside, reviewing their books and praying for inspiration, or an easy question.

"As the arc increases from pi over 2 to pi, what happens to the sine?"

"It . . . ah . . . increases from 0 to 1."

"*No!*" The girl squealed in dismay and hit her forehead with the heel of her hand. Escalante turned to the next in line.

"F of x equals sine $4x$. Give me the period."

"Two pi?"

"No way, Johnny. Study." The boy's shoulders slumped.

"I give you one more chance, ten more minutes, otherwise you're going to have to come the whole day, three to six o'clock."

For once on schedule, he reappeared ten minutes later and tried again. He gave the squealing girl the same question as before, but this time she had the answer—decreases from 1 to 0. "Oooooo, weeeeeee," she said.

"Take a seat," Escalante said. "I loooove you!"

In fifth-period calculus, a student struggling to delay a quiz on a Friday tried the usual gambit, a sports question. The California Angels had just wasted, in spectacular fashion, an opportunity to win the American League pennant. "They blew it, right, Kimo?"

"Yes, they blew it, just like some of you may blow it. They had the last chance, one strike away."

"What do you mean?"

"You have a last chance here, to go to college, to get a good job, and some of you are blowing it."

The questioner said no more. Someone tried another approach. "Did you hear that [Angel second baseman] Bobby Grich retired? When are you going to retire, Mr. Escalante?"

Escalante gave his crocodile smile. "No, no, no. *I'm* the one who decides who will retire."

"What you mean?"

"I can flunk you, and you will retire very early."

Gradillas now had a waiting list of 400 students who lived slightly outside the boundaries but whose parents wanted them to attend Garfield. Many lied about their addresses, or sent a child to live with a relative inside the Garfield area.

His dropout rate was still high, perhaps 30 percent. Since his advisory council, the rough equivalent of the PTA, had endorsed his new three-year mathematics requirement and the other basics of his accelerated program, he could now concentrate on dropouts. Coca-Cola provided $50,000 for a school-within-a-school to try to curb the dropout rate. Students with poor records were put in special classes with teachers who stayed with them throughout the program, giving close attention to each individual's problems. Another new program promised jobs or college admission to anyone who graduated with a C average and good attendance.

Another principal once asked Gradillas how he could justify tougher discipline and more difficult courses if they led more students to drop out. "Kids do drop out," Gradillas said, "but no one has shown it is because the school has rules or requires homework. And the kid who fails algebra: Is there any guarantee he would not have failed simple basic math if we had let him take just that?"

He had prepared a chart that some people did not like. It showed that he had reduced the number of shop and home economics classes from 112 to 42 in just one year. He had been principal at Garfield longer than anyone else in recent memory. Maybe he had burned too many bridges Downtown to expect anything more. So be it. He could at least put Garfield on solid ground.

Beltrán had written a note at the bottom of a daily quiz: "Help! I Need Help!" He had gotten only two out of eight right. Jiménez initially dismissed it as a joke. Beltrán was the first to groan in sarcastic agony whenever Jiménez declared a night without homework, or to pretend great glee when the load of nightly problems climbed over the fifty mark.

Jiménez usually assigned ten to forty problems a night. Like Escalante, he did not have time to check them all, but kept track of who turned the work in and who did not. The daily quizzes were his monitoring device. A student who performed poorly on a quiz had not done the homework or had copied it from a friend.

Beltrán had missed school for three straight days. He habitually cut school when he began to fall behind. He told himself he would use the time to catch up at home, rather than sit in class and pretend to listen to boring lectures. Sometimes he actually did some work, but lately he had been feeling sluggish. He felt like he had spent his whole life doing homework. He came home and lay on his mother's bed watching "People's Court" or "CHiPs" or "Little House on the Prairie." He fell asleep, arose for dinner, jogged at ELAC, played basketball or lifted weights, and then went home to bed.

In class he appointed himself Jiménez's principal tormentor. He never let the muscular, wavy-haired instructor forget he had once been proclaimed best-looking male teacher in the yearbook. *"Sexo! Sexo!"* Beltrán shouted if Jiménez wore one of his laser-bright Hawaiian shirts. To a Jiménez request, Beltrán responded politely, "Yes, Your Buffness," a reference to the deep-chested Jiménez physique. Jiménez blushed. "How *cute!*" a girl said. "He's *embarrassed.*"

Beltrán had to ration his fun. Jiménez became very testy if interrupted too frequently. He prided himself on presenting the subject matter in a logical way, each equation large and clear on the board, followed by neat note taking by his students and orderly examinations and quizzes. Jiménez could see, from the work he received at the beginning of the term, that other mathematics teachers were willing to accept a great deal of slop. Some students grasped a few threads of the concept but could not weave them together because no one had ever insisted they write neatly, or sketch diagrams. He was not surprised, having seen the way some teachers wrote on the board.

He could not blame them too much. There were only so many hours in the day and so many dollars in the paycheck. He himself taught basic mathematics to adults three nights a week. Margie Zavala and Mai Phung were still slipping into his room sixth period for their underground calculus BC class. He had no time even for his beloved workouts, unless he pried himself out of bed at 4:00 A.M.

There were also the demands of playing middleman between Escalante and Shiroishi. Escalante had been complaining about what he considered Shiroishi's latest atrocity—she had let a student drop Calculus BC because, Escalante thought, the boy's father feared it would hurt his grade-point average. Actually, the boy had suffered a nervous breakdown, something Shiroishi felt she could not disclose.

Jiménez thought Shiroishi, a fellow graduate of Roosevelt High, did a fine job. The magnet kids were no smarter than the regular student body. They had family problems and academic weaknesses like everyone else, and Shiroishi was familiar with every last one of them.

His nonmagnet students were another story. Beltrán was hurting, and Jiménez did not know if anyone else noticed. The cry for help, he concluded, was not a joke. Beltrán livened up the class. The other kids liked him. He talked to everybody. But something had gone wrong, and his teacher was going to have to fix it.

Orozco handed the cross-country coach his calculus ten-week failure notice and stood back. Orozco was a terrible cross-country runner. He was too tall, too heavy, and too prone to muse on the meaning of life or work on his Reagan imitation when he was supposed to be concentrating on the man ahead of him. But the cross-country coach did not like surprises, and the F at the ten-week marking period would force Orozco to drop cross-country altogether under the rules of eligibility for extracurricular activities.

The coach used words so new to the boy's vocabulary that he made a mental note of them. Orozco thought he deserved it. He could not absorb the basic concepts of calculus. It was his first-period class. He could not concentrate that early in the morning.

Escalante had been friendly when he handed him the slip. "I am sorry," he said. "But you're doing lousy." But in class he was very stern.

Olga García noticed the same mood in fourth period, Calculus BC. Escalante did not joke. He was all business. Orozco, having just read about Italian fascism, began to refer to him as Escalini, but the calculus teacher was not the only sour face in Orozco's life. Woessner had just tossed one of his history chapter outlines back at him: "This isn't worth a damn, Raúl."

Escalante stroked his problem children. He teased them, tugged them, scolded them, did everything he could to get their attention. At 3:00 P.M. several students appeared for disciplinary detention, supervised homework, or another Escalante trademark—the "correction action." Anyone who missed four or more on a standard quiz of fifteen questions had twenty-four hours to present a paper showing each incorrect problem correctly solved, twice, with a written explanation of the mistake. Only when dealing with the tenderest egos did Escalante fail to suggest, usually with a smile, that the student was on the brink of disaster.

Margarita Herrera, a counselor at ELAC, visited his fifth-period class. After adjusting to the youthful shouts of "Late! Late!" that greeted anyone arriving after the bell, she surveyed the posters and the inspirational sayings on the walls and remarked how proud everyone in the class must be of their achievements.

A boy whispered loudly from his seat near the back of the room, "Everybody in this class is *failing*."

Escalante told other mathematics teachers to send discipline problems to him. Dispatch the kid to MH-1 with a note that said simply "Coke" or "Pepsi"—he would not discriminate against any brand—and he would know it was time to motivate that student.

Teachers outside the department had heard of Escalante's generosity and occasionally sent over some of their own problems, if they thought the student knew Escalante. Gabriel León, a 6-foot-1, 225-pound football linebacker, had called one teacher a "greaseball" and soon found himself in MH-1.

"Gabriel, this is a big mistake you made. You see?"

"I know."

"You trying to make a good impression but you losing ground. If he flunks you, period, I'm gonna flunk you too."

"Why? You can't do that."

"That's true. *You* can't do that. My kids never do that. You gonna flunk this class."

"Come on, no."

"Yeah, that's it, Gabriel. You made the big mistake. I gonna talk to the teacher. You maybe apologize, maybe she give you something better than a fail."

Adolfo Mata was an effervescent senior basketball guard and Alex Zayas a quiet, tall junior forward. They were close friends. Zayas had missed a month of trigonometry during the summer because of a family vacation in Mexico. Mata—he liked to be called "Magic" Mata—usually had two or three girls on a string and found it difficult to leave a basketball game, any basketball game, to do homework. Escalante told them frequently they would never make the NBA, so why bother? They laughed and went back to dreaming about raising their scoring average, although undersized Garfield lost most of its games.

What they liked about Escalante's class was the spirit of cama- raderie, the jokes, the pep talks about the AP, and especially the warm- up. Zayas and Mata were both in period 5 and tried to shake the foundations and let the entire school know they were warming up. Queen's rendition of "We Are the Champions/We Will Rock You" vibrated from the stereo, a signal to begin.

Thump, thump. Clap.

Thump, thump. Clap!

Thump, thump. Clap.

Thump! Thump! Clap!

The entire class pounded desktops and the concrete floor in rhythm at Escalante's signal. When that built to a crescendo, they attempted a wave, standing and then sitting row by row to create the impression of a spurt of ocean foam moving over the surface of the class.

"Yip, yip, yip, *eeeeeeeeeeeyyoooooouuu*," Escalante shouted.

"*Eeeeeeeeaaaaaaayyyyyyooooooouuu*," the class replied, pointed fingers sweeping across the room. "Kill 'em! Kill 'em!"

"*Bulldogs! Bulldogs! Bulldogs!*"

Dorothy Fromel had gone through some rocky moments in her life. Back home in North Carolina her parents divorced when she was three. Her own first two marriages failed. A student had once grabbed and terrorized her in an empty Garfield classroom. But by the fall of 1986, she liked just about everything about her life, except the burden of doing Jaime Escalante's job for him.

Her third husband, an evangelical Christian like herself, was doing well in the automobile repair business. Their marriage was solid. They had a nice house in Tujunga, up in the dry semirural hills of north-western Los Angeles.

She felt her skill as a high school mathematics teacher had reached a satisfying level, particularly in dealing with students struggling with basic mathematics. Her job at Garfield, mathematics resource teacher for the Chapter 1 program, did not give her a regular classroom, but she had much time and money to help other teachers. She tried to develop new programs and work with students with special problems.

That left Escalante, and what she felt had become her role as the de facto chair of the mathematics department.

Escalante still hated meetings. As certainly as the x-axis intersects the y-axis, he did not attend them. The regular monthly mathematics department meetings had ended the day he became chair. He refused to leave his students for the monthly gathering of all department heads in the library. No one bothered to inform him anymore of the district-level meetings held every few months; they knew he would not go.

Some members of the mathematics department, as well as other departments, applauded his resolve. Jiménez noted that before Escalante had become chair, there had been much talk but little action. Now it was the opposite. Fromel wondered if this was an entirely good thing.

The Chapter 1 program provided federal money to inner city schools with large numbers of poverty-level students. The money allowed Garfield to support a few unusual nonclassroom jobs, like Fromel's, whose duties were sometimes difficult to define. The mathematics resource teacher could, if she chose, sit and shuffle papers and wait for the occasional student referral. Fromel recalled one predecessor who seemed to do little more than play chess—a way, he said, to stimulate student interest in sequence, geometry, and other mathematical concepts.

Fromel had taken the job with the approval of Gradillas, Escalante, and everyone else involved. She had a demonstrated talent for teaching basic mathematics. She thought she could help the many inexperienced, emergency-credential teachers joining the department. She did not like to see a student receive a B and still not know how to divide. She wanted a standard curriculum for basic mathematics and Algebra 1.

Since Escalante refused to go to meetings, or read the mountain of reports, district memos, state work sheets, contest announcements, and promotional materials addressed to the mathematics department, Fromel felt obliged to pick up the slack. The meetings and correspondence filled up so much of her time that her own projects lagged.

She had her doubts about the long-range impact of the calculus program. She wondered if those kids had the talent to compete at the college level in higher mathematics. In the long run, would calculus in high school do them any good?

If Escalante was going to spend all his time with them over in MH-1, somebody should be reading the mail and going to meetings. And she did not want that somebody to be her.

Escalante had been receptive in early 1986 to her suggestion that they look for someone to take over the chair. He said he would ask Jiménez, but reported back that the younger teacher said he was too busy. When school began again in September, he still seemed agreeable to handing over the title, so she asked Jiménez again. He still declined. Lydia Trujillo was the only other teacher in the department with the appropriate experience and professional background, but she also said no.

This was too much, Fromel thought. She was even scheduling classes for Escalante now. She was the one who pointed out to him that one of his teachers seemed to be missing class because of a family problem. She decided to call an election.

Fourteen of the seventeen department members, including Escalante, signed the petition. A meeting date was set. Then Brian Wallace showed Escalante a copy of the note Fromel had written giving her reason for the meeting: "He is not fulfilling any of his responsibilities as d.c."

Mount St. Escalante erupted. This, he suddenly realized, was the ultimate sabotage by someone he considered a bored administrator. She wanted all the fractions reduced and the decimals carried out to nine places, but she did not know how to motivate kids in a classroom. If he let an administrator kick him around like this, the whole program could grind to a halt.

He chose his favorite option: He resigned as chair. Then, still agitated and depressed, he waited to see what would happen.

260

Shortly before the scheduled election, Fromel had persuaded one woman, an outgoing, if inexperienced, algebra-geometry teacher named Roberta Hernández, to consider taking the job. Escalante would not have it. He liked Bobbie, he said, but she was not a mathematics major and had no regular credential. The other department members learned that Escalante was upset and signed a petition supporting him. The minute the story reached Gradillas, he told Fromel to back off.

She gave up and returned to her office, wondering how anyone could run a school that way. It would not be her last clash with Escalante.

17

It was about nine o'clock in the evening, early in February, when Esparza heard her mother coming up to her room. What was going on? The converted attic was Esparza's refuge, the place where she did the homework and earned the grades that made her mother so proud and hopeful. The woman usually did not disturb her daughter's concentration.

Life with two AP classes had hit Esparza a little harder than she had expected. Woessner handed out enormous assignments, always due in two weeks, with a warning that she ration her time, like a college student. She rarely did. Escalante assigned homework every day, but some essential concepts of calculus were eluding her.

Escalante liked her because she tried. Despite a rash of failing quiz grades, she received a B for the semester. A gift, she thought. If only fate had been so generous in some other parts of her life.

"Désirée, you don't look too well, is something wrong?" Her mother had come into the room. Oh God, she had asked the question. Esparza was not ready for this.

"No, I'm fine, Mama."

"Well, I think we better have a doctor look at you."

"Really, Mama, it's just I have all this work."

"It won't hurt to check."

All right, Désirée, she said to herself, you were going to tell her soon anyway. She wished Ramiro was there.

"Mama, there is something."

"Uh huh?"

"Mama, I'm pregnant. We went to the clinic. They checked already."

"I see." The woman was very calm and quiet, frighteningly so. "Well, that's it, I guess. I guess you're not going to graduate. We'll just have to make other plans."

Esparza began to cry. That was precisely what she did not want to hear.

"If you want to stop this happening to you, let me know. We could get something done about it."

The girl shook with sobbing. "No, Mama, I *want* it. I want the baby."

Her mother could not find any more words. She quietly walked back down the stairs.

Esparza continued to weep as the shock gradually wore off. Then she stopped and thought. She looked at the calculus textbook in front of her. She still had homework to do. She looked at a problem, and tasted something: adrenaline, anger, pride?

She could at least do her homework. And maybe she could prove something to her mother, and to Escalante, and to everybody.

She plowed through work, staying up until 1:00 A.M., much longer than she had been able to concentrate in some time.

When at home, in the light green wooden house with the big plants and enormous plastic awnings, Orozco rarely left the living room. There were not too many other places in the house to go. This seemed to him an efficient use of time and space.

Besides the three red couches, the small room had a blue rug, light blue flowered wallpaper, and a record player. A medium-sized television that worked sat on top of a huge console television that did not. There was a small electric clock to wake him and the refrigerator to sustain him in the kitchen just across the tiny front hall. He could use the kitchen table to study, if he got there before one of his older sisters did. Orozco slept on the living room floor, usually with a sleeping bag or blankets to cushion or cover him. He thought the hard surface was good for his back. Often he nodded off while his sisters were still watching television.

He was struggling in school. Everybody expected so much of him. He joked in class, and that was supposed to mean he was bright. But he had never been on the gifted list. He remembered the test they had given him in the second grade: make or break, genius or dunce. There was a picture of a man on a bicycle beside a picture of a truck. The truck was smaller, at least in the picture.

"Which one do you think is heavier?" the lady asked.

Orozco recalled being overwhelmed by the possibilities. The bicycle might have been made of lead. The truck could be papier-mâché. The man on the bicycle resembled Fats Domino; that would certainly make a difference.

"The man on the bicycle," he said. He assumed that was why they never put him in the gifted program.

His life seemed to move in cycles. Even-numbered grades were bad. Middle grades—eighth grade in junior high, eleventh grade in senior high—were worse. Ill health bothered him in the eighth grade, or at least that was what he told his mother when he did not want to go to school. Now, in the eleventh grade, he really had been sick— a bacterial infection of the throat that pushed his temperature up to 104 degrees.

The fever had gone but he still felt listless, and having calculus first period did not help. The class was relatively small for Escalante, only twenty-nine students, and quiet. Everyone complained about period 5, a noisy animal house of fifty-one students, but that might have helped keep him awake.

They were knocking on her door again. Juanita Gutiérrez had her own room, the one advantage of being the only daughter, but she was also the eldest child, and that brought many responsibilities. If Octavio, fourteen; Jacinto, twelve; Israel, eleven; Oscar, nine; or Said, six, had difficulty with their homework, they went to her. She comforted her friends in their unhappy romances. She did the grocery shopping and took her brothers to the doctor—her mother had no driver's license. Yet her father insisted on knowing where she was going if she extended a toenail outside the front door. She was mortified when, at the June "Farewell to School" dance, she looked up and saw him standing behind the disc jockeys. He was watching her like a proctor during finals week.

It was getting to be too much. Her brothers demanded help with five different homework assignments. Her friends telephoned for advice. Her hair had to be put up in rollers every night. She tried to start on her homework by 8:00 P.M., but the house did not quiet down until 10:00, when the boys went to bed.

Escalante was pushing her, although gently. She leaned on Cong Lam, another junior in period 5. He would get a 5 for sure on the AP test, she thought. Usually he would make suggestions and then insist she work the problem herself. Once she had the answer, he would force her to describe the process to him, to make certain she understood.

She was staying up until midnight now, sometimes beyond. It had been so hard to grasp the basics, and once she had, everyone else had jumped ahead. She gritted her teeth every time she missed a negative sign lurking outside a function. The secret agent, Escalante called it. She hated it.

Pulgarin had been dismissed as a religious nut by most of the people he knew at Garfield. He was also considered something of a foreigner with his slight Colombian accent. He remained pleasant and friendly, if painfully quiet. Other students sensed he was lonely, and they were right.

Each evening he sat in the wreck of an easy chair, his designated spot, and did his homework. A tiny lamp table was his only desk. His mother might have been able to afford a better place if she had found work outside the garment industry, but undocumented aliens had to take what they could get.

Both she and her son had arrived before 1982. They qualified for amnesty and legal status under the Immigration Reform and Control Act of 1986, but she trembled at the thought of approaching the immigration authorities after all those years of avoiding them. Her job and their cramped living room were what God had provided, and they would make the best of it.

In calculus, Pulgarin felt himself slipping. He was taking trigonometry at the same time. The two classes reinforced each other to some extent, but in calculus he noticed his lack of a solid foundation. Some of the top-of-the-period quizzes were so far removed from what he understood that he did not turn them in. All the little F's began to pile up.

Escalante, sensing Pulgarin's shyness, treated him like a delicate rose. The boy often came after 3:00 P.M. to do his homework in MH-1 and seek help from tutors or friends. He would leave at five or six o'clock, take the bus home and study for three or four hours in his chair, glancing at the little black-and-white television only when there was a game on.

At 11:00 P.M. he stopped. For ten minutes he read the Bible—an old *Reina Valera* edition his mother kept on a shelf. He stretched out on the floor, prayed to God for strength and wisdom, and fell asleep.

Beltrán did not see the point in working so hard in calculus any longer. He did not plan to use mathematics in the future. Some concepts came clear; some did not. Even taking a few days off from school never helped him catch up. At the end of the first semester, Jiménez gave him a D.

He told his friends, Conrad Dungca and Gilbert Valenzuela, that he was through. He was ranking out—meaning, he had had enough. They were stunned. "You've put a whole year into this, man," Dungca said. "You can't quit now."

Margie Zavala was doing her Calculus BC and correcting papers for Jiménez when she noticed Beltrán's distress. This was a job for a cheerleader. "That's the way I felt," she told him, "but it goes away. Don't give up." Beltrán appreciated the encouragement. He realized how little he would be sharing with his friends if he dropped calculus. But it was a real pain, and he did not think it would get better.

Escalante had one pregnant student in Algebra 2 and a teenage mother in trigonometry. He scheduled sex education talks at the beginning of the year, one for boys, one for girls, but not everyone listened. He blamed the priests. They filled these girls with church doctrine and never considered the awful reality of having a baby at sixteen. Esparza sensed his attitude and did not tell him her news.

Norma Huizar and Juana Valdez and her other close friends understood, but word leaked out to the rest of the school. Huizar clucked in dismay at the stares Esparza received when they walked across the mall together to AP history.

Esparza approached the teachers who could make or break her: Dennis Campagna, who taught the American literature half of the AP history two-course unit, and Tom Woessner. Campagna said he would not hold it against her, but he had to be honest, he thought she had made a serious mistake. Woessner enfolded her in his large, sad eyes and told her everything would be all right. You can do it, he said. You can pass this test and have your baby too. It was exactly what she wanted to hear.

Ed Martin, her counselor, stopped to ask what summer school courses she planned. When she told him why she could not go to

summer school, he flinched in surprise. Then he rallied. He promised
to inform Escalante, a chore she dreaded, and suggested she might
like to meet a Garfield graduate he knew. The young woman had had
a baby in her junior year also, but had gotten a 3 in AP calculus the
next year and was now a premed at UCLA. Her little boy was in the
university day-care program, and everything seemed fine.

Escalante reacted just as she feared. Another one had blown it, he
thought. She felt him ignoring her, talking to Norma as if there was
no one else there. She would show him.

Gradillas shaved off his mustache, a sign of peace and love in the
second semester. Usually he grew it toward the end of the school year.
He felt it gave him an air of unassailable authority just as tempers
ran short and parents sensed that the picky rules laid down by that
high-handed Gradillas might keep their child from graduating.

People who saw his mustache, he was convinced, called him Mr.
Gradillas, not Henry; gave him compliments, not teacher grievances.
Or they just stayed out of his way.

He had grown the thing over the summer because he thought most
of his problems would come in the first semester this year. There had
been a fair number of them, but now his teachers were getting restless
about the endless district salary renegotiations. One of his coaches,
in a fit of rage over some missing baseballs, had set fire to part of the
gym.

Mustache or no mustache, Gradillas was determined to enjoy the
year. It might be his last in this job.

Escalante prowled MH-1 like a caged bulldog. He hated vacations.
They gave too many of them in the middle of the year—Christmas,
Martin Luther King Day, semester break. Whenever he thought he
could get away with it, he scheduled a class on a holiday. He assigned
homework the last day of the first semester that was due the first day
of the second semester. He planned two full mornings of school during
spring vacation. He had stored twenty weeks of work in these kids'
dark-haired computers, and he could not bear to let a long fallow
period wipe it out.

He was, as usual, telephoning the parents of missing or faltering
students. The threat of a call was more useful than the call itself,
particularly if he reminded the students of his weakness for hyperbole.
"I hate to go to your house and talk to your mom and so on, because

267

I always say everything negative," he told his trigonometry class. "I don't know why I have that tendency. For instance, if you miss one class, I will say, 'I remember he missed two or three classes.' If you don't pay attention one day when I ask a question, I'll say, 'He never pays attention,' and that is one of my weak points."

Escalante cornered a group of his after-school quarantine students and checked their detention slips, issued for various misdeeds. "Okay, I'm going to look over these papers one more time. What happens if I get one more of these papers?"

"To the dean?"

"Right. And if I get another one after that?"

"To Jordan."

"Right! I like that. Very good."

He began to focus, in a desultory manner, on raising money to subsidize his students' AP fees. He had promised they would only have to pay five dollars of the required twenty-nine dollars. The actual fee was fifty-three dollars, but Bennett always requested the reduced fee for disadvantaged students for everyone at Garfield. The College Board never objected.

Bennett had experience with Escalante's fund-raising schemes. He objected to the calculus teacher promising his students such a large subsidy, but Escalante ignored him. He had several boxes of chocolate bars left over from a previous fund drive. Students in need of a snack, and in the vicinity of MH-1, stopped in, handed him fifty cents, and helped themselves.

Orozco studied the long hairs crosshatching Escalante's balding skull. "With all that money you could get a hair transplant."

Escalante stared back. "With all this money I could send some kids from here to South America. Just like what happened to Che Guevara. They sent him to Bolivia by accident, and in two shots, no more Che."

Emily Hernández made her usual afternoon appearance in Escalante's office and promptly fell asleep. She was Jiménez's calculus student, but Escalante had a much more comfortable chair. She awoke, again her bright and bubbly self, to find Orozco there. "Walk with me to ELAC, Raúl," she cooed, but he was engaged in a battle of wills with Escalante. Orozco insisted he had done a problem correctly. Escalante disagreed. Orozco began to shout across the room, "Conspiracy! It's a *conspiracy.*"

Escalante looked toward Hernández, who shrugged and gave the teacher back his chair. "I don't know anything about it, Kimo. I'm an innocent child of God. Failing, but innocent."

In its April Fools' Day issue, the *Garfield Log* headlined Gradillas's campaign for the U.S. presidency "to fight Communism and defend the American way." Colonel Oliver North would serve as campaign manager, the newspaper reported.

A second article appeared under a picture of Calculus AB student and graduation speaker Rolando Cerna. The boy appeared to be holding his hands protectively over the thick hair on his head. "Escalante has been figuring out calculus for nearly all his life, and now he is losing his hair from pulling it out while trying to solve problems made up by himself. . . . He is at the present time looking for a hair donor. Anyone interested in donating hair should report to MH-1 after school. If studying can't help you pass the class, maybe a little of your hair might do the trick."

Escalante saw he was going to need more money. A lady from the cafeteria had dumped the invoice on his desk and the arithmetic seemed almost right:

Cafeteria Account no. 8679
Invoice prepared by: Lucille Washington
Customer: Jaime Escalante
Type of event: for Saturday feeding

Quantity	Unit Price	Amount Due	
750 apples	093	69.75	
750 milks	015	11.05	
		80.80	subtotal
		8.08	sales tax
		88.88	total

   Mr. Escalante: Cafeteria needs a check for this invoice payable to Garfield High School cafeteria. Thank you.

His salary at Garfield was now about $32,000 a year. With $4,000 for teaching summer school at ELAC and about $6,000 for his night school classes, he made $42,000 before taxes.

His mortgage was low. Jaimito was on his own. Fernando had not yet started college. An occasional donor helped with lunches and breakfasts for the summer program. The ARCO Foundation was giving $25,000 to support the summer sessions, and Jack Dirmann at the Foundation for Advancements in Science and Education still found grants here and there. He was very fortunate in his friends, he thought, but it was still a struggle. When Dirmann wangled a $10,000 grant from Anheuser-Busch, Gradillas objected to any link between schoolchildren and a beer company.

Escalante felt he needed money to motivate. It was something these kids understood. In his Algebra 2 class at the beginning of the second semester, he discussed the summer classes, a way for them to accelerate their program and be on the calculus team the following year. "Here is the application. If you qualify, your family income low enough, you gonna get a job, make a thousand dollars over the whole summer." He hinted at more money in tutoring jobs for those who succeeded in Calculus AB.

He was not entirely pleased with how the money was spent. A week after his Calculus BC students received their tutoring checks, they appeared at school in new blouses and shirts. Sandra Muñoz waged only occasional war against her weight problem; he was certain much of her money disappeared at McDonald's.

The nursing building classroom at ELAC rattled and buzzed on Saturdays with the sounds of students checking work with each other, consulting tutors, chewing Laura Scudder's caramel corn, corn chips, barbecued potato chips, and tortilla chips. Escalante motivated them with the prospect of a midmorning break—a chance to purchase more crunchy carbohydrates. They would have no snack unless they did what he wanted them to do.

Escalante wished it was that easy to influence the teachers he wanted in the program. He and Madrid and Gradillas had combed the junior highs for help, with little luck. Most teachers did not like the idea of staying in class after 3:00 P.M. They seemed distressed that the late afternoon work brought no more money, just a chance to teach in the summer. They could do that anyway, and in an easier subject, without Escalante looking over their shoulder.

There was one exception, a man who had *insisted* Escalante take him on. His name was Angelo Villavicencio. He taught mathematics at Bell High School. His principal and department chair would not listen to his ideas for new courses, he told Escalante. They did not think pushing Advanced Placement mathematics would do anybody any good.

Villavicencio grew up in Managua, Nicaragua, and came to the United States when he was twenty to study engineering at California State Polytechnic, Pomona, Jaimito's school. He found more satisfaction in teaching. He saw how much more of the modern world a student could appreciate and how much better a job he could find if he grasped early the mysteries of a curved line. But the mathematics department chair at Bell told him, "I don't believe high school students should take calculus."

At Escalante's insistence, Gradillas nudged aside several bureaucratic obstacles and arranged Villavicencio's transfer to Garfield.

Jiménez dropped seven of his fifty students after the first semester. He would have dropped eight, but Beltrán objected so strenuously that he left him alone, despite a score of four out of twenty-five on his last test.

Escalante found it difficult to drop anyone after the trouble he had taken to keep them from dropping themselves. He let three go in first period, and five in fifth period, still leaving him eighty-three to prepare for the Calculus AB examination. One student, always a problem despite his 3 in Calculus AB, was forced to leave the BC class as well as the school after his arrest for car theft. He had finally discovered an offense that really could get a student sent to another high school three bus transfers away.

Calculus could not cure all the world's ills, but that did not diminish its reputation at Garfield in early 1987. Yuen Chau, a senior struggling in Calculus BC, editorialized in the *Garfield Log*:

ARE YOU FOLDING UNDER PRESSURE?

Students in other countries such as Japan and the Soviet Union attend school six days a week, along with night classes. The average U.S. student's time spent in front of the television exceeds the time in school over 2000 hours a year.

Without pressure on students, the educational system is only denying students of the reality of the competitive world we live in. . . . Many drop out of school while others try to run away from their problems. Being able to work out the stress of growing up in society can be assisted by a counselor or school administrator. . . . [But] if students can not compete at the same educational level with students in other countries, our human resources will diminish.

When Escalante and Jiménez joined a one-day picket and walk-out in February to dramatize the union's fight for a 15 percent pay raise, the *Garfield Log* put their pictures on the front page. A student gave Escalante a sign: I 4 CALCULUS.

Esparza pulled the hooded sheet back off her face. In her best approximation of a molasses-thick Georgia accent, she addressed Woessner's history class.

"We aren't gonna be overtaken by those niggers. Since World War I, a lot of foreigners have been coming over to the United States. We true Americans must protect our land from foreigners, as well as from Negroes, Jews, Orientals, and Roman Catholics. It is foreigners and Negroes who make my life and the lives of all other Anglo-Saxons intolerable."

The harsh words of the Ku Klux Klan seemed odd, almost comic, coming from the mouth of a tiny Latina half hidden behind the lectern. It was Roaring Twenties day in Room 723. Each student in AP American history picked a group or personality of that era, assumed their persona, and presented a report that illuminated a social issue. Woessner heard from Gutiérrez on the flappers of the 1920s and women's rights. Esparza's friend Norma Huizar did Bartolomeo Vanzetti in an old brown coat and hat and a slight Italian accent.

Woessner watched Esparza detail the history of the Klan and marveled at the venom issuing from this sweet, gentle mother-to-be. "You all can hiss and boo if you wish," he told the class. He could have done without her final theatrical touch—a black Cabbage Patch doll hanging by the neck from a rope dangling over the front blackboard. He had it taken down the minute she was done.

Orozco came next. "You can't be Ronald Reagan, Raúl," Woessner said. The boy wore an old black coat, white dress shirt, black bow tie, blue jeans, and gray Reeboks. He had a pencil stuck behind one ear. He abandoned the lectern and perched on his desk or strolled the aisles as he spoke. His southern accent was better than Esparza's.

"My name is E. K. Hornbeck, correspondent for the *Baltimore Herald*. I was present at the Scopes Trial in Dayton, Tennessee, otherwise known as the Monkey Trial, because one John Scopes was prosecuted for teaching evolutionary theory in the public high schools."

He described the dramatic courtroom presence of William Jennings Bryan, attorney for the prosecution, former candidate for president, and "fundamentalist preacher who would go around saying, 'Hallelujah, hallelujah. You're saved!'" Orozco dashed from desk to desk. He placed both hands on each student's head and repeated the blessing.

The trial, he said, was a symbol of changing attitudes toward science. He spoke of Clarence Darrow's procedural defeats and his great inspiration in putting Bryan on the witness stand.

"John Scopes was a modern man. The trial symbolized the change in the 1920s: Should we go back to old-fashioned ways, or should we change?"

Orozco was done. He sighed in relief as he sat down and pulled something out of his coat pocket.

"Well, I don't know about you," he said, "but as for myself, I have a strange craving for one of these." He devoured a very large, ripe banana.

It was the crunch point, six weeks before the May 11 AP calculus examination. Escalante put entire rows of students on quarantine. Jiménez cut his sleep down to four hours a night. They turned the Saturday morning sessions into mini-AP tests. Students struggled with questions from old tests and listened intently while their teachers explained their mistakes.

At the same time, seniors worried about college. This ritual had less of the frantic quality found in more affluent neighborhoods. Olga García laughed when friends came back from visits to her first choice, Occidental College, and complained about the small dorm rooms. Perhaps they would like to see my room at home, she thought, and the three people I share it with.

Pulgarin felt himself sinking into a pit of unholy depression. He sat in his cramped living room, idly listening to the radio, letting his mind wander while his notebooks lay stacked neatly nearby, untouched.

No one liked him. Despite his curly hair and delicate features, he was convinced girls thought him ugly. The only people who showed any interest in him were gang leaders or coke dealers, and he had had enough of them. He found it hard to concentrate. Escalante had handed out a three-page paper listing the basic concepts of calculus. He thought he knew only half of them.

He had told his mother how he felt, and she cried. He would have to stop telling her things like that. He spoke to Pastor Galino at the Hispanic Baptist Church. They explored the inferiority complex he carried with him from his first days in America. He put his faith in the Lord, and that made him feel a little better, but that did not mean he knew enough calculus. He was not sure Escalante would even let him take the test. He would have to do his work, and show what he could do.

Gutiérrez felt Escalante gently goading her, warning that she was slipping too far behind. Woessner told her she was performing far below her capabilities.

Beltrán began to turn in his quizzes, even the bad ones, when Jiménez explained he gave some credit for even one question right. Spanish was giving him trouble—that annoying Castilian vocabulary. But he had Wallace's economics class, where he enjoyed the free exchange of opinion and the feeling that there, at least, right and wrong could not always be worked out to the last decimal.

Orozco missed Escalante's spring vacation review classes, as well as the first two days of the following week. He thought he understood now how the 1982 cheating charge arose. Escalante piled on these old examination questions, over and over and over until you could not help but do them all the same way. It was boring. He played with Laser, his pet bulldog, jet black with a stripe down the middle. He shot baskets.

The year before, when he thought of taking the AP Spanish test, his mother had noted his general listlessness and refused to give him the money. This year he needed thirty dollars; five dollars for his share of the calculus test fee, fifteen dollars for history, and (he would not tell her this part) ten dollars for the yearbook.

He tried a different approach: "Mom, if you don't lend me the money something terrible might happen to the car."

In the last six weeks before every AP examination, Escalante developed an urge to teach some concept he thought had tripped his students the year before. This year it was domains and range, and also volumes—the formula that had brought on the troubles of 1982. And he wondered if he had not neglected relative rate of change. And absolute value, and limits, and continuity. Even the basics needed a light brushing off.

But every year he missed something. The solution was to ensure everyone was prepared, and then keep them loose. He did not want anyone paralyzed by fright like poor Leticia Arambula in 1979.

Nicknames seemed to build confidence. The several Elizabeth Taylors and Jacqueline Onassises christened each year liked their notoriety and the sense of a special place in Escalante's heart. One tiny girl with bleached blond hair, third row, four back in Algebra 2, had been dubbed Madonna—the rock singer, not the Holy Virgin—and rushed home to tell her mother.

Escalante also tried to leaven the mood of the final drilling sessions with a few stories. "I don't know if you remember, last week we had an open house. And few of you brought anybody over here because you all know you're failing. But anyhow, that day a grandmother came and said, 'I know my grandson is failing, he's not doing his homework assignment. I want you to know that he is not living with his mother.' I asked why, and she said, 'His mother beat him.' "

A few in the class gasped.

"And I said, 'Wow, does the father know that?' And she says, 'Yeah, he knows that and he beats him too.' I said, 'Golly, well, this is no choice, you have to take care of your grandson. What's wrong with him living with you?'

" 'He doesn't want to live with me either. He wants to live with the Dodgers.'

" 'What? The Dodgers? Why?'

" 'Because, the Dodgers don't beat anybody.' "

After the aborted chairmanship election, Escalante and Fromel observed a frosty truce. Reports and studies and surveys from the state and Downtown still flowed into the mathematics resource office. Escalante continued to ignore them. He was convinced that twenty-five years of personal trial and error had shown what worked and what did not. Fromel was equally determined to share the work of professors who felt that research—running surveys, collating data, weighting results for race, sex, income, and national origin—would bring truth.

Escalante had never forgotten the day in 1974 when he discovered some basic mathematics teachers were allowing students to carry pocket-sized, laminated copies of the multiplication tables to assist on their examinations. In March 1987 he walked into the classroom of a new basic mathematics teacher, a midsemester replacement, and found the man had given every student a calculator, purchased with Chapter 1 funds by Fromel.

At a faculty meeting he made a rare appearance and expressed his astonishment forcefully. "These kids don't even know the *times tables*! How can they be doing this? I saw some of the problems on the board, 32 times 4; 33 times 6, and they *used the calculator*!" He pointed out that calculators were banned from the AP calculus examination. He did not even permit them in trigonometry. Students had to use the tables in the back of the book, just as students had done for decades.

Fromel sat stunned in the back of the room. This was the last straw, she thought. She photocopied some of the latest reports from the California Math Framework and the school district mathematics advisers and gave them to Gradillas, Escalante, and some other mathematics teachers. Analysis of seventy-nine research projects showed calculators had a positive effect from kindergarten through twelfth grade, with the exception of grade 4. The National Council of Teachers of Mathematics, the Conference Board of the Mathematical Sciences, the Mathematical Sciences Education Board, and the National Science Board had all recommended that calculators be used throughout mathematics instruction and testing.

Experts and national panels did not impress Escalante. People like that had told him he had no chance teaching calculus to Chicano kids. Students had to learn to use their brains. The California Test of Basic Skills (CTBS), the SAT, and every other important standardized test used to measure Garfield students prohibited the use of calculators. The AP calculus test had allowed them in 1985, then reimposed the ban when calculators became capable of performing the most complex operations. Escalante did not want crutches in his school.

Gradillas listened, and called Fromel in. He told her he had decided to remove her as Chapter 1 mathematics resource teacher and assign her to a new support resource center, a special classroom for students with severe learning problems.

She pleaded with him to let her finish the year in the mathematics department. She wanted to leave Garfield and find someplace where she could teach mathematics, but she did not want to sit in a room and struggle with kids she would only see for a few weeks. When Gradillas insisted, she quit and retreated to her home in Tujunga.

She had left a memo, her last word on the calculator controversy, in Gradillas's office mailbox. "I was unaware," she said, "of some unwritten law at Garfield that Mr. Escalante's opinion is the only opinion there is."

Escalante and Jiménez felt they were slipping and sliding while they pulled a very large weight up a hill. About 130 students—you could never tell who might lose nerve at the last minute—appeared ready to take Calculus AB or BC. Some, of course, were thinking more about the senior prom than AP mathematics. A young woman sought Escalante's opinion on several swatches of pink and lavender material. Adolfo "Magic" Mata, less confident off the basketball court, asked Escalante if he should take Gabby or María to the dance. Throughout weekday and Saturday classes, notes circulated speculating on the likelihood of various pairings. Hoots and giggles echoed through MH-1 when María flinched as Escalante shifted the overhead projector toward her desk. "Do not be afraid, María," the teacher said loudly. "I am not Adolfo."

George Madrid dreaded this time of year. Escalante seemed ready to castrate him if he did not come up with enough money to subsidize the AP student fees. He dislodged a $1,500 contribution from ELAC Chicanos for Creative Medicine, but before he could congratulate himself, he heard Escalante complaining about the fund-raising car wash he and the kids had organized. Sure, it was just two days before the examination, but it would be fun—a chance to work off some tension and size up members of the opposite sex in skimpy, soggy clothing. He realized that no one at San Marino High School ever had to rub down a car to earn money for an AP test, but he thought it important to the self-esteem of East Los Angeles youths that they knew all the money was not charity.

Escalante sent his students off the Saturday morning before the test with his standard speech:

They were the best team he'd ever had. They had to play defense (organize their time and watch for silly mistakes). They had to remember they were helping build a mathematics program that someday would have 200 kids sitting down to do AP calculus. If they watched the Lakers game, he said, they should keep their mathematics texts at their side and do a couple of problems during each commercial.

Jiménez went home to catch up on his sleep. Escalante left to help Fabiola prepare for a Mother's Day barbecue. He would prepare his best top sirloin for Fabiola's mother, a widow living in Santa Ana. He thought she had long since forgiven him for failing to keep his promise to be baptized, but you never could be sure.

Bennett had his 329 AP exams, nearly 100 more than the previous year's school record, locked up safely in the storage closet of Room 520. Garfield students would be tested during a two-week period for college credit in calculus, American history, Spanish, computer science, physics, biology, English, European history, French, and government. There were so many calculus students that those examinations alone would have to be divided among four rooms, including MH-1. Escalante cursed the rules that required him to cover some of the helpful reminders on his wall (such as "$n/0$ = not defined") in the interest of test security.

The examination began at 8:00 A.M. Orozco had never before taken so important a test so early in the day. His metabolism was going to handicap him. He had had enough trouble staying alert during Escalante's morning lectures. He had to do something about it.

Saturday he reviewed his history notes. Sunday he sat in his mother's tiny kitchen and worked out old calculus problems. About mid-afternoon he went out to purchase a one-liter bottle of Coca-Cola, rich in caffeine, and placed it in the refrigerator. He issued orders that it not be touched, then stretched out on the floor about 10:00 P.M. and tried to sleep. He set the electric alarm clock on the lamp table.

Brrrrzzzzzzzzzzzzzz. The clock buzzed at 4:30 A.M., right on time. In the dark stillness he staggered to the refrigerator and pulled out the liter of Coke. He sat down hard on a plastic-covered couch and drank the entire bottle, every last drop, until he produced a satisfactory belch. He rubbed his eyes, tucked the empty bottle in a corner of the couch, and lay back down for two more hours of sleep. By 7:00 A.M. he was not exactly wired, but at least conscious. His thoughts seemed clearer than usual for that hour. If this did not work, he thought, nothing would.

Esparza appeared at the library at 8:00 A.M. wearing a loose blouse and pants with an elastic top. She did not look six months pregnant. She did not look pregnant at all. Carlos Cobos, the assistant principal, assisted by counselor Joe López, frantically counted examination booklets and worried over what to do with students appearing who were not on their list. Esparza took her assigned seat and pondered her future.

She was going to have to move out soon. Her mother still barred Casillas from the house. They met at predesignated rendezvous spots, though in the last week, as she pored over history notes and calculus problems, they had not met at all. When the baby came something would have to change.

She did not want to marry yet. She saw divorce all around her and wanted to be absolutely sure. Casillas was proposing they live together. She liked that idea.

Beltrán rubbed his eyes and joined the long line into the library. He had had only three hours of sleep. He had spent the weekend at the glass-topped table in his dining room. His friends Dungca, bound for the U.S. Naval Academy, and Valenzuela, Cal Poly, San Luis Obispo, might be geniuses who did not need to alter their routine, but he had to cram. He stayed up until 2:00 A.M. Monday, then lay down for a few restless hours before heading to school.

Cobos scattered about forty students in widely separated alcoves and tables and began to work his way through the instructions: "In filling out this answer sheet, there should be absolutely no talking. If you have an emergency and it is essential for you to go to the rest room, please raise your hand.

"Listen carefully. You may not use slide rules, calculators, or reference materials during the examination. If you have brought any of these with you, please bring them up to the front of the room at this time.

". . . If you have no other questions, no talking, open your white section one booklet and begin work."

Esparza had not experienced much morning sickness. A little dizziness in first period occasionally, nothing more. She was well past that stage now. She fought back a small surge of nervousness. It was very important, after all she had gone through for this moment, that she remain calm. She opened the booklet and ran her eye quickly down the problems, as Escalante had recommended. Yes, she thought, we've done that before, that one too.

Beltrán tried the same procedure, in a casual way. The teachers suggested students mark each question, a plus for ones that looked easy, a minus for ones that did not. Beltrán just made a quick mental tally, without marking anything. It did not look too bad.

Cobos and López walked quietly up and down the aisles. After the 1982 troubles, Bennett insisted on carefully randomized seating, wider spacing, and at least two proctors in every AP testing room. The library was the largest test site, but the proctors prowled diligently. Beltrán noticed that when he looked up from his paper and stretched, Cobos or López stared at him until he returned to work.

Cheating, he knew, was not uncommon at Garfield, although it usually occurred only on quizzes and in the end did the participants little good. Both Escalante and Jiménez ignored the buzz of conversation that accompanied their own quizzes. They would have a pretty good idea soon enough who understood and who did not. Cheating on the AP was too difficult. Not only was everyone watched, but no one was quite sure that anyone else's booklet would be worth copying.

At the break between the multiple-choice and free-response sections of the test, the proctors in Room 111 had a crisis. One of Jiménez's students discovered her period had begun. She dashed to the gym, on the other side of the campus, for a sweatshirt to cover the results. The proctor asked Bennett if she could continue with the free-response section even though she returned late. That was fine, Bennett said. Jiménez would later proudly note she received a 3.

The examination resumed. Esparza opened the free-response section and studied the first problem:

1. A particle moves along the x-axis so that its acceleration at any time t is given by $a(t) = 6t - 18$. At time $t = 0$ the velocity of the particle is $v(0) = 24$, and at time $t = 1$ its position is $x(1) = 20$.
   (a) Write an expression for the velocity $v(t)$ of the particle at any time t.
   (b) For what values of t is the particle at rest?

Write an expression for the position $x(t)$ of the particle
(c) at any time t.
(d) Find the total distance traveled by the particle from $t = 1$ to $t = 3$.

She suppressed a surge of delight. Calm, stay calm. She could do that one. Escalante had put them through enough velocity and acceleration problems to qualify for astronaut training. She scanned the others. Number 2 was not bad, number 3 a little harder. Number 4 would be very tough. Number 5 presented one of those troublesome water troughs. Number 6 looked like something in another language.

Never mind. She was confident she had at least thirty of the forty-five multiple-choice questions right. Good answers on half the essay questions would mean a 3.

Beltrán had worried about the multiple choice, his weak spot in Jiménez's drills. Free-response questions, on the other hand, were like outside fastballs—he could hit them to all fields. He did all the work on the first four and made educated guesses on the last two.

Gutiérrez fought back panic. It had been a terrible week. Her father had argued violently with her mother. She could not seem to get a good night's sleep. Now the numbers she puzzled over seemed to run together, and she could not find anything at all in the last two free-response questions that looked familiar. She was hungry. She was also resigned to her fate. She waited for the test to end.

"Put down your booklet and leave it closed on your desk. Mr. López will collect your booklets and also your green sheets. Everyone stop writing. Pencils down."

Orozco walked out of Room 111 with a worn expression. He had stayed awake, but the examination had been difficult. He felt tired and dizzy. And he was not done. The AP history exam came the next day. He was flirting with an F in English, which would kill Bennett's plans to make him the grade C star of next year's Academic Decathlon team. The interschool scholastic competition required at least two C students in each team. Underachievers like Orozco were treasured, but they could not play with an F.

Pulgarin followed Orozco out of 111. He felt oddly elated, refreshed. It had not been as hard as he had expected. He did not do the last two free responses, but he did thirty-five of the multiple choice, and the answers made sense.

On Sunday he had gone to church and then sat in his chair from 4:00 to 9:00 P.M. reviewing his notes. He read the Bible as usual before putting down his head to sleep without interruption until 5:30 A.M. Just before the test began, he closed his eyes and asked God to help him find the answers. The good Lord would determine if he was worthy of a 3.

Banned from their classrooms full of test takers, Escalante and Jiménez held court in the cafeteria and the athletic stadium bleachers. Feeling drained, Jiménez began lunch early. He piled his plate high with fries, rice, and chicken nuggets, washed down with iced tea. Escalante poured from a thermos of Bolivian vegetable soup, prescribed by Fabiola for a lingering cold.

Room by room, the examination ended and test takers who had been sent elsewhere filtered back to MH-1 and MH-2. They provided varying accounts:

"It was *hard*."

"It wasn't too bad."

"The last two were a bitch."

Escalante answered questions directed to him but declined to work out the free-response questions. Let them enjoy their relief and play a little Ping-Pong—he had a table set up in MH-1.

Each student was allowed to keep a copy of the second half of the test. They compared notes among themselves, while the teachers talked about the impossible strain of fifty-student calculus classes, and what they planned to do about it.

Escalante had drawn up a different schedule for the next year. He would teach three Calculus ABs instead of two. Jiménez would have two ABs instead of one. Each would be limited to thirty students. Escalante would keep an Algebra 2 class, the place where he did his calculus recruiting. He would drop his trigonometry–math analysis class, giving it to Litvak. Escalante and Shiroishi clashed briefly when he failed to clear this arrangement with her and Jack Knight, Litvak's immediate superior, but the crisis passed.

Gradillas sat in his office with his application for a sabbatical leave in front of him.

Pinned to his wall was a huge Spanish expletive on computer paper—"*CHUPA!* [Suck!]." It was a favorite slogan of the young

282

men who cruised by the school at closing time. It reflected his mood. He had just heard another principal ask why courses at the special high school day program at ELAC had to be so difficult. "A little art, a little PE" should be enough, the man said. Gradillas's staff embraced the words with glee, quoting them whenever they wanted to see the old anger flash in the boss's eyes.

Next year would be the last in which he could complete his doctoral dissertation under the BYU program. He wanted to take the sabbatical, then come back and look for an area superintendency that would allow him to pester the junior highs into raising *their* standards.

He had told Bennett, "I think I need the Ph.D. if I'm going to climb higher in the district."

"You sure that's a valid assumption, Henry?"

"Well, maybe in some other district."

Bennett and most of the rest of the faculty thought Gradillas was stuck. He was an airborne ranger, not a bureaucrat. He never paid much attention to detail. He charged through red tape as if it were part of a Fort Benning obstacle course. Sometimes he discovered he had to go back and splice some of it back together.

Yet Bennett the gentle draft avoider thought Gradillas the trained killer had been wonderful for Garfield. The principal had given the AP program nearly everything Bennett asked for. Bennett had been at the school twenty years. Based on test scores and campus cleanliness and student punctuality and all the other things principals were measured by, he thought Gradillas should have been promoted long before. Bennett had seen many people, less competent people, moved up sooner.

Three days after the calculus examination, Gradillas gave Bennett a characteristic farewell. The afternoon before the AP physics test, one of the last of the year, there was a small rebellion. Several physics students, most of whom had just taken calculus, told AP physics teacher Themistocles Sparangis that they had had enough AP and would not show up for the examination. They were magnet students. Shiroishi tried to dissuade them, but they were adamant. Gradillas cursed. He missed his mustache.

His temper way above boiling point, he resolved to go and confront personally every last rebel. Assistant Principal Catherine Brown; his secretary, Rose Kennedy; Bennett; and others considered this a terrible idea—something akin to declaring thermonuclear war. They persuaded him to circulate a memo instead:

JAMES A. GARFIELD HIGH SCHOOL
INTER-OFFICE CORRESPONDENCE

TO: AP Physics Students
FROM: Henry C. Gradillas
      Principal

I am very disturbed to find that some students in the AP Physics class are not planning to take the AP exam. The teacher feels that the students are ready and so do I. This exam is mandatory. Too much time, effort, and money have been spent on curriculum materials, teacher time, and books. You, as students, are hereby directed by me to take this exam today. Failure to do so will jeopardize your grade in the class. This procedure is not new and I, as principal, have the authority to require you to take the exam. If [financial] waivers are needed, you may obtain them from me. The exam does not have to cost you anything. I expect you to do your best.

Not everything in the memo, Gradillas and Bennett both knew, was precisely true. There was no district rule making AP examinations mandatory. Gradillas considered that *his* policy, although he never before had had to insist on it.

All twenty students, some still unhappy, took the physics test.

Whatever Bennett thought of such methods, it was clear to him that they worked. Push, push, push.

The teachers' union was still threatening to strike. He could not afford it, but he would walk the picket line if the union said to. It defended teachers, and demanded higher pay for higher standards. All that made sense.

But he had learned something at Garfield, watching Escalante and other teachers perform. If the public schools were a business enterprise, and they were all judged by how their students did, many more teachers would be dying of ulcers.

But they would also have much better schools.

PART THREE

—

INTEGRATION

|| 18 ||

American teachers have become understandably wary of new ideas. Few human enterprises, with the possible exception of the Chinese Communist Party, have endured as many bewildering changes over the last three decades as American education. The *Sputnik* challenge, new math, open classrooms, relevancy, computer education, back to basics, and critical thinking have ridden in on attractive waves of publicity, often followed by awkward silence when teachers discovered again the fragility of theory exposed to human nature.

The unexpected and unprecedented success of Garfield High School grew out of the personal beliefs and ambitions of one man, with help from a handful of men and women who shared some, but not all, of his views. None of them proposed any grand theory when they began the venture. Few dreamed of the remarkable results.

In some cases, their ideas about how to go about what they were doing could not have been more different. Jaime Escalante detested Jo Ann Shiroishi's willingness to let students lighten their academic loads when feeling pressured. Ben Jiménez considered Henry Gradillas's relentless promotion of rising test scores to be an empty public relations gesture that did nothing to improve the lot of his calculus students. Many Garfield teachers were annoyed or hurt by the media attention Escalante received after the 1982 triumph.

Yet these often aimless passions and frustrations produced something spectacular. How did that happen?

It is difficult to resist the urge to go back and search for an enveloping theory. Sadly, that is an exercise that often reveals more about the theorist than about the truth he seeks.

Some general observations will be made here. I am no more able to resist the temptation than anyone else. But if educators have any hope of making use of what happened at Garfield, they must interpret the facts for themselves.

For the first lesson of Garfield is: Teachers who bring students up to high standards are precious commodities. Leave them alone—as Escalante insisted be done when his schemes violated protocol or conventional wisdom. If good teachers ask for help, give it to them, but only the way they want it.

The second lesson is: If left alone, teachers who work hard and care for their students will produce better results than ten times their number dutifully following the ten best recommendations of the ten latest presidential commissions on education.

Commission recommendations and, to cite a more recent innovation, teacher objectives committee reports, sometimes do some good. Good teachers read them and get good ideas. Other good teachers, like Escalante, ignore them and find their own experience serves best.

Trouble starts when new ideas are imposed from above, through federal grant conditions or state edicts or local school board policy. If a particular system works, good teachers will hear about it—the teachers' associations and unions will see to that—and they will try it. More government money helps, but often it has too many strings. Escalante used HCOP and Chapter 1 funds to best advantage only by finessing federal guidelines. Even the best ideas to come out of the Garfield story probably would have turned rancid if they had first been cooked in a school board committee and reduced to short numbered paragraphs.

A third lesson seems to apply just to minorities, but it ought to work with nearly all human children: Demand more than they think they have to give. Spend every available moment convincing them they can do it if they simply make an effort. The largest slogan on MH-1's wall is CALCULUS NEED NOT BE MADE EASY; IT IS EASY ALREADY. Importantly, the door to that classroom was open to nearly everyone, even students with weak records. Escalante loathed tracking systems—putting quick and slow students in different classes or barring students from courses unless they passed entrance tests.

In 1987 Garfield High School produced more than 26 percent of all Mexican Americans in the country who passed Advanced Placement Calculus AB or BC with a 3 or better. That is a victory for

Garfield but also a troubling indictment of the thousands of other American high schools who have failed to persuade their Latino and other minority students that they can succeed at this level, or who have not even let them try.

A number of commentators have underlined this principle. Successful educators in the barrio, wrote *Los Angeles Times* columnist Frank del Olmo, "share one thing in common . . . —they truly believe that Latino students can succeed in school, and they act on that conviction." Thomas P. Carter of California State University, Sacramento, after a lengthy study of Latino schoolchildren, concluded that teachers of Mexican Americans "don't expect much and, lo and behold, they don't get much."

The Carnegie Foundation for the Advancement of Teaching, in its 1988 report, "An Imperiled Generation—Saving Urban Schools," said: "The first priority is to affirm that every student can succeed. While Americans talk of providing a quality education for all children, we found that many people, both in and out of schools, simply do not believe this objective can be reached." Richard Rodríguez, in a newspaper essay, warned that "education is personal and individual and eccentric," and should not be reduced to labels that set a different standard for minorities than for everyone else.

That is a very difficult rule to follow, because it requires a teacher to fight inertia and human sympathy and some popular political views. Successful educators at Garfield battle these feelings every day, within themselves and within their community. Teachers who handle classes full of average and remedial students, and try to make the hours count for something, may have the hardest jobs of all. It would not take much for the entire effort to subside into mediocrity if too many of them lost heart, as Escalante on occasion has seemed about to do.

There are some teachers at Garfield with a different vision for the future. Brian Wallace argues only full-scale ethnic integration of all the city schools will raise standards over the long term for the majority. Michael Litvak favors teaching methods that emphasize movement, variety, and visual images to stimulate the creative processes on the right side of the brain.

These are visionary proposals, but most teachers in most American schools must for now work with the materials at hand and the time allotted.

Some teachers fear that methods like Escalante's can never work with the great majority of underprivileged students. That remains to be seen. Escalante and Jiménez have never even met most of the 3,500 students at Garfield, but the school's overall effort to toughen its mathematics courses, stimulated by the success with calculus, seems to have had some impact outside MH-1 and MH-2. From 1983 through 1986, standardized mathematics scores for nearly all Garfield juniors increased from the 39th to the 53rd percentile, and that did not include the scores of students in the magnet computer science program. The percentage of Garfield seniors admitted to college, including ELAC, grew from 60 percent in 1982 to 70 percent in 1987.

Much that has happened in the last forty years of American education—desegregation, busing, magnet schools, ethnic studies—has knocked at least some of the hard edges off the structure of racism. This seems like a good time to shed some of the understandable worry about the impact of high standards and difficult homework on those unaccustomed to them. There is a destructive bias, no matter how well intentioned, in making more demands on rich children than on poor ones.

A teacher who makes demands is always under assault, friendly or otherwise. Single-mindedness, one of Escalante's more obvious traits, is essential.

But there is a subtler way to sustain the effort, which might be lesson four: Pick some unusually difficult goal, such as an Advanced Placement examination, and organize students as a team to reach it.

Peer pressure claims significant power on every high school campus in America. On some it leads students to compete for academic honors. It may produce spectacular football teams. Sometimes it works at cross-purposes, rewarding both academic effort and academic nonchalance.

Garfield would not have come as far as it did if the calculus and AP programs had not infiltrated important student cliques and attained a critical mass of student interest. It became fashionable to be in calculus, in part through the dramatic events of 1982, and in part through the showmanship of Jaime Escalante. Popularity begot pride and productivity. And by encouraging quick students to help slow ones, and hiring Calculus BC students to tutor lower classes, Escalante demonstrated the advantages of cooperative learning. He echoed the work of theorists like Roger and David Johnson of the University of Minnesota and turned the family spirit of East Los Angeles into an academic tool, one that skillful educators might find useful elsewhere.

It was not so much the test itself that made a difference. Standardized tests, even those as challenging and relevant as AP calculus, have their flaws. What changed lives was the disciplined act of preparing for the test and the thrill of passing it. Students learned beyond any doubt that such obstacles, if taken seriously, could be overcome. Even students scoring 1s or 2s felt they had made progress.

Are teachers like Escalante made or born? His own talents are unusual enough to suggest some innate quality present long before he enrolled at the Normal Superior or at Cal State, LA. That may be true of most good teachers, but some key skills can be learned. Jiménez learned from Escalante how to control a class. That practical knowledge made a critical difference in the younger teacher's career. Jiménez's success proves that many of the methods that worked for Escalante can also work for individuals whose backgrounds and personalities match those of the average American educator.

Escalante and many other Garfield teachers learned their most useful techniques on the job, not in the education courses they were required to take for certification. The psychology, political science, and sociology they studied often did not apply to their situations. They received little useful instruction in discipline or, more important, in proven methods of motivating disadvantaged students.

To be fair to those who educate teachers, university courses rarely cover all the needs of any profession, be it law, medicine, or journalism. The educational philosophy and theory Garfield teachers learned at places like Cal State, LA—today the largest teacher training institution in the country—probably removed the mystery from many education school notions and made them easier to discard when they did not work in practice. Perhaps discipline can only be learned by doing. But university education departments, as they have already heard many times, need to reexamine their curricula. And school districts should continue to be receptive to older teacher applicants like Escalante and Gradillas, who bring something extra from dealing with the outside world.

How can a community encourage good teaching, and leach out bad? This was the principal political focus of a series of reports critical of American education which sprouted in 1983, just as Escalante's calculus program was beginning to blossom. "A Nation at Risk," the Carnegie "Report on Secondary Education in America," and others sparked an interest in education among politicians, particularly presidential candidates, that gives no sign of slackening. The 1988 presidential campaign rang with calls for action in the classroom, as will, more than likely, many campaigns that follow. Given the limited federal role in education and the difficulty any federal office seeker would have with the first lesson of Garfield—leave good teachers alone—it remains to be seen how useful any of this story can be to men and women seeking such offices.

To take one example of a politically popular educational reform, the merit teacher plans of the early 1980s have had very mixed results. They have channeled more money to some very good teachers, which is fine. Other very good teachers—including Jaime Escalante—have been denied the same rewards or have rejected the system as too wedded to the needs of principals and teachers' unions and too removed from the process of teaching students.

In California, most of the merit teacher programs depend on favorable comment from supervisors and other teachers—an instant handicap for anyone of independent spirit. John Bennett's application to become a mentor teacher failed to pass even the first level of review—apparently because one previous principal remembered the day Bennett refused to let Geraldo Rivera, the television journalist, into his classroom. Escalante rejected the mentor program because it required many hours away from the classroom preparing instructional materials he doubted other teachers would use.

Most teachers deserve higher salaries, if for no other reason than to remove financial annoyances that distract from good teaching. More money, nearly everyone acknowledges, will not make them better teachers. That motive comes from within. If the Garfield story has a lesson here, it is that preparing students for an unusually difficult goal like an AP examination can bring personal satisfaction and community recognition with far more psychological impact than the $4,000 extra a year a mentor teacher earns in California. It is also important to remember that an exceptional teacher like Escalante, if left alone, may create a whirlwind that will vacuum up money from sources no one thought existed.

Escalante benefited from public notice, in local newspapers and television, at a crucial moment in his calculus program. If American media paid closer attention to successful teachers, some of the problems of morale and reward might be overcome. A report by Claire

L. Gaudiani and David G. Burnett of the American Association for Higher Education suggested the creation of new "academic alliances"—which could include journalists—to give good teachers the attention that they deserve and that their programs need.

But you have to start with good teachers, and leave them alone.

19

Immigrant communities in American cities are overcrowded. Social services have broken down. Homeless people sleep on the streets. In fiscal year 1986 an unprecedented 1.6 million aliens, mostly Mexicans with very little education, were apprehended trying to cross the border illegally, and it was thought that at least that many entered the United States undetected.

New immigration laws and housing programs have been passed or proposed to keep U.S. cities from spinning out of control, but the events of the last decade have led many economists and sociologists to predict a U.S. society permanently split between suburban affluence and urban chaos. Nowhere has that division seemed deeper or more depressing than in education.

In that same year that illegal immigration to the United States reached an all-time high, Henry R. Levin, professor of education and affiliated professor of economics at Stanford University, prepared for the National Education Association a disturbing summary of American schools' failure to educate poor and minority children. In his paper, "Educational Reform for Disadvantaged Students: An Emerging Crisis," he said if these children were not helped, and soon, the "consequences include the emergence of a dual society with a large and poorly educated underclass, massive disruption in higher education, reduced economic competitiveness of the nation as well as of individual states and industries that are most heavily impacted by these populations, and higher costs of public services associated with impoverishment and crime."

Without action, he predicted "increasing numbers of the disadvantaged will gain college entry but a large proportion of them will experience academic failure and leave without a degree." Among students who entered college in 1972, he noted, only 13 percent of Latinos, compared with 34 percent of Anglos, had completed a bachelor's degree by 1976.

Garfield's story suggests only some of the many steps that have to be taken to reverse the course Levin describes. But his report does set up one measure of the school's success that merits closer attention.

When I mentioned Garfield to teachers and principals at other schools, they often asked: So what happened to those kids when they went to college? I sensed a stubborn assumption, fed by other miracle stories gone sour, that the progress under Escalante and Jiménez would turn out to be an aberration. They felt that Garfield students carried such heavy sociological baggage from a childhood in East Los Angeles that it would eventually wear them down.

The need to find and interview Escalante's 1982 calculus students provided, as an unexpected by-product, an interesting first answer to those who doubt Escalante's lasting influence. Thirteen graduates of that class told me what happened to them after high school and provided some information on four of the five graduates I was not able to reach.

At least fifteen of the eighteen went to college, though some of them slipped and stumbled, as do most college students. Leticia Rodríguez, once so at odds with her family, found when she reached Princeton that she missed them. She transferred to Cal State, LA. Fernando Bocanegra left Columbia a year short of graduation because of financial pressure. Alex Guerrero graduated from Columbia and made plans for architecture school. Both María Jiménez and Roy Márquez graduated from Loyola Marymount University. Jesse López had to drop out of that same college due to a serious head injury, but he also later enrolled at Cal State. Hortensia Sánchez taught mathematics to freshmen while earning a psychology degree at the University of California, Santa Cruz, then immediately began working for her master's in social welfare at Berkeley.

Of the three Escalante students who went to the University of California, Berkeley, as undergraduates, Luis Cervantes stayed and graduated in microbiology and immunology, Gustavo Hernández switched to Cal State, LA, for a bachelor's degree in anthropology, and Martín Olvera dropped out after a series of depressing and distracting family tragedies—including the brutal murder of his sister's two children.

Olvera himself became one more inexplicable tragedy. On September 24, 1987, he was found hanging by the neck from a yellow nylon rope tied to a metal beam in a shed behind his family's house in East Los Angeles. The Los Angeles County Coroner's Office ruled his death a suicide. He left no notes or other significant clues. His father told the coroner's investigator that Martín was a "good kid" who had made no previous threats or attempts at suicide. He said Martín had mentioned a disagreement with a girlfriend a few weeks before, but it had not appeared to be serious.

When I had interviewed him nine months earlier, he had seemed in excellent spirits. He met me in MH-1 wearing white tennis shoes, white pants, white suspenders, and white jacket over a blue UC Berkeley T-shirt. He was talkative, funny, and extremely helpful. He brought me an entire file of letters and other information pertaining to the 1982 test controversy. All the 1982 students I spoke to were friendly and cooperative, but he went far beyond the demands of politeness.

At the very end of the interview he talked about a fifth-grade teacher who once told him he would be a great man and lead his people. It was a messianic notion that I did not understand and wrote off as youthful high spirits. He said he planned to work as a construction foreman while earning credits at UCLA toward a business degree. Later in the year he told Escalante of his distress over his parents' impending divorce, and also mentioned his feeling of failure for dropping out of college. "He's in bad shape," one of his friends told me. I never had a chance to interview him a second time about the controversy over question 6 in 1982.

By the end of 1987 at least nine of Escalante's eighteen calculus students from 1982 had earned bachelor's degrees, far above average for Latinos and close to the national average for all college students after five years. Most of the degree holders were working full-time as teachers, accountants, business executives, or medical technicians or were pursuing graduate studies. Four others, including the one 1983 graduate, Josie Richkarday, were still attending college and were within one or two years of graduation on schedules that allowed them to work and study. They had made what appeared to be sensible compromises between their career goals and financial needs.

Bocanegra was the only 1982 graduate other than Olvera known to have dropped out of college and not returned, but he was said to be planning completion of his degree at Cal State, Fullerton. Sandra López enlisted in the army in 1982 and remained in the service. Another 1982 graduate, René Cano, appeared to have been picked up by the U.S. Immigration and Naturalization Service while working in a local factory several months after scoring his unchallenged 4 on the AP calculus examination. Teachers at Garfield heard he had been deported to Mexico as an undocumented alien. A final member of the calculus class of 1982, Juan Cuadras, could not be located.

Some of the 1982 group's achievements in the last few years border on the remarkable. Five years to the month after she took the AP calculus exam, Aili Tapio had not only a bachelor's degree but a master's in business administration and a job as an auditor for a major oil company. In June 1988 she married René Gardea, the quiet boy she met in the Garfield band. Margaret Zamarripa had earned her college degree and passed her CPA examination by the fall of 1987, and was thinking of law school. Roy Márquez joined the Garfield faculty as a computer science teacher in September 1986. Nine months later his students scored the best Garfield results ever on the AP computer science examination.

Elsa Bolado tutored other students in mathematics at UCLA while working toward a degree in history and a junior or senior high school teaching career. Raúl Haro earned degrees in both aerospace engineering and computer science at Cal Poly, Pomona, while working part-time at the Jet Propulsion Laboratory and actively promoting the engineering profession in the Latino community. Luis Cervantes was working in a diagnostic medical laboratory while saving his money for graduate school. María Jiménez had joined a local financial firm. Leticia Rodríguez was close to an engineering degree.

I did not have the time or resources to check the college careers of the hundreds of Escalante students who have graduated since 1982. The subject demands detailed university research, something the Garfield phenomenon has failed to attract so far.

A clue to what such a study might find was contained in a February 1986 letter from Armand Ramos Reynolds, minority engineering program director at the University of Southern California: "For the past two years, students from Garfield constituted the largest group of entering minority freshmen and, in fact, outnumbered the students from all the other high schools in [East Los Angeles] combined. Even more important, the Garfield students with a median GPA of about

3.0 are academically doing far better than the average USC Engineering student and have an excellent retention rate."

In the spring of 1988, Escalante celebrated the graduation of seven of his students from the USC engineering program. Other veterans of MH-1 and MH-2 were graduating from several Ivy League and University of California campuses.

Nearly all had been born into the American lower class. By all indications, they should have spent their lives in the bottom half of a troubled dual society. But Jaime Escalante had shown a way out.

The air-conditioning in the dormitories had already expired, as expected, when 194 readers arrived at Trenton State College, Trenton, New Jersey, to spend six muggy days in mid-June 1987 grading 59,123 AP calculus examinations. Slapping hands with old friends, complaining about the weather, inquiring discreetly about the beer supply, the secondary school and college mathematics teachers assumed their usual role of boys and girls at camp before heading for their assigned grading rooms on the second and third floors of Forcina Hall.

The boxes of examinations were everywhere, stacks upon stacks of them, but few in the group would complain about the rapid growth of a program to which they had given so much time and sweat. The number of students taking either the AB or BC calculus examination had nearly doubled since 1982—part of a steady 12 to 15 percent annual growth for the entire AP program. Advanced Placement students still constituted only a tiny fraction of American youth, but AP was growing faster than the Scholastic Aptitude Test. A few reformers were suggesting that AP, or something like it, ought to replace the SAT.

The month before, 262,081 students from about 7,500 schools—about one-third of all American secondary schools—had taken 369,207 AP examinations in American and European history, government and politics, art, art history, biology, chemistry, physics, computer science, English, French, Spanish, German, Latin, music, and calculus. English and American history were the most popular examinations, but calculus was in third place and growing rapidly. College professors had become so enamored of the AP program that additional disciplines were being considered. Economics, the College Board had announced, would be offered in 1989, and a psychology test was being considered.

At some point, such rapid expansion of a once elitist academic tool would begin to sink into the public consciousness. Critics would begin to ask inevitable questions: Did the small groups of high school and college teachers who write the AP examinations constitute a semisecret brain trust? Were they creating, with little or no public review, a national standard high school curriculum? What would that do to the healthy diversity of American education? Was the fifty-three-dollar test fee too much, and where was all that money going? Could human graders be trusted to maintain a fair standard across the board? Was AP creating a national tracking system—a new elitism in which every school in the country would find itself divided between those teachers and students who enjoyed the benefits of AP and those who did not?

For the moment, the readers gathered at Trenton State, the thousands of AP teachers across the country, and the AP officials in New York and New Jersey were too absorbed in this fundamental transformation of their program to anticipate future debates. High schools most of them had never heard of before, places where the majority of the students were poor and their parents undereducated, had begun to send in dozens, sometimes hundreds of completed tests.

No such school had yet come as far as Garfield, but there were some likely candidates. William C. Bryant High School in Long Island City had given ninety-four AP calculus examinations to an amalgam of Anglo, Latino, Asian, and black students from blue-collar neighborhoods of Queens. Southside High School in San Antonio had only 550 students, mostly Latinos from disadvantaged homes, but 10 percent of them were enrolled in various AP courses. District of Columbia school administrators, convinced that AP's higher standards could galvanize faculty morale and motivate difficult students, had launched a program to put at least one AP course in every high school in the city.

Six states—Utah, Alabama, Florida, Kentucky, Louisiana, and South Carolina—had decided to provide tax dollars for special support of AP programs. Clemson University mathematician John Kenelly, an early convert to the AP program, was convinced that its aggressive introduction into the struggling Greenville County, South Carolina, school system had helped bring about the area's economic renaissance. Promotion of the program by several prominent educators persuaded South Carolina to begin a million-dollar program putting AP classes into every high school in the state. School administrators who had laughed at the thought of even attempting an AP program began to wonder if it might provide, at the very least, a helpful jolt.

The calculus readers assembled at Trenton State could see the results of this new enthusiasm in the grinding schedule before them. Dressed in shorts and sundresses like a crowd of vacationing tourists, they sat in folding chairs at long tables and plowed through the piles of test booklets—300 free-response questions a day each. They looked forward to an evening of gossip and drink and the often incomprehensible humor characteristic of their discipline.

Some complained about a free-response question with too much fancy arithmetic in it. It gave both test taker and test reader unnecessary headaches, without really probing ability to handle the theorems involved. But as the ETS analysts checked the results at the end of the week, everything seemed to be in order. Despite the rapid expansion of calculus into new, uncertain territory, the quality of the students' work had not fallen off. If anything, thought Kenelly, it was a little better.

For the first time in his life, Jiménez reached the Garfield mailbag with the AP grade roster at the same instant as Escalante. The older teacher checked every day each early July and usually found the thick envelope first. The calculus scores would be highlighted in yellow marker and exhaustively analyzed before Jiménez ever saw them. But by chance on July 7, Jiménez stopped by the main office just as the mail, and Escalante, arrived.

His good fortune gave him little advantage. Escalante had the envelope out of the bag and ripped open before Jiménez could even check the return address. They adjourned to Escalante's office and Xeroxed more copies so both could read and ponder. This was *their* report card, a measure of their talent and energy unlike anything most American teachers ever received. It excited and unnerved them.

They could not know, even with a careful look at the eight-page document, how astonishingly well they and the other Garfield AP teachers had done. The first seven pages listed each student who had taken an AP examination, his or her birth date or Social Security number, intended college (designated by a code number), and AP test grades. The eighth page totaled the number of Garfield students who were attending each of the listed colleges and, in a narrow strip along the bottom, totaled the school's results in each AP category.

They could determine quickly how many of their own students had passed each examination, but it would take several weeks for me to survey other schools around the country and calculate the extent of Garfield's achievement on a national level.

The school had done better than any other normal enrollment, inner city high school in the history of the country. About 74 percent of the 329 AP examinations taken by Garfield students received grades of 3 or better, above the national average of 69 percent. The 129 Garfield students taking Calculus AB or BC examinations exceeded the total of every U.S. public school except three: Alhambra High School (177) of Alhambra, California, where nearly every calculus student was from a middle- or upper-income Asian American family; and the two New York City superschools, Stuyvesant High (162) and the Bronx High School of Science (156), where students were admitted only after competitive examinations. (See Appendix 2.)

Garfield had sent more students to the calculus examinations than Exeter or Punahoe, New Trier or Evanston, Hunter College High or Lowell High, or many other competitive secondary schools of American legend. The only private school that did better was Andover (154). Garfield produced 27 percent of all Mexican Americans in the country who scored 3 or higher in Calculus AB, and 22 percent of Mexican Americans who scored at that level on the BC. Thirteen calculus students had 5s and nineteen had 4s. More than 87 percent of the Garfield test takers were Hispanic; the rest were Asian American. No inner city school with such an overwhelming percentage of poor minority students had ever had so many take Advanced Placement, or score so well.

The root of the success was the calculus results, although from Escalante's point of view they were mildly disappointing. About 66 percent of the 129 calculus students scored 3 or higher on the calculus examination. This was close to the national average of 71 percent, but a substantial drop from the previous year. In 1986, 84 percent of ninety-three Garfield calculus students had scored 3 or better.

Escalante guessed whose fault that was very quickly. The summary sheet showed eleven 1s in Calculus AB. "Those are all mine," he told Jiménez. "My basketball players, a few others." Both Mata and Zayas, the varsity hoopsters, received 1s, along with six other students in Escalante's crowded fifth period. One of them was Juanita Gutiérrez, ashamed that she had let her panic wash away eight months of work. Her 3 in AP American history helped her feel better. Both she and Zayas would take Calculus BC and resolve to screen out all distractions.

Escalante had tried to handle too many students in general, and too many in period 5 in particular. Only 50 percent of the forty test takers from period 5 received 3 or better, compared with 83 percent of the eighteen from Escalante's smaller class in period 1. His BC class also dropped below previous years: Fifty-seven percent of the twenty-one students had 3 or better. None of Jiménez's forty-five students had a 1. Nearly 87 percent had a 3 or better. His clandestine BC class did fine: a 4 for Phung and a 3 for Zavala. One Asian American student scored a 3 after taking Calculus AB at a local college.

Escalante suffered from the huge size of his classes. But both teachers were handling too many students at a time. They would have to keep to the reduced class size the next year, Escalante thought, and something would have to be done to free him from the visitors and observers and the other demands on his time.

There was always something or someone to worry about. Escalante had suffered under his father. In turn, perhaps in consequence, he had paid loving attention to the children of a few thousand other fathers, as well as to his own two sons. His father had not helped him with his dream of becoming an engineer, but he and Fabiola had sent both Jaimito and Fernando on their way to that profession.

Jaimito now worked in Santa Barbara for a firm handling complex problems of electronics and medicine. Fernando still lived at home, but was about to enter the engineering program at Cal Poly, Pomona.

Fernando had insisted that the family keep the old Volkswagen for his use, although as history's tallest Escalante, 6 feet 2, he had to fold himself into the driver's seat. Even with the old bug's pinstripes now painted over, he loved the car as much as his father did.

Escalante now drove a blue 1975 Chrysler with an "I ♥ calculus" license-plate holder presented by the class of '82. He turned the Volkswagen over to Fernando only reluctantly, and reserved the right to complain about the boy's American-style gear shifting, his heavy foot on the accelerator, and other perceived failings of the next generation.

302

It was his habit to complain about youthful indulgence. He was too old to change now.

Armando Beltrán came home from a basketball game and saw the envelope on the glass top of the dining room table. He sucked in a deep breath, picked up the envelope, and opened it. He needed a 3. He had decided to go to Cal State, LA, in physical education, but he wanted to take more mathematics. He did not want to mess with beginning calculus.

The thin sheet of paper slipped out easily. He looked, and looked again, and exhaled in relief. A 3! So near the brink, and he had pulled himself back out. Jiménez was right. He just had to try, a little at a time. He had to stick with his friends.

Hoping to start an engineering course at Cal State, LA, but desperate for money, José Pulgarin found a job as a messenger shortly after school ended. His life seemed more stable now. His mother had submitted their papers applying for legal residence. Her check stubs from the garment factory and his school records showed both had arrived before 1982 and qualified for the amnesty program.

It had been such a difficult year, taking two mathematics courses at once. Escalante had pushed him and, toward the end, he'd thought he was beginning to comprehend. He had prayed. Now he had to wait.

One night when he returned from work, he found the envelope on the little lamp table where he usually kept his notebooks. He saw the return address: "The College Board." This was it. He opened it and looked.

He smiled. A 3.

Gloria a Dios. Praise the Lord!

He had done it.

It had to have been, Raúl Orozco concluded, the worst academic year of his career, proof of his junior-year, middle-year jinx. A C in chemistry, a C in calculus, a C in English. That last grade made John Bennett happy. He thought Dennis Campagna was going to flunk Orozco and cost the Academic Decathlon team a prize C student. Tom Woessner, out of step, had given him a B.

And how was he spending the summer after such a disastrous

year? Was he resting? Rebuilding his strength? Working on his Michael Dukakis and George Bush impressions? Nah, he was down at school every week, drilling with Bennett's decathlon team on aviation and the Renaissance, or over at ELAC tutoring in Escalante's summer program, or playing Horse on the basketball court with Chenglim Ear, the class genius, and Art Ramírez.

Perhaps the AP grades would save the day. He should have a 5 on the history, a 4 in calculus. So what if he had missed a lot of school? He learned the stuff, his way.

He saw the envelope on the kitchen table and felt a twinge of fear. He tried to figure which side of the paper the grades would be on, and open from the *other* side. He needed time to gather his courage. Ooops! He guessed wrong. There they were.

Shit. A 3 in calculus; a 4 in American history. Escalante and Woessner would tell him that was great. He thought he deserved better. He would show them. He would ace European history. He would kill Calculus BC. They would see.

In June Désirée Esparza finally left home. Escalante had become her friend again in the month before the examination, when he saw she was still trying. Ramiro Casillas stuck with her all the way. He had attended Lamaze classes with her and promised to be in the delivery room, even after the live-birth videotape nearly made him lose his dinner. But her mother had never accepted the idea of having Casillas anywhere near the house. Esparza had decided she could not live like that anymore.

Casillas and she, along with his sister and her husband, found an apartment on Florence Avenue in Bell, a four-mile drive down the Long Beach Freeway from East Los Angeles. It was not fancy—two bedrooms in a dirty beige stucco two-story building with an empty pool and trash in the courtyard. But it was a place to live, at least for a while.

After the baby was born and school began again, Casillas's sister would watch the child until she came home in the afternoon. Casillas would take the evening watch while she studied. The midnight duties they would share.

By early July, the baby had moved into a breech position and showed no signs of turning. The nurse said not to worry. Esparza tried to follow that advice, and telephoned her friends in search of distracting gossip. Juana Valdez was mildly depressed: "Ah, I didn't pass calculus. Just got a two."

"Did you get your grade already?"

"Yeah, two in calculus, three in history, five in Spanish."

It was time to go see her mother and check the mail. All that pride and anger that had kept her going through the winter now focused on an envelope four miles up the freeway.

"Any mail, Mom?"

"Yeah, right on the table."

The woman had already opened it, but had said nothing. Perhaps she did not know what it meant. Esparza pulled it out, looked at it, and jumped a few millimeters into the air, hoping the baby would not mind. She had 3s in both calculus and history.

She looked up to discover her mother was staring at her. "I passed them both, Mom."

The woman nodded, as if she had never expected anything else.

By the time she and Casillas reached Beverly Hospital on July 27, the baby had gotten itself permanently stuck in a feet-first position.

The hospital was a featureless, modern, brown-brick structure on a busy avenue in Montebello, just east of East Los Angeles. Across the street was Frumento's Italian Market, the Marufuku Restaurant, and Ordoñez Mexican Food, and not far away was a Jack-in-the-Box, symbol of the dreary future awaiting any Escalante student who did not do his or her homework.

Esparza knew her baby could not be very big. She did not look more than six months pregnant. She fought back some fear as the doctors discussed this and told her they would do a cesarean. They let Casillas stay. It was only right. He had practiced so hard.

The doctors seemed to be working very hard down there. She felt mild discomfort, then saw blood. "Here she is!" someone shouted.

She felt her head being raised. She blinked twice to clear her eyes. She saw what she had been waiting for: Robin Nichole Casillas, 6 pounds, 12 ounces, a perfectly formed little girl with a full head of black hair.

She was beautiful and, like her mother, just a little ahead of her time.

APPENDIX 1

ESCALANTESE: A GLOSSARY

Doghouse: Synthetic division

Face mask: A mistake at the problem's beginning

Give and go: Breaking down of absolute value

Gravy: Simple substitution

Green light: Easy factoring

In love: Factoring by grouping

Marching band: A simple solution following usual procedures

Nosey: Need to study the problem and find the key words

Red light: Difficult factoring, stop and study

Secret agent: The minus sign in front of a parenthesis, with the power to change the signs inside

Three-second violation: Similar to give and go: $|x| < a$, $|x| > a$, $|x| = +$ or $-a$

Thumb up: A or B

Thumb sideways: C

Thumb down: Failing

Burro: A stupid student, used in a humorous way

Hyatola: A student who comes into the classroom and just sits

Johnny: Any student whose name or nickname Escalante cannot remember

Kanguros: Students from other schools

Pedazo de retaso: A little kid, or a tiny girl

Rajneesh: A student who wants to get an A in the class without doing anything

Intensive care: When a student is failing test after test, he or she must see Escalante after school every day until the improvement shows.

Quarantine: When a student has poor attendance and does not do the required work, he or she must stay after school.

Warm-up: Students pound hands on desktops and pound feet on the floor in rhythmic fashion to prepare themselves for class.

The wave: Students stand or raise their arms and yell at their desks by rows. Also used to increase alertness.

People of Rome: When students continue the warm-up or wave without authorization.

Mickey Mouse: Such classes as woodworking, plastics, marching band, cheerleading, or any sport that takes time from math

Students are sent to see:
Dr. White: For light review

Dr. Green: For after-school study

Dr. Black: For emergency treatment and lengthy quarantine

Take your break and don't come back: Get out of class

Rifle pass from Magic Johnson: Represents another function

Qué me miras? [**What are you looking at?**]: To a student who doesn't understand and just looks around

All seniors turn crazy: Reminder of where trigonometric functions are positive (Quadrants I, II, III, IV)

Good morning. How are you? You're still failing: Greeting to encourage good study habits

APPENDIX 2

TOP U.S PUBLIC HIGH SCHOOL
ADVANCED PLACEMENT CALCULUS PROGRAMS

Results based on examinations given in May 1987

School	AP Calculus Exams Given	Percentage of Students Scoring 3 or Better*	Characteristics
1. Alhambra High School Alhambra, Calif.	177	67	3,400 students, 54% Asian, 31% Latino, in four grades. Nearly all test takers were from middle- or upper-income Asian American families.
2. Stuyvesant High School New York, N.Y.	162	80	2,700 students in four grades selected after a competitive examination.
3. Bronx High School of Science Bronx, N.Y.	156	90	3,000 students in four grades selected after a competitive examination.
4. Garfield High School Los Angeles, Calif.	129	66	3,500 students in three grades from a predominantly Latino lower- and middle-income area.

School	AP Calculus Exams Given	Percentage of Students Scoring 3 or Better*	Characteristics
5. New Trier High School Winnetka, Ill.	125	90	3,700 students in four grades from a predominantly Anglo† middle- and upper-income area.
6. Evanston Township High School Evanston, Ill.	124	74	3,200 students in four grades. 54% Anglo, 39% black from a lower- to upper-income area.
7. Syosset High School Syosset, N.Y.	104	80	1,900 students in four grades from a predominantly Anglo middle- and upper-income area.
8. Plano Senior High School Plano, Tex.	99	95	2,600 students in two grades from a predominantly Anglo middle- and upper-income area.
9. William C. Bryant High School Long Island City, N.Y.	94	47	3,400 students in four grades. 42% Anglo, 27% Latino, 17% Asian, 14% black from a middle- and lower-income area.
10. Gunn Senior High School Palo Alto, Calif.	93	97	1,250 students in four grades from a predominantly Anglo middle- and upper-income area.
11. Scarsdale High School Scarsdale, N.Y.	92	97	1,460 students in four grades from a predominantly Anglo middle- and upper-income area.

311

School	AP Calculus Exams Given	Percentage of Students Scoring 3 or Better*	Characteristics
12. Oak Park and River Forest High School Oak Park, Ill.	92	78	3,200 students in four grades from a predominantly Anglo middle- and upper-income area.
13. Hunter College High School New York, N.Y.	91	84	1,300 students in five grades selected after a competitive examination.
14. Midwood High School Brooklyn, N.Y.	91	58	2,700 students in four grades, half from middle-income area, half from rest of city under magnet program; 48% Anglo, 37% black, 9% Latino, 6% Asian.
15. New Rochelle High School New Rochelle, N.Y.	89	43	1,840 students in three grades from a predominantly Anglo middle-income area.

*The highest grade on an Advanced Placement examination is 5; the usual minimum grade for college credit is 3.
†Non-Hispanic whites.

Note: Private schools with successful programs include Phillips Academy of Andover, Mass. (154 test takers), Punahoe of Honolulu (117), Northfield Mt. Hermon of East Northfield, Mass. (107), and Phillips Exeter Academy of Exeter, N.H. (104). Stuyvesant, Andover, Exeter, Gunn, and Hunter had a majority taking the more difficult Calculus BC examination.

Source: Survey by the author.

INDEX

313

314